Barcode on Title Page!

Child Abuse and Child Protection:

Policy and Practice

Stephen Antler, Editor

National Association of Social Workers, Inc.
Silver Spring, Maryland

This compilation was funded in part by grant No. 90-C-1727 from the
National Center on Child Abuse and Neglect, Children's Bureau,
Administration on Children, Youth and Families, Office of Human
Development Services, U.S. Department of Health and Human Services.
The contents should not be construed as official policy of the National Center
on Child Abuse and Neglect or of any agency of the federal government.

 3

CONTENTS

FOREWORD

These articles, which were selected and introduced by Stephen Antler of the Boston University School of Social Work, provide a comprehensive overview of various issues in child abuse from the perspective of practice and policy. They are being published by the National Association of Social Workers (NASW) as a project of the National Professional Resource Center on Child Abuse and Neglect for Social Workers and Public Welfare Workers, funded from 1978 to 1981 by the National Center on Child Abuse and Neglect of the U.S. Department of Health and Human Services. The objectives of the resource center include raising professional awareness of child abuse and neglect, cultivating skills, fostering interdisciplinary collaboration, promoting cultural responsiveness, and enchancing resources in the field. Publication of this collection of articles fulfills most of these objectives. NASW hopes that it will be a useful addition to the sparse literature on the topic generated by the social work profession.

It is a paradox that the social work profession no longer is the leader in the field, even though social welfare agencies were the first to be concerned about the plight of maltreated and neglected children—long before the concept of the battered child syndrome was introduced in the 1960s. Social work has lost its leadership of the field because of the "medicalization" and "legalization" of the problem and because of the emergence of the occupational category of "protective service worker"— one result of the trend toward the declassification of public social service positions. It is time to reassert what Antler, in the Introduction to this collection calls "so-

cial workers' long hegemony over child welfare theory and practice."

The articles in this collection demonstrate how well equipped professional social workers are to deal with the dual perspective of *practice* with individuals, families, and groups and of *policy strategies* in communities and society at large to facilitate the most satisfying transactions between persons and their situations or environments. The collection documents the need for multilevel intervention and for a variety of community resources to assist families because of the many factors involved in abusive situations. Yet although it is true that the bulk of abusing families do not require intensive psychotherapy, social workers should not abandon the concept of the interpersonal helping relationship as central to the process of serving vulnerable children and families.

Social workers have the special skills to create or combine sensitive service to troubled people with an imaginative coordination of resources, such as material assistance, homemaker services, or volunteer support groups. Child protection is a complex field that imposes conflicting demands on its practitioners. Social work is proud and able to meet the challenges of practice and policy in this field.

Isadora Hare, *Former Project Manager*
Leila Whiting, *Project Director*
National Professional Resource
Center on Child Abuse and
Neglect, NASW

Washington, D.C.
January 1982

v

INTRODUCTION

In the past decade, child abuse and neglect, as well as other forms of domestic violence, have been recognized as widespread social problems that warrant intensive social intervention. Because scientific knowledge of the identification and treatment of child abuse has improved and been disseminated to the public, professional and lay people alike have been sensitized to the existence of this problem and have felt compelled to protect abused children. As a result, public and voluntary child welfare agencies are now obligated to dedicate most of their efforts to the investigation, screening, and treatment of cases of child abuse. Thus, the functions and typical caseloads of most child welfare agencies are markedly different from what they were twenty years ago; child protection is now the gateway for receiving traditional child welfare services.

BACKGROUND

In related fields of service, such as mental health care, health care, and family services, heightened awareness of the manifestations and indicators of abuse and neglect has increased the likelihood that children and their families will receive protective social services. At the same time, it has created numerous critical conflicts in programs and practice, particularly in regard to the imposition of formal authority on reluctant clients and the ambiguities surrounding parents' rights to confidentiality.

Protective services for children are among the most difficult social programs. They have been made more complex by the introduction of mandatory reporting laws that require the social worker to submit a report to an official agency as well as to judge whether the allegation of abuse is founded before the client may receive services.

In most mental health agencies, the voluntary client-worker relationship is essential to the helping process. A critical element of the relationship is the maintenance of trust and confidence between the caseworker and the client. However, in all states, reporting laws *require* an official report by mandated professionals of abuse and neglect. Thus, the confidential relationship of clients and caseworkers is tarnished; clients must anticipate that the information they give to the caseworker while receiving help may be used against them in protective reports or in court hearings. Most professionals are aware of these problems and are struggling to develop strategies that use the official requirements to support the objectives of treatment. However, in some states, particularly those in which the police or the district attorney are routinely involved in child protective cases, it is difficult to work toward conventional social work goals since the judgments and strategies of social agencies may be arbitrarily overridden. Consequently, workers may find it difficult to follow through on commitments to clients and clients may feel betrayed by the workers.

In addition, many agencies base their decisions to accept clients for scarce services on specific definitions taken from state child abuse laws that include narrow criteria such as "severe harm to the child" or "physical danger."[1] Yet, child protective

---

[1] These criteria are examples of an unintended consequence of well-intentioned and seemingly ra-

workers have long recognized that a wide variety of practices are harmful to children and that these practices can be altered by the aggressive intervention of social agencies.[2] However, the flood of child protective reports generated by new laws and revived public interest leaves little time or energy for providing services to families with less serious or urgent problems. Indeed, to control the growth of caseloads, some states have sought to relax their definitions of abuse and neglect, thus reducing the number of families they are required to assist.

The complexity of child welfare practices is best illustrated, however, by the diverse, often contradictory, roles that protective workers must enact while assisting families in trouble. This multiplicity of contradictory roles—investigator, judge, diagnostician, and clinician—often confuses clients as well as professionals. Unless the worker is unusually secure and a superior communicator and effectively uses authority, the proliferation of such roles can hamper his or her capacity to provide help.

The worker must assume the roles of investigator and judge because neither the child nor parent ordinarily requests protective services. Another member of the family or perhaps a physician, teacher, social worker, or neighbor usually notifies the protective agency that a problem exists. The worker's first responsibility under current practice is to ascertain whether the child has been abused or neglected. To make such a determination, the worker enters the home as an investigator and judge, combining two roles that are normally separate. The court system, unlike social services, separates the investigator or police role from the judicial role for obvious reasons: no accused person should be judged by an individual or institution whose objectivity is tainted in any way. Separating investigation or fact gathering from the final determination of the meaning of facts assures a more impartial hearing. In the social services, however, professional supervision and ethical commitments are deemed sufficient protection from arbitrary judgments. Yet, ethical standards devised for services delivered and received voluntarily may not be adequate in the context of protective services in which workers have substantial legal power over the lives of families.

The roles of diagnostician and clinician are generally more consistent with the professional self-image of social workers. However, precisely because these roles are similar to more formal judicial roles, protective workers may alternate between perspectives without knowing consciously which role they are assuming at any time.

As a consequence of the professional's role conflicts, the client is placed in an ambiguous situation because he or she is given a double message. That is, the client is threatened with having his or her children taken away and, at the same time, offered help in maintaining the family.[3] Yet, if the social worker is to be useful to the family, this is precisely the message that he or she must convey: help and support are available, but, if the family situation does not change, so is more dramatic legal action that can lead to the severance of family relationships. The decision often rests largely on the worker's skill and a suspicious and frightened client's willingness and ability to enter a relationship when the potential for helping is unknown and the outcome is not certain.

Of course, other areas of ambiguity con-

tional agency processes. As a result, workers may also be motivated to err on the side of defining a condition as child maltreatment simply to facilitate service to an ineligible family.

[2] See, for example, Joyce Antler and Stephen Antler, "From Child Rescue to Family Protection: The Evolution of the Child Protective Movement in the United States," Children and Youth Services Review, 1 (1979), pp. 177–204.

[3] In his research on the treatment of child abuse, Nagi revealed that casework was the most common service offered and it was also the most resisted by clients. See Saad Nagi, Child Maltreatment in the United States (New York: Columbia University Press, 1977).

found the efforts of workers to maintain families who may be able to stay together. In addition to facing reluctant and often hostile clients, workers, supervisors, and administrators often fear that their decisions about abusive families may be reviewed by a crusading press or an irate district attorney, particularly if serious harm occurs to a child known to the protective agency. For workers and agencies, the least risk-laden alternative in cases of severe abuse is frequently to place the child in foster care. Yet, ethics and efficacy demand that the decision reflect the circumstances of the case rather than the prejudices and fears of the community. As a consequence, protective work demands that the worker not only have skill, judgment, and compassion, but courage, confidence, and the ability to be obstinate in behalf of clients.

The social work literature reflects many of these concerns, most of which arise from the profession's proprietary interest in and long hegemony over child welfare theory and practice. Indeed, the leadership of professional social workers in child welfare has been challenged by the current widespread revival of concern about abuse and neglect and the movement of these issues to the forefront of contemporary social concerns. Physicians and other health professionals and lawyers and law enforcement personnel are playing increasingly important roles in treatment as well as in policy development.[4]

It was with these issues in mind that this collection of articles was selected. All but one of the articles first appeared in *Social Work, Social Casework,* and *Child Welfare* and therefore reflect the thinking of authors interested in communicating with social work audiences. Indeed, several arti-

cles register concern about the need for other professions to become involved in problems of child abuse and neglect and about the impact such new influences will have on child welfare practice.

The articles in this collection illustrate the historical dimensions of social work's concern for abused and neglected children and their families as well as a broad spectrum of practice issues and dilemmas that have been debated in the social work literature. Discussions in the first group of articles range from broad conceptual questions about the nature of abuse and neglect to the specifics of location, causation, and significance. In the next two clusters of articles, various treatment perspectives and methods are elaborated, from highly professionalized casework systems to informal services provided by self-help groups of parents. Emerging problems are then discussed, followed by several articles on burnout. Although burnout is a problem for all social workers, it is especially relevant for protective workers because their clients are often the most resistant to being helped and hence create additional personal pressures on these workers. In the final group of articles, solutions to child protective problems are offered. The solutions require broad changes in social policies, including income maintenance and the guarantee of services to support family life. Although social work agencies usually consider intervention with individual families the way to resolve child welfare problems, social work has a dual focus that requires broader changes in social policies as a backdrop for assisting individuals.

BROAD ISSUES

No matter how widespread the recognition of child abuse and neglect as serious social problems, the extent to which parents inflict cruel and serious injuries on defenseless infants and young children is always appalling. In the early 1960s, however, when Elmer wrote "Abused Young Children Seen in Hospitals," public and pro-

---

[4] *See,* for example, Eli Newberger and Richard Bourne, "The Medicalization and Legalization of Child Abuse," *American Journal of Orthopsychiatry,* 48 (October 1978), pp. 593–607; Stephen Pfohl, "The Discovery of Child Abuse," *Social Problems,* 24 (February 1977), pp. 310–323; and Stephen Antler, "Child Abuse: An Emerging Social Priority," *Social Work,* 23 (January 1978), pp. 58–61.

fessional knowledge of child abuse was still limited.[5] Elmer noted that abuse and neglect were so repugnant to medical and social service personnel that these professionals had a "blind spot" that prevented them from accurately assessing the degree to which injuries inflicted on young children were willful or accidental. She was among the first social workers in the medical field to identify the problem and to urge a more systematic and general approach to helping families. Although her article received much attention in the social work community, it did not have as great an impact on the public sector or on physicians.

The reasons for this lack of impact are touched on in Antler's article "Child Abuse: An Emerging Social Priority." Antler noted that physicians such as C. Henry Kempe and others at the Denver Medical Center were "aided by their high status, professional credibility and political sophistication" and were, therefore, able to capture the imagination of the public and to pressure public agencies to take a deeper look at this emerging problem.[6] Aided by the Children's Bureau and other national agencies, physicians gained acceptance for the idea that child abuse is a *medical* problem which requires medical intervention. The medical approach also affected social work; child protective agencies responded to it with expanded casework services designed to complement the new reporting laws that were rapidly adopted by virtually all states at the urging of the Children's Bureau. These reporting laws stimulated public involvement and awareness, increased the caseloads in child protective agencies, and required agencies to determine, during the initial assessment phase, if abuse or neglect had occurred. Because of this requirement, the emphasis of protective practice shifted subtly from service to investigation.

In addition, Antler stated, a general lack of supportive services, such as day care and homemaker programs, stimulated agencies and workers to concentrate on clinical casework as the preferred helping method. This emphasis conformed to the medical theory that stresses the need to reform individuals and was consistent with the general thrust of casework practice, but it retarded recognition of the broader social changes required to ease the situation of parents with problems in child rearing.

Antler's article raises an important question: To what extent should strategies to reduce child abuse and neglect balance casework with individual families against efforts to improve social policies directed toward all families? How one answers this question rests, in part, on one's beliefs about what works best to prevent and treat abuse or neglect.

Jayaratne assessed the research on child abuse and its cliniical implications in "Child Abusers as Parents and Children: A Review."[7] He noted that the child abuse literature abounds with the unproved and empirically untested assertion that abusive behavior occurs among all social groups and that variables of social class such as education, income, and occupation have no bearing on the propensity to abuse children. Jayaratne's comprehensive critique of the research revealed the degree to which additional clinical research is needed to provide firm guidelines for practice. It also suggested the magnitude of the uncertainty that practitioners must feel in this complex area of service.

In support of Jayaratne's observation that abuse and neglect are not common among the middle class, Pelton ("Child Abuse and Neglect: The Myth of Classlessness") contended that the available evidence calls for the opposite conclusion.[8] Noting that the poor are exposed to

---

[5] Elizabeth Elmer, "Abused Young Children Seen in Hospitals," *Social Work*, 5 (October 1960), pp. 98–102.

[6] Antler, op. cit., p. 58.

[7] Srinika Jayaratne, "Child Abusers as Parents and Children: A Review," *Social Work*, 22 (January 1977), pp. 5–9.

[8] Leroy H. Pelton, "Child Abuse and Neglect: The Myth of Classlessness," *American Journal of Orthopsychiatry*, 48 (October 1978), pp. 608–617.

great stress on the family as well as severe environmental conditions, such as substandard housing, nutrition, and health care, Pelton asserted that abuse and neglect are directly and inextricably linked to economic status. Pelton navigated through numerous research studies in his critique of the theory that middle-class children are abused in the same proportion as children of other social classes but that cases are not reported because middle-class families are insulated from community scrutiny and are less likely to come in contact with public agencies. Rather, his analysis suggested that the most severe cases of neglect and battering occur among the most profoundly deprived. This conclusion was also reached by the American Humane Association.[9]

Pelton also constructed a vigorous critique of contemporary strategies for protecting children, noting that they all presuppose some type of psychic maladjustment that requires clinical intervention. Following the reasoning of his earlier assertions, Pelton proposed interventions focused on reducing stress and deprivation.

In a landmark two-part review of the literature, Zalba delineated areas in which the research provided helpful information and offered some practice guidelines based on the available data. In "The Abused Child: I. A Survey of the Problem," Zalba criticized the use of the term "battered child syndrome," concluding that the use of "syndrome" implied an "identifiable sociomedical identity" with known etiology and a typology for diagnosis and treatment.[10] As his extensive review of the literature illustrated, however, there are many reasons for both abusive and neglecting behavior; although many of the reasons may be related to mental illness or to character disorders in family members, no discernable, unique features could be

derived from the literature to provide an explanatory framework for the emergence of abuse in any family.

Zalba indicated some of the characteristics of abusive families and practice with them. For example, families who abuse or neglect their children deny the existence of any family problem and are thus uncomfortable in working with social agencies. Moreover, the American tradition of privacy and individualism often provides a rationale for not observing or noting the problems of neighbors and acquaintances and for not encouraging outside, particularly public, intervention even when serious problems are discovered. Zalba further noted that verifying the existence of an abusive situation is usually difficult. Even when severe abuse is disclosed, removal of children from their home may not be desirable because children often are fragile and tightly bound to their family arrangements. Zalba concluded the first part of his two-part article by stressing the need for a typology that identifies the danger to children and provides a basis for predicting the outcome of treatment.

In "The Abused Child: II. A Typology for Classification and Treatment," Zalba offered a conceptual framework for choosing the appropriate protective strategy and treatment modality in cases of child abuse and neglect.[11] The assumption behind the typology is that the causes of child abuse can be located in the personality system of the parents, the family system, or the person-environment or family environment system. In addition, Zalba divided abuse into two major varieties: controllable and uncontrollable. When abuse is held to be uncontrollable, as it is with psychotic or "pervasively angry" parents, the typology suggests removal of the abused child. However, most other types of abuse are placed in the controllable category, and removal is eschewed in favor

---

[9] *National Analysis of Child Abuse and Neglect Reporting* (Denver, Colo: American Humane Association, 1978).

[10] Serapio Richard Zalba, "The Abused Child: I. A Survey of the Problem," *Social Work,* 11 (October 1966), pp. 3–16.

[11] Serapio Richard Zalba, "The Abused Child: II. A Typology for Classification and Treatment," *Social Work,* 12 (January 1967), pp. 70–79.

of intensive treatment. Although Zalba's categories have still not been empirically tested, they at least offer the perspective that the outcome of intervention may not be satisfactory for some types of individual or family dysfunctions, which require more drastic action by protective agencies.

Zalba's insightful review of the literature underscores a major problem in making casework judgments about an appropriate action when potential damage to the child is a significant factor. Because few paradigms are available on which to base decisions and assess the risk to the child, caseworkers often have to choose between unsatisfactory alternatives. The decisions are particularly difficult when there are few agencies that provide comprehensive social and mental health services. Indeed, the availability or lack of availability of services to assure the safety of vulnerable children may be a significant determining factor in decision making about cases. That is, in communities with a wide variety of services and a long history of community involvement, protective agencies and the courts may decide to place fewer children in foster care.

Knowledge of the effects of treatment remains incomplete despite the expenditure of many millions of dollars on a wide variety of demonstration programs funded by the National Center on Child Abuse and Neglect. Cohn's assessment of federally funded demonstration programs in "Effective Treatment of Child Abuse and Neglect" provides beginning guidelines for developing effective program strategies.[12] Although the results of the study must be used guardedly because of the study's numerous methodological limitations, they raise issues about the delivery and content of effective programs. Perhaps the most disturbing finding was that some demonstration programs (which are not equivalent to all protective treatment) had a reincidence rate as high as 51

percent. Cohn concluded that abusers with the most serious symptoms were most likely to be recidivist. In all the programs, workers were guarded in their assessment of how much help they had been able to provide; however, they thought that families receiving a combination of services which included Parents Anonymous or lay counseling appeared to fare better. It should be noted that Cohn considered these two services equivalent for the purpose of reporting research. Yet, there is a great difference between going to a paid lay therapist and participating in a voluntary group experience. Nevertheless, Cohn's research suggests that the provision of concurrent services works better than counseling alone. It also suggests that when intake, assessment, and case planning are performed by trained and experienced professionals, children are more likely to be protected. Presumably, experienced workers with an extensive background of "case wisdom" are more likely to assess accurately the degree of risk to children.

CLINICAL METHODS

Shorkey, in "A Review of Methods Used in the Treatment of Abusing Parents," described and compared various clinical methods for the treatment of child abuse and offered guidelines for their use in different types of family situations.[13] In summarizing the available frames of reference and techniques, Shorkey noted that virtually all the methods involve supplemental services, such as day care and homemaker services, as well as clinical treatment. He further noted that programs that used all the methods reported successful outcomes; however, the literature included no evaluations of carefully selected control groups. Thus, conclusive evidence cannot be mustered to support any method. Shorkey concluded

---

[12] Anne Harris Cohn, "Effective Treatment of Child Abuse and Neglect," *Social Work,* 24 (November 1979), pp. 513–519.

[13] Clayton T. Shorkey, "A Review of Methods Used in the Treatment of Abusing Parents," *Social Casework,* 60 (June 1979), pp. 360–367.

that the paucity of good research on outcomes is not surprising because few communities have the wide range of comprehensive alternative treatment programs that would encourage investigation and comparison.

Although severe mental illness is not present in most protective cases, treatment programs continue to offer therapeutic counseling. Indeed, in 1977, the American Humane Association's national study of child protection found that the most widely available service was social casework.[14] Tracy and Clark proposed an alternative theoretical framework—learning theories rather than psychopathology—for diagnosis and treatment in "Treatment for Child Abusers."[15] That is, aberrant parental behavior would be diagnosed as a lack of skills in child rearing and family management; treatment would be oriented toward improving the ability of parents to function in the adult world. The program described by Tracy and Clark was tested in a hospital. However, the guidelines offered by the authors are applicable to any major treatment innovation in a social service agency. The authors noted, for example, that retraining staff, particularly in the interdisciplinary context of child-abuse treatment, was complex because the conceptual categories that each discipline used to describe behavior had to be rethought. Hence, the introduction of learning theory into a setting geared to psychodynamic theory must have strong institutional and staff support.

Cantoni's article "Clinical Issues in Domestic Violence" provided a framework for assessing and treating violent families and suggested that all domestic violence, no matter to whom it is directed, stems from similar family dynamics.[16] Moreover,

Cantoni argued, violence in some families may be endemic, involving abuse of the spouse, siblings, children, and, ultimately, elderly or helpless adult family members. Using the observations of clinicians, Cantoni described a variety of personality traits—role reversal and role confusion, problems in sexual adjustment based on early experiences with adult family members, isolation, mistrust, imperfect social relationships, and the lack of self-control—that appear to be associated with domestic violence.

Noting that stress can trigger violent episodes among abusive parents, Cantoni contended that few parents are seriously mentally ill. Indeed, as a preconditon for receiving help, the family must recognize that the threatened family member must be protected from further attack. Consequently, the family members must adopt nonviolent means of resolving problems if they are to remain together. Claiming that intrafamily violence is learned behavior, Cantoni advocated therapy, reeducation of family members, and "education and advice" about family life and child rearing when appropriate to the relationship between the caseworker and client.

In an earlier article, Shames described an approach whose conceptual framework and treatment methods were similar to those described by Tracy and Clark even though the approach was not formally based on learning theories.[17] In "Use of Homemaker Service in Families that Neglect Their Children," Shames noted that the women involved in the program were lonely, unmotivated, unacculturated, and unfamiliar with normative standards of household management, budgeting, and child rearing. These families were so unskilled that even though they lived in a crowded urban area, they were unable to establish reciprocal child care arrangements with other families. The ap-

[14] *National Analysis of Child Abuse and Neglect Reporting.*

[15] James J. Tracy and Elizabeth H. Clark, "Treatment for Child Abusers," *Social Work*, 19 (May 1974), pp. 338–342.

[16] Lucile Cantoni, "Clinical Issues in Domestic Violence," *Social Casework*, 62 (January 1981), pp. 3–12.

[17] Miriam Shames, "Use of Homemaker Service in Families that Neglect Their Children," *Social Work*, 9 (January 1964), pp. 12–18.

proach of the child neglect unit of the California Department of Welfare, designed by Shames, was to use skilled, experienced homemakers to provide intensive services to the families. Rather than relationship therapy, the homemakers supplied physical services such as laundering clothes, housecleaning, and attending to the needs of the children while offering acceptance, friendship, and support to the mothers. Shames claimed there was significant and lasting improvement in almost all the cases after intervention. It is particularly noteworthy that although the mothers thought the most important feature of the program was the homemakers' provision of companionship, the gateway to the relationship was the observable changes that occurred in the family environment because of the homemakers' intervention in physical chores. The author theorized that the mother's self-image and feelings of hope were enhanced in the new atmosphere engendered by the work of the homemaker. As a consequence, service could be terminated in a short time with some assurance that the children would receive better care.

Holmes delineated still another model for helping abusive families in "Parents Anonymous: A Treatment Method For Child Abuse." Parents Anonymous, a national self-help organization with branches throughout the country, was modeled after Alcoholics Anonymous. It focuses on the loneliness and lack of mutual support frequently identified as characteristics of abuse-prone individuals. New members are helped to develop relationships in the group and "an adequate support system for themselves within their own families and communities."[18] Although a mutual support group such as Parents Anonymous is a viable alternative for some abusive clients, Holmes noted that many clients, particularly those who are unable

to form relationships in the context of the group, would not benefit from it.

Helfer and Kempe's Denver model was one of several alternative program models of direct help to individuals who need more than group support.[19] It involved trained lay therapists who gave personal support to clients often at any hour they required it. The lay therapist model is similar to the homemaker services described in this collection, which are available in limited supply through public protective services.

Withey, Anderson, and Lauderdale described still another model in "Volunteers as Mentors for Abusing Parents."[20] They reviewed several programs that used volunteers as mentors to parents whose knowledge and skills were deficient and presented guidelines for selecting volunteers and for pairing them with families in need of help. In effect, the parents were placed in the role of apprentices, and the mentors modeled appropriate, successful behavior. As a result of the modeling, "reparenting" occurred. The clients received affection, nurturance, and acceptance and acquired the skills they did not achieve as children. Thus, they were able to learn and adopt better child-rearing practices.

The paucity of public attention and social services to older children, particularly adolescents, was the subject of "Meeting the Needs of Mistreated Youths" by Garbarino.[21] Older children, who constitute about one-third of the cases reported to state child abuse registries, usually come to the attention of social agencies and the courts because they exhibit such deviant behavior as running away or truancy. As a result, they are not treated as victims, but

[18] Sally Holmes, "Parents Anonymous: A Treatment Method for Child Abuse," *Social Work*, 23 (May 1978), p. 245.

[19] Ray E. Helfer and C. Henry Kempe, eds., *Helping the Battered Child and His Family* (Philadelphia: J. B. Lippincott Co., 1972).

[20] Virginia Withey, Rosalie Anderson, and Michael Lauderdale, "Volunteers as Mentors for Abusing Parents: A Natural Helping Relationship," *Child Welfare*, 49 (December 1980), pp. 637–644.

[21] James Garbarino, "Meeting the Needs of Mistreated Youths," *Social Work*, 25 (March 1980), pp. 122–126.

as if they were the cause of the family's problem. Garbarino suggested that the public is outraged about the abuse of defenseless infants and young children who cannot be thought of as contributing to their own victimization. Thus, he urged social workers and others to investigate whether the troubled adolescents they work with have been abused because it must be assumed that teenagers who run away or otherwise exhibit deviant behavior are reacting to long-standing patterns of parental abuse or rejection. Recognizing that treatment of adolescents is linked to social attitudes, he advocated that social welfare professionals should engage in sustained community action on behalf of victimized older children to bring about a more accepting climate for helping them.

Shamroy, in "A Perspective on Childhood Sexual Abuse," concluded that the sexual exploitation of preadolescent children is more pervasive than caseloads would indicate.[22] Shamroy described a hospital-based program to identify and help young victims (usually girls) and their families. Although the primary objective was to protect the child from future sexual abuse, Shamroy's sympathetic description of the dilemmas faced by child-victims is a moving testimonial to the ambiguities of protective work in this sensitive area. When a child is sexually exploited, it is usually by a close relative or another person she knows, and frequently she cooperates with her abuser. If the offender is prosecuted, the child may feel guilty for having been the instrument of a loved one's punishment or may be blamed by other relatives or by her mother. Thus, for the child, the event is colored by her involvement in punishing someone for whom she has a strong, often loving, attachment. Although many abused children are emotionally attached to those who hurt or even maim them, the dilemma is even

more pronounced in cases of sexual exploitation because many victims are not forcibly assaulted. Often they were compliant and accepting, since the act was initiated by someone for whom the child felt great affection and trust.

The issue of sexual abuse raises questions about the conditions under which offenders should be prosecuted, given the potential for sustained damage to the child if she has to testify and undergo cross-examination in an open courtroom. The court action and its consequences for the family (such as incarceration of the father or close relative) may punish the child and make her feel she is the cause of the family's problem. Especially in these cases, protective workers should try to help the family contain the sexual acting out and reconstruct the family on a more healthy foundation. When this is not possible, the child must be protected, either by removal from the home or through separation from the abusive adult.

The procedures regarding access to child protection records by clients and their lawyers have shifted radically in the past few years. Increasingly, the courts are permitting lawyers of clients engaged in court actions under child protection statutes to obtain access to agency records. Protective workers, who are often unfamiliar with the rules of evidence and uncertain in their relations with lawyers, generally have resisted these trends and have attempted to limit access under professional and agency rules of confidentiality. In "Child Protection Records: Issues of Confidentiality," Levine reviewed these trends and suggested that social workers and lawyers must learn to work with each other if the best interests of clients are to be safeguarded.[23] Levine concluded that child protection may actually benefit from greater judicial scrutiny of agency decisions. Nevertheless, such changes in child

---

[22] Jerilyn A. Shamroy, "A Perspective on Childhood Sexual Abuse," *Social Work,* 25 (March 1980), pp. 128–131.

[23] Richard Steven Levine, "Child Protection Records: Issues of Confidentiality," Notes for Practice, *Social Work,* 21 (July 1976), pp. 323–324.

welfare will not be effected without conflict, adding additional tensions to the already difficult problems that protective workers confront. These problems, which tend to be associated with working with hostile clients in an unsupportive agency environment, generate severe stress for protective workers that may lead to burnout—the subject of the next three articles.

EFFECTIVENESS AND BURNOUT

Daley's " 'Burnout': Smoldering Problem in Protective Services," discusses the causes of burnout and proposes ways that supervisors and administrators can reduce the problems associated with high tension in protective practice.[24] Daley noted, for example, that burnout leads to the reduced effectiveness, high rates of absenteeism, and increased turnover of workers. To combat the problem, he advocated a comprehensive program that would include supervisory support, time out from work, rotation of roles, staff training, and better opportunities for promotion.

Bandoli described an additional method to combat burnout: peer support groups. In his article, "Leaderless Support Groups in Child Protective Services," he observed that the concept of leaderless support groups among professionals is derived from similar mutual aid groups of clients.[25] Thus, leaderless groups can be seen as an analogue to organizations such as Parents Anonymous in that they are designed to facilitate relationships, learning, and mutual aid.

A related cluster of issues was raised by Fauri. In "Protecting the Child Protective Service Worker," Fauri observed that the problems of child protective workers are coming to resemble those of police officers.[26] The requirements to comply rigorously with the law, to observe rules of due process in child protective cases, and to present evidence in court make new demands on social workers who are normally not accustomed to working in a legal framework. Fauri noted that unlike the police (who have police review boards), social agencies do not have adequate internal procedures for reviewing the performance of workers or the policies of the agency when a case situation goes awry. This lack of review procedures leaves individual workers vulnerable to charges of mismanagement without access to due process. Because protective work is increasingly linked to legal procedures, public and voluntary agencies will need to confront the question of how they can protect workers from unjust accusations and provide a formal means for clients and others to request a review of the worker's and agency's performance.

The problem of accountability becomes more salient when social workers are called on to exert authority in the context of the helping process. The debate over the place of authority in the delivery of social services and in social work practice has intensified in the past decade. Many fields of practice have found that more of their work is being linked to court-related activities or to publicly funded services required by law. Referrals from the schools, treatment decisions in the mental health system, child welfare actions, and even work with the aged often have a court-related component. Not only do social workers need sophisticated legal knowledge, but they must learn to apply their clinical skills to involuntary clients—persons who face serious legal consequences if they do not seek help.

The use of authority and an understanding of the effects of coercion, although difficult for many social workers, is essential in protective services. Indeed,

[24] Michael R. Daley, " 'Burnout': Smoldering Problem in Protective Services," *Social Work,* 24 (September 1979), pp. 375–379.

[25] Larry R. Bandoli, "Leaderless Support Groups in Child Protective Services," Notes for Practice, *Social Work,* 22 (March 1977), pp. 150–151.

[26] David P. Fauri, "Protecting the Child Protective Service Worker," Points and Viewpoints, *Social Work,* 23 (January 1978), pp. 62–64.

even clients who have not been ordered by the court to accept counseling recognize that failure to cooperate or at least to seem to cooperate may lead to further sanctions from the agency.

Gourse and Chescheir, in "Authority Issues in Treating Resistant Families," described a study of social work strategies using authoritative measures to promote service for involuntary clients. As they put it:

> . . . ultimately to engage in or avoid socially unacceptable behavior or to engage in or avoid problem-solving efforts is the client's decision. Any authoritarian action taken by a social worker . . . cannot be simply rejected as total violation of the client's right of self-determination, for there are many decision points for the client along the way to such worker actions.[27]

The argument may not satisfy all practitioners, particularly since the authors used the term "authoritarian" when "authoritative" may have been more appropriate. However, the research suggested that social workers, although uncomfortable with authoritative actions, are prepared to use them for appropriate reasons. Indeed, the responses indicated that workers will attempt many strategies before applying legal sanctions, but if the client remains unwilling, they will eventually use legal authority.

Use of authority in practice is likely to become even more salient as public social services are reduced because of budget cuts. Thus, there will be little possibility of offering preventive help and concrete services such as day care that have heretofore served as a support for families in distress. The point of intervention will, under reduced funding, be a crisis in which the family is legally required to receive services.

SOCIAL POLICY

The need for adequate child protective programs and for maintaining the skills of those who provide them should not obscure the larger factors that affect family life in this country. There is no conclusive evidence to suggest a direct relationship between neglect and abuse and the lack of social services for children and families. However, many believe that a more benign and supportive environment for families, characterized by universally available social services, would lead to improved conditions for all children, including those who might otherwise be neglected or mistreated.

In "Primary Prevention of Child Mistreatment: Meeting a National Need," Miller discussed the implications of current policies designed to prevent child abuse and neglect.[28] She observed that the incremental approach to developing child welfare policies has led to the provision of services after evidence of maltreatment has been established. Thus, primary prevention is not practiced.

Whatever prevention is practiced is secondary prevention: services designed to protect children from further attack. As Miller observed: "The establishment of eligibility criteria works contrary to the principle of preventive service" in that it limits the population accessible for service.[29] In analyzing the effect of these programs and policies, the author concluded that universally available services are required to provide support to all families as a normative feature of community life.

Universal social services for families with young children is hardly a popular political topic. Yet, the subject is receiving scholarly and public attention as a result of fundamental changes taking place in the roles, structure, and functions of families. For example, as of 1978, 47.9 percent of the

---

[27] Judith E. Gourse and Martha W. Chescheir, "Authority Issues in Treating Resistant Families," *Social Casework*, 62 (February 1981), p. 69.

[28] Carolyn Clark Miller, "Primary Prevention of Child Mistreatment: Meeting a National Need," *Child Welfare*, 50 (January 1981), pp. 11–23.

[29] Ibid., p. 14.

mothers of children aged 3–5 were in the labor force—a trend that is not likely to be reversed, given today's economy.[30] The rapid increase in divorce and in the number of single parents has also shifted the social needs of families with children. At the same time, identification of young single mothers with young children as the "new poor" has generated concern about the ability of many families to provide a reasonable economic and emotionally nurturant environment.

Although the need to control violent behavior in families has received much attention in recent years, social workers and other concerned professionals have stressed the importance of improving social services to all families at every life stage as well as to families in which both parents must work. The current emphasis on controlling the worst forms of family misbehavior without altering the climate in which parents must raise children is tragically misguided. Emerging evidence suggests that child abuse and neglect correlate with such factors as poverty, unemployment, single parenthood, and poor housing and are not widely distributed throughout the population. Thus, social policies designed to ease the situations of the poor and of single parents may help reduce the incidence of maltreatment and improve family life.

In the past two decades, Americans have investigated the use of a comprehensive family policy to determine governmental programs for all types of families. In the current climate of hostility toward new governmental initiatives, one can expect little immediate improvement for families through public programs. Yet, the movement to increase programmatic and financial support for beleaguered American families cannot be relaxed, as many industrial societies have learned. Indeed, as Moynihan noted in 1968: "A nation without a conscious family policy leaves to chance and mischance an area of social reality of the utmost importance."[31]

The articles by Authier and Kamerman and Kahn suggest some approaches to family policy that would assist families in child rearing. Authier, in "Defining the Care in Child Care," observed that nostalgic formulations about family life in the past, which are based on conventional models of female domesticity, mask the disabilities that many families experienced. Indeed, for many young children, particularly poor children, the experience of family life ended by age 6 when they were sent out to work or were left in the care of other siblings.[32] Other children were merely neglected or abandoned to accommodate the needs of parents, both of whom worked just to survive. After tracing the history of the day nursery movement, Authier concluded that even though day care is not a panacea for errant families or a solution to social problems, nevertheless, it is an important form of temporary substitute care. Authier advocated a flexible federal approach involving a variety of child care models that would fit the needs and parenting styles of the increasing number of working mothers both in two-parent and in one-parent families.

"Comparative Analysis in Family Policy: A Case Study," by Kamerman and Kahn compares the different approaches to child care for children under age 3 in five European countries. Reasoning that all adults are likely to be "full, participating, productive members of the labor force," the authors delineated a variety of "benefit service packages" that European countries have adopted to provide for the needs of families with young children.[33] With the exception of France, virtually all countries with comprehensive programs for young

[30] George Masnick and Mary Jo Bane, *The Nation's Families: 1960–1990* (Cambridge, Mass.: Joint Center for Urban Studies of Harvard & M.I.T., 1980).

[31] Daniel Patrick Moynihan, Introduction to Alva Myrdal, *Nation and Family* (Cambridge, Mass.: M.I.T. Press, 1968), p. x.

[32] Karen Authier, "Defining the Care in Child Care," *Social Work,* 24 (November 1979), pp. 500–505.

[33] Sheila B. Kamerman and Alfred J. Kahn, "Comparative Analysis in Family Policy: A Case Study," *Social Work,* 24 (November 1979), p. 506.

children respond to variations in labor market conditions and to concerns about the birthrate. Moreover, European child care planners are less concerned about specific programs to prevent family deviance than about identifying the best mix of subsidies and services that would provide young children with the optimal possibilities for socialization. Kamerman and Kahn were careful to note that no one service can reasonably fulfill the demands of a family policy. Their discussion, therefore, focused on the mix of services, programs, and incentives that have been identified as options for parents and children. Practitioners who are concerned about the care of neglected and abused children will find the article useful for considering the wide variety of programs that could be provided to all American families.

CONCLUSION

The protection of young children from abuse, neglect, and other forms of maltreatment is a serious challenge to American society. As is true of other serious social problems, the incidence of abuse and neglect tends to rise dramatically during periods of declining resources, high unemployment, and uncertain financial security. That personal stress increases during times of economic decline needs little validation. Without public programs to cushion the effects of such economic stress, marginal families, who are most vulnerable to changes in a volatile economic climate, suffer. The stress experienced by the family is communicated to children, either through aggressive or violent family reactions or through more subtle, less physically damaging forms. Consequently, agencies and practitioners dedicated to protecting children also have an interest in promoting broader social policies to assist and support families.

It is hoped that the readings assembled in this collection will provide a basis for understanding the important considerations involved in the field of child protection. The articles represent only a small fraction of the available literature in this burgeoning field but should provide practitioners and policymakers with an excellent overview as well as important new ideas concerning the types of programs, policies, and practices that should be encouraged.

STEPHEN ANTLER, EDITOR

Associate Professor
School of Social Work
Boston University
Boston, Massachusetts
January 1982

PART 1
Defining the Problem

BY ELIZABETH ELMER

Abused Young Children Seen in Hospitals

HOSPITAL SOCIAL WORKERS, along with their colleagues in other professions, appear strangely unaware of a rare hospital phenomenon that cries dramatically for attention—evidence of unbelievably primitive transactions that take place beyond our gaze, safe from our curious questions, and thus an index of social pathology which would seem to merit more attention. This is the fact that a small number of infants and children are hospitalized every year with injuries sustained through the ignorance, gross negligence, or deliberate abuse of the parents or other responsible adults. The possible extent of abuse was forcefully illustrated for the author several years ago when six infants became patients in Children's Hospital of Pittsburgh because of injuries thought to be due to abusive treatment. All were under 16 months of age, and all were admitted within the short span of one week. Fortunately, later study did not confirm the initial impression of abuse in all six cases. However, so grimly impressive was the number of the infants and the presumed reason for their admission to the hospital that the author was spurred to learn more about this category of children and their families. It can now safely be said that very little is known about any facet of the problem and that methods for dealing with it are random and inadequate. The purpose of this paper is to point out the problem and to suggest the major professional blind spot that seems to prevent us from attacking it in a forthright way. One approach to expanding our understanding of these families will also be suggested.

It will be helpful first to inspect another phenomenon that beclouds the issue at every turn: the repugnance felt by most of our society for the entire subject of abused children. Such a reaction may be partially understood on several scores. First, we are led in many subtle ways to believe that our society is an enlightened one which offers to every child at least the bare minimum of care and protection. It is a rude shock to come up against the evidence that this is not so, and we prefer to shut from our minds such disquieting evidence. Second, so strong is our current cultural emphasis on the rights of children and the responsibilities of parents that many parents will not even admit to the occasional spanking they administer. A parent who might be guilty of assault against a child is therefore invested in our eyes with an unnatural quality that adds to our general discomfort. These two factors do not fully explain the strength of the universal repugnance that is so easily observed. Concerning this subject there are undoubtedly powerful unconscious feelings that deeply affect the attitudes of most people. Whatever the conscious or concealed components, the emotion of repugnance is common enough to warrant the label of cultural norm, at least in middle-class American society. In the opinion of the author, this repugnance is the chief reason that so little systematic study has been devoted to abused children and their families.

ELIZABETH ELMER, M.S.S., is assistant professor of casework at the Graduate School of Social Work, University of Pittsburgh, Pittsburgh, Pennsylvania.

Reprinted from SOCIAL WORK, 5 (October 1960), pp. 98–102.
Copyright © 1960 by the National Association of Social Workers, Inc.

MEDICAL RECOGNITION

Neglectful or abusive treatment may take many forms, of course. The six infants mentioned above and the other hospitalized children of concern in this paper suffered multiple skeletal trauma. Gross neglect or assault is suspected when roentgen survey reveals several fractures dating from different times and there is no clinical disease that accounts for them. For example, there may be a fresh fracture of one bone, a healing fracture of another, and an old healed fracture of still a third. Any one such fracture may be the result of an accident, but the presence of several at various healing stages reduces drastically the possibility of natural explanation. For the sake of simplicity this paper will use the term "abuse" to cover gross neglect as well.

The medical literature affords sparse but authentic documentation of the existence of this category of children. The first published article appeared in 1946 when Caffey noted that subdural hematoma in infants was often accompanied by fractures of the long bones.[1] No history of injury could be elicited from the parents and Caffey did not offer an explanation of the observed concomitant physical conditions. In a later publication Caffey speculated that such injuries in infants were due to the negligence or mistreatment of the parents.[2] Very gradually this possibility gained attention from other physicians. In 1953 Silverman referred to physical trauma as the most common bone "disease" of infancy.[3] He also noted the strong resistance of pediatricians and orthopedists to the interpretation of

parental mismanagement as the basis of the infant's injuries. Woolley and Evans related the injuries of twelve infants with fractured bones to an "injury-prone environment." All were found to come from unstable homes with a high incidence of neurotic or psychotic behavior on the part of one or both parents.[4] Bakwin agreed that skeletal changes in infants and young children were frequently due to trauma, in contrast to disease.[5] Thirty-seven cases from the literature, plus five of their own, were reviewed by Jones and Davis in 1957. The importance of early recognition of the possibility of trauma was emphasized; unnecessary and costly diagnostic procedures might thus be curtailed and the child removed from the offending environment when necessary.[6] A prominent orthopedist, Miller, identifies parental assault as a common cause of fractures in infants and young children. He urges a particularly careful history when fractures in young children are accompanied by multiple soft tissue injuries at other sites of the body. He warns the medical examiner not to adopt an accusing attitude toward the parents because they might later make the child the target for their vengeance.[7]

This brief survey of the medical literature indicates the existence in hospital practice of a number of small children who have suffered severe injuries through the adults responsible for their care. The possibility of purely local explanation is ruled out by the fact that the authors mentioned are engaged in practice in various parts of the

[1] J. Caffey, "Multiple Fractures in the Long Bones of Infants Suffering from Chronic Subdural Hematoma," *American Journal of Roentgenology*, Vol. 56, No. 2 (August 1946).

[2] J. Caffey, *Journal of Pediatric X-ray Diagnosis* (2d ed.; Chicago: Year Book Publishers, Inc., 1950), pp. 684–687.

[3] Frederic N. Silverman, "The Roentgen Manifestations of Unrecognized Skeletal Trauma in Infants," *American Journal of Roentgenology*, Vol. 69, No. 3 (March 1953).

[4] P. V. Woolley, Jr. and W. A. Evans, Jr., "Significance of Skeletal Lesions in Infants Resembling Those of Traumatic Origin," *Journal of the American Medical Association*, Vol. 158 (June 18, 1955), pp. 539–543.

[5] Harry Bakwin, "Multiple Skeletal Lesions in Young Children Due to Trauma," *Journal of Pediatrics*, Vol. 49, No. 1 (July 1956), pp. 7–16.

[6] Henry H. Jones and Joseph H. Davis, "Multiple Traumatic Lesions of the Infant Skeleton," *Stanford Medical Bulletin*, Vol. 15, No. 3 (August 1957).

[7] Donald S. Miller, "Fractures Among Children. I. Parental assault as causative agent," *Minnesota Medicine*, Vol. 42, No. 9 (September 1959), p. 1209.

country, such as New York, Cincinnati, Detroit, Chicago, and Palo Alto.

These reports in the medical journals may be viewed in another aspect. After Caffey's first report seven years elapsed before another author wrote on the same subject. Since 1955, when Woolley and Evans reported their study, several papers have appeared, but as yet there has been minimum attention from pediatricians and other practicing physicians. One might speculate that the small number of reports on the subject reflects distaste and discomfort on the part of physicians, feelings similar to the repugnance noted in society at large toward this topic. Such general feelings may logically account for the resistance to this kind of diagnosis, as reported by Silverman.

ATTITUDES OF DOCTORS AND SOCIAL WORKERS

The experience of the author as supervisor of social work students in Children's Hospital of Pittsburgh bears out the impression that many physicians do have strong feelings in this area. While some deal with the abused child and his parents in a very professional manner, this seems to depend largely on the personal qualities of the individual physician. Sometimes great resistance is shown toward the diagnostic impressions of the radiologist, and the attending physician may proceed quite independently without considering the implications of the radiologist's findings. Other physicians accept the conclusions of the radiologist but find it difficult to deal with the parents in an objective manner. Precipitate accusations may be made, which heighten the parents' defensiveness and make it virtually impossible to learn the facts in the situation. By tradition, social workers decry such attitudes on the part of the physician in this area and tend to blame him if he refers parents to social service in a threatening manner. Actually they, too, are much affected by the prevailing repugnance in relation to these children and their families.

Like the pediatrician and the orthopedist, the social worker may refuse to perceive the social significance of the roentgen survey that indicates repeated trauma over some period of time. Or he may distort the significance of the data he himself collects, accenting the positives and discounting pathological signs in the parents which are predictive of acting out against the child in impulsive and uncontrolled ways. Such distortion can lead to unrealistic planning for the child, which may result in grave danger for him. Again, it is occasionally possible to find cases involving suspected mistreatment that have been referred to the social worker but have not been pursued by him. There is always a plausible reason for this, but one begins to suspect that the ubiquitous repugnance is again being demonstrated.

Thus it appears that both the physician and the social worker are subject to the same kinds of feelings that can be observed in other segments of society in regard to these families. Two observations come to mind. First, strong feelings that operate outside conscious awareness can cause serious errors in the evaluation of the families and in planning for them. It follows that the more the feelings of professional people can be recognized, assessed, and dealt with, the greater will be their freedom of action in any sphere affecting the families and children involved.

RADICAL CHANGES IN CHILD-REARING

We think of these families as abnormal because they appear to have no qualms about excessively aggressive actions against children too young to understand the parents' rules. A different dimension is obtained if we recall that throughout most of recorded history these aggressive actions would have merited no more than passing attention from other members of society. It was only about a hundred and fifty years ago that the stirrings of public conscience in regard to children began to be expressed by a few enlightened persons.[8] Consider the lot of the child up to that point—in primitive groups and early civilized communities the object of widespread infanticide. So extensive was this practice that at one period of history from half to two-thirds of all infant lives were snuffed out at birth.[9] In ancient Rome the concept of *patria potestas* gave to the father absolute power over his children. Even in adulthood, when the children were in the father's house they could be sold into bondage, tortured, or killed.[10] Later, children were commonly bought and sold, exhibited in circuses, maimed to make them more appealing as beggars. In the seventeenth century the governess of a future king of France was instructed to whip him so he could be a better man; flogging began when the prince was barely two years old.[11] In our own country the early colonists regarded incorrigibility as just cause for the death penalty for children over 16.[12] And Calvinism dictated that only by complete breaking of the will could the young child be "saved" from his inborn evil spirit. Thus, we see in a parents' magazine of the early nineteenth century a report that smacks of the triumphant as the young mother describes how she whipped her 16-month-old daughter until the child would repeat the phrase, "Dear Mama."[13]

There were of course other elements in the relationships between parents and their

children, such as tenderness, affection, and concern for the children's welfare. The more barbaric side is emphasized here to point up the radical change in thinking about children that has occurred in the past hundred to a hundred and fifty years. This has been remarked by various writers. Margaret Mead notes the striking change in American thinking in this area between the nineteenth century, the early twentieth, and the present. She also reflects upon the tendency of Americans to push out of consciousness whatever customs they have outgrown.[14] In the matter of physical measures instituted against children, we seem indeed to have forgotten much of our own history as well as the history of the child in other parts of the world.

WHAT KINDS OF FAMILIES ARE INVOLVED?

So thoroughly have we incorporated present-day concepts regarding the importance of nurturing the young child, protecting him, and stimulating him toward maximum development, that it is startling to reflect on the differences of only a few score years ago. The second observation to be noted in this paper is really a question: How does it happen that certain families have remained insulated from these tremendous and crucial cultural changes? Might the study of the absence of acculturation in these families yield increased understanding of the positive acculturation process? It goes without saying that such increased understanding is much to be desired, for it would immeasurably enhance our ability to attack problems of mental health on a broad scale.

The presence in our society of a small number of grossly abused or neglected children is a challenge to the social work profession, one that justifies the most painstaking attention. There are many complicated ramifications of the problem which have not been touched on in this paper. To mention a few: How can these families

[8] I. Pinchbeck, "State and the Child in Sixteenth Century England," *British Journal of Sociology*, Vol. 7 (December 1956), pp. 273–285.

[9] James H. S. Bossard, *The Sociology of Child Development* (New York: Harper & Brothers, 1948), p. 596.

[10] Edward Gibbon, *The History of the Decline and Fall of the Roman Empire* (New York: The Macmillan Co., 1898), Vol. 4, pp. 473–474.

[11] Robert H. Lowie, *Are We Civilized?* (New York: Harcourt, Brace and Co., 1929), pp. 138–139.

[12] Alice Morse Earle, *Child Life in Colonial Days* (New York: The Macmillan Co., 1899), p. 7.

[13] Robert Sunley, "Early Nineteenth Century American Literature on Childrearing," in Margaret Mead and Martha Wolfenstein, eds., *Childhood in Contemporary Cultures* (Chicago: University of Chicago Press, 1955), pp. 150–167.

[14] Margaret Mead, *ibid.*, p. 3.

be helped to provide a safe environment for their children? What is the responsibility of the physician in these cases which, after the initial medical attention, are primarily social in nature? Does the care of these children in the hospital pose particular questions regarding the kinds of information to be included in medical charts? What are the complications for the family, the social worker, the physician, and the hospital in those instances where legal intervention is sought? What are the community resources to deal with this kind of family and their children? Perhaps the most important question is the kind of family, or more precisely, the kinds of families, with whom we are dealing. These and many more questions await further study. In the opinion of this author, sober attention needs to be paid to the professional blind spot noted in this paper before we shall be in a position to answer any of the important questions regarding abused children in the hospital, and their families.

Child abuse: an emerging social priority

Stephen Antler

In recent years, child abuse has emerged as a social priority of national importance, largely through concerned physicians' efforts to make it so. Grafting a medical approach onto what has been a social work concern, though, has had serious, perhaps unfortunate, consequences for social work policy, practice, and education.

Stephen Antler, DSW, is Associate Professor and Chairman, Social Policy Sequence, School of Social Work, Boston University, Boston, Massachusetts. A longer version of this paper was presented at the 22nd Annual Program Meeting of the Council on Social Work Education, Philadelphia, Pennsylvania, February–March 1976.

IN THE PAST 15 YEARS, through the efforts of a small group of concerned physicians, child abuse—particularly child battering—has emerged as a social issue of seemingly great significance. Although medical interest in child abuse was first stimulated by radiologists who reported multiple bone breaks in very young children in the 1940s and 1950s, it was not until 1961, when Kempe and his associates at the Denver Medical Center coined the diagnostic term "battered child syndrome," that public and professional interest in child abuse began to develop.[1]

Aided by their high status, professional credibility, and political sophistication, these physicians mounted a successful campaign to focus public attention on child abuse as a problem whose incidence was growing to epidemic proportions. The strategy of dramatizing the issue through publicity in the lay and professional press, the use of the emotionally charged term "battered child syndrome," and the claim that child abuse was a problem not solely the province of the poor, galvanized a national coalition of physicians, social workers, legislators, federal officials, and the public in the interest of combating child abuse. However, grafting a medical approach onto what has been recognized traditionally as a social work concern has had serious, perhaps unfortunate, consequences for social work policy, practice, and education.

Years ago, social workers who were concerned with child protection realized that to prevent abuse and neglect they had to become involved not only in strengthening the family through social casework, but also in alleviating the causes of social problems by establishing a broad program of legislative change, community action, and family reconstruction. The community action approach to child protection was pioneered at the turn of the century by the Massachusetts Society for the Prevention of Cruelty to Children (SPCC) under the leadership of Carstens. It superseded the law enforcement emphasis of the first child protective agencies. According to law enforcement criteria, SPCC workers had to contend with infant mortality, birth registration, child labor, pauperism, dependency, and venereal infection—all seen as directly related to "cruelty." By 1920, the New York SPCC had also begun to broaden its program to include family and community reconstruction.[2] This broad-based approach to the problem of child protection, which developed over a 50-year period, has been dramatically altered in the past few years.

With the conquest of most major causes of infant and child mortality, improved public health services, and a rising standard of living, child abuse presented itself as a new frontier for involvement by the medical profession—to fill a leadership void created by the failure of public and voluntary social service agencies to develop innovative preventive and treatment programs needed to assist troubled families.

INFLUENCE OF PHYSICIANS

A noteworthy hospital-based child abuse treatment program was pioneered by Kempe and associates at the Denver Medical Center in the early 1960s. The Denver program incorporates an interdisciplinary treatment team, led by a pediatrician, that includes a psychiatrist, nurse, social worker, attorney, and lay therapist—all available 24 hours a day.[3] Although it is an innovative attempt to deal with the complexities of helping families in trouble, the Denver program has been criticized for its limited applicability. The program requires large investments of professional staff time but can serve only a small number of clients. In addition, unlike publicly operated protective services, hospital-based treatment programs can select or reject those who come to use their facilities. Hospital-based programs, moreover, tend to emphasize cases of severe abuse, a small minority of the total incidence of abuse and neglect.

As a consequence of involvement by physicians in the early 1960s, for the first time in the history of child protection, child abuse was identified as primarily a medical problem requiring the leadership of physicians for its resolution. Despite criticism, hospital-

Reprinted from SOCIAL WORK, 23 (January 1978), pp. 58–61.

based treatment programs have become models for treatment and have garnered public attention. Further evidence of the influence of physicians in the area of child protection is also suggested in statements by physicians calling for treatment programs to operate in medical facilities under medical leadership, leaving child protective agencies the responsibility of receiving and investigating reports.[4]

Physicians have also been prominent in developing the strategy of "reporting," the framework on which most legislative activity on child abuse has focused.[5] However, the reporting-law concept, conceived to encourage the involvement of physicians, has had unforeseen consequences.

First, because the reporting-law idea was adopted in some form by virtually every state within 5 years of its introduction, a momentum was created that contributed to a sense of urgency. The existence of reporting mechanisms has triggered an increased number of reports, estimated to have reached 600,000 per year (a significant proportion unsubstantiated), but has not resolved the question of whether child abuse really is a growing problem of crisis or epidemic proportions.[6]

Second, the increase in legislative activity promoted the illusion that treatment and helping resources were available in sufficient quantity to meet the demand; in fact, these programs were few in number and limited in scope.

And third, the emphasis on reporting, focused on identification and investigation, reflects 19th century child protective concerns that stressed locating parents and establishing their guilt or innocence. In combination with the child-battering label, the reporting laws contribute to a general public sentiment that child abuse is caused by essentially vicious and depraved parents who should not be permitted to raise children.

IMPLICATIONS

Because of the influence of physicians in child abuse cases, the tendency to view child abuse as a disease has been exaggerated. This view was stated by Fraser of the Denver program who noted that child abuse is "an infectious disease" whose carrier is the parent, with the child as victim.[7] The metaphor is reinforced by evidence that the abusing parent is recreating conditions experienced in his or her own childhood. The child abuse virus lies dormant in an abused child until, as an adult, the appropriate growth medium is provided.

Further emphasis affords considerable attention to the disease concept by identifying characteristic psychopathologic factors in child abuse situations. Pollock and Steele, for example, indicate that abusing parents have infantile personalities, while Morris and Gould find that abusing parents reverse roles with their children and seek reassurance and mothering from them.[8] Kempe and Helfer also note that the characteristic problem of abusing parents, as identified by the Denver program, is a need for sympathetic mothering denied them in their own childhood.[9] Gelles, criticizing child abuse research and theory, has diagrammed it as a linear psychopathological model: childhood deprivation leads to a variety of psychopathic states, that then lead to child abuse.[10] Despite the tendency to emphasize the psychopathology of abusers, there is general agreement among physicians and social workers that fewer than 10 percent of parents who abuse children are psychotic, sociopathic, or otherwise severely mentally ill.

The programs designed by teams of physicians working in child abuse have often been more broadly based than the disease concept suggests. For example, the Denver program and other hospital-based services provide short-term relief from child rearing, and social services and psychotherapy for families requiring help. This emphasis on offering concrete social services is based on a growing understanding that child abuse often occurs when parents are under severe and unremitting stress. Events causing this stress are generally understood to be associated with social problems outside the families' immediate control (unemployment, poverty, poor housing, lack of adequate health care, and so on) and not based on individual psychopathology.

Though the association of abuse and neglect with poverty and unemployment is unmistakable, medical commentators point out that abuse crosses class lines (though this claim is unsupported by reports actually made by registries). Exposing middle-class abuse is in one sense laudable, since it relieves the beleaguered poor of the total societal burden. However, such revelations also strengthen the impression that abuse is caused simply by poor parenting, thus further deflecting attention from the socioeconomic factors.

The involvement of physicians in the identification and treatment of child abuse has helped focus attention on a problem previously hidden from medical, and often, public view. More attention is now paid to the need for protective intervention, though, unfortunately, this has had little impact on the availability of other helping services. The recent resurgence of interest in child protection, however, has generated new problems. In spite of the tendency of hospital-based programs to respond to child abuse situations with social services, few physicians discuss the broad social policy implications suggested by the maltreatment of children.

Instead, their involvement in child protection has reinforced the notion that the solution to child maltreatment lies in the rehabilitation of the parent.

ABUSE VERSUS NEGLECT

In emphasizing physical abuse, the medical model has diverted attention from neglect, the less obvious though more widespread form of maltreatment. Also, the emphasis on child abuse as an epidemic may have created an atmosphere of suspicion of families that experience nondeliberate accidents or deaths of children and are genuinely distressed by them. Furthermore, civil liberties organizations, concerned that life-style could become a variable in evaluating neglect, have begun to question the appropriateness of requiring mandatory reports of both abuse and neglect and are seeking to narrow the range of reportable events.[11]

Social work practice, which is traditionally vulnerable to shifts in public emphasis, has become identified with the medical model of child protection. Protective units of public child welfare agencies now emphasize the physical effects of maltreatment, as does most current practice literature. In the past, because of experience in child protection, social work recognized neglect as the more prevalent problem and called for a broad attack on its underlying social causes; however, this view has itself become a victim of "professional neglect."

Medical and social work emphasis on child abuse has diverted energies from constructing a congenial environment for family life. Such an environment requires fundamental social supports—such as the provision of adequate income, health care and child development programs—to the development of each family member. The growth of policy and programs on child abuse, however, has not proceeded from a conception of strategies designed to accomplish these goals, but rather reflects calls for immediate action generated by a crisis atmosphere.

Child abuse has in effect entered the "issue-attention cycle," in which dramatic events of a seemingly emergency nature are catapulted to public attention. However, attention rapidly diminishes as the public, bored with repetition of the issue and distressed when the real social costs of solving the problem become known, moves on to a newer social problem.[12]

APPROACH MUST SHIFT

Solving the problem of child abuse and neglect requires a fundamental realignment of public priorities, one that accepts the necessity of attacking the social and economic conditions associated with abuse and neglect, such as poverty, unemployment, and inadequate housing.[13] These conditions are disproportionately represented in the ranks of abusing parents. An attack on these problems must be high on the agenda of any program designed

to improve the capacities of families to provide a positive nurturing environment for their children. Programs designed to provide better health care and to educate parents for child rearing, in addition to day care services and aids to relieve young parents of some of the pressures of child rearing, are required as part of a massive effort to strengthen the capacities of families to rear children.

Although abuse and neglect are associated with poverty and unemployment, other more subtle erosions of family life can be found in the rising rates of divorce, juvenile delinquency, and runaway children, and the growing importance to the young of the peer group as a substitute for the family. These problems point to the need for a more holistic concept of the needs of the child and the family, rather than single-purpose, fragmented, problem-oriented programs.[14]

Family needs, however, are now a residual rather than a central concern of public policy. Consequently, the system for investigating, reporting, and treating child abuse does little to change conditions that are at the root of child abuse—the deteriorating status of the family in society.

Improving the condition of the family requires a national policy that provides for a full measure of social welfare programs and personal and health services designed to integrate the family into the community and offer help to all families, particularly during the critical child-raising years. Although many western European nations have developed such programs, the United States remains in this sense "underdeveloped."[15]

It is important that social work education build a broad understanding of policy questions affecting the family. Preparation for practice must balance the tendency of the profession to define practice narrowly, thus losing sight of the broader policy issues with which the child welfare movement has historically concerned itself.

Years ago social workers concerned with child welfare focused their efforts on a dual strategy of family rehabilitation and social action to foster social and economic change. By forging

coalitions with labor unions, voluntary organizations, and other professions, they were able to obtain numerous reforms now integrated into public policy. Since that period social services and social work education have emphasized child-helping and rehabilitative activities and deemphasized social action.

Emphasis on the importance of various forms of advocacy in social work education suggests movement toward practice objectives that place social justice on a higher level of importance. This emphasis must be buttressed by the development of skills in policy analysis to assure that practitioners will develop the conceptual skill to pursue broader social welfare agendas.

Social work program development is particularly vulnerable to the issue-attention cycle, since program priorities are established in the marketplace and in the media. In a democratic society this is desirable and unavoidable; therefore, social work training must also emphasize an understanding of this process as well as skill in utilizing it to achieve policy ends.

The case of child abuse illustrates the need for social work to publicize and defend its unique conceptions of human needs, developed from the experience of practice, the insights of social science, and the values of the profession. By applying professional values, insight, and experience, social work can recapture the inspiration of early social work leaders and build on their special view of practice.

NOTES AND REFERENCES

1. *See,* for example, Paul V. Wooley, Jr. and William A. Evans, Jr., "Significance of Skeletal Lesions in Infants Resembling Those of Traumatic Origin," *Journal of the American Medical Association,* 158 (June 1955), pp. 539–543; C. Henry Kempe, Frederick N. Silverman, Brandt Steele, William Dregmuller, and Henry Silver, "The Battered Child Syndrome," *Journal of the American Medical Association,* 181 (July 1962), pp. 17–24; and Samuel X. Radbill, "A History of Child Abuse and Infanticide," in Ray E. Helfer and Kempe, eds., *The Battered Child* (Chicago: University of Chicago Press, 1968), p. 16.

2. *See,* for example, Carl C. Carstens, "The Development of Social Work for Child Protection," *The Annals of the American Academy of Political and Social Science,* 98 (November 1921), pp. 135–142; Carstens, "The Prevention of Cruelty to Children," *Proceedings of the Academy of Political Science,* 2 (1911–12), 613–619; Carstens, "Who Shall Protect the Children," *Survey,* 51 (1923–24), pp. 92–96; William J. Schultz, *The Humane Movement in the United States, 1910–1922* (New York: AMS Press, 1968); Roswell McCrea, *The Humane Movement* (College Park, Md.: McGrath Publishing Co., 1910); and George Mangold, *Problems of Child Welfare* (New York: Macmillan Co., 1914).

3. *See,* for example, C. Henry Kempe and Ray Helfer, "Innovative Therapeutic Approaches," *Helping the Battered Child and His Family* (Philadelphia: J. B. Lippincott Co., 1972), pp. 41–54; and Kempe and Helfer, "The Responsibility and Role of the Physician," *The Battered Child,* pp. 43–57.

4. *Child Protection Report,* 1 (November 1975).

5. *See* Monrad Paulsen et al., "Child Abuse Reporting Laws: Some Legislative History," *George Washington Law Review,* 34 (March 1966), p. 488. *See also* Carroll Lucht, "Providing a Legislative Base for Reporting Child Abuse," *Fourth National Symposium on Child Abuse* (Denver: American Humane Association, 1975).

6. Saad Z. Nagi, "Child Abuse and Neglect Programs: A National Overview," *Children Today,* 4 (May-June 1975), pp. 13–17.

7. *Child Protection Report,* 2 (January 1976), p. 2.

8. Brandt F. Steele and Carl B. Pollock, "A Psychiatric Study of Parents Who Abuse Infants and Small Children," in Helfer and Kempe, eds., *The Battered Child;* and Marian G. Morris and Robert W. Gould, "Role Reversal: A Necessary Concept in Dealing with the Battered Child Syndrome," *American Journal of Orthopsychiatry,* 33 (March 1963), pp. 298–299.

9. Kempe and Helfer, "Innovative Therapeutic Approaches," *Helping the Battered Child and His Family,* pp. 41–54; and Kempe and Helfer, "The Responsibility and Role of the Physician," *The Battered Child,* pp. 43–57.

10. Richard J. Gelles, "Child Abuse as Psychopathology: A Sociological Critique and Reformulation," *American Journal of Orthopsychiatry,* 43 (1973), pp. 612–621.

11. Personal communication with Vincent de Francis, former director, Children's Division, American Humane Association. *See also, Child Protection Report,* 1 (November 1975).

12. Anthony Downs, "Up and Down with Ecology, The Issue-Attention Cycle," *Public Interest,* (Summer 1972), pp. 39–50.

13. *See,* for example, David G. Gil, *Violence Against Children* (Cambridge, Mass.: Harvard University Press, 1971), for a penetrating analysis of cultural influences on child abuse.

14. For a more detailed presentation of the public policy questions, *see* Urie Bronfenbrenner, "The Challenge of Social Change to Public Policy and Developmental Research." Paper presented to the Society for Research in Child Development (Denver, Colo.: April 12, 1975) (mimeographed); and David G. Gil, "A Holistic Approach on Child Abuse and Its Prevention." (mimeographed, 1974).

15. *See* Alfred J. Kahn and Sheila Kamerman, *Not for the Poor Alone: European Social Services* (Philadelphia: Temple University Press, 1975). ◀

Child abusers as parents and children: a review

Srinika Jayaratne

Are the assumptions about child abuse based on valid evidence? The author analyzes the documentation in the literature concerning two widely held beliefs about child-abusing parents and suggests further study that is needed.

Srinika Jayaratne, Ph.D., is Assistant Professor of Social Work, University of Oklahoma, Norman. The preparation of this article was facilitated by the bibliography collected under HEW Grant No. 84-P 96805/0–01, directed by Diane Green, MSW, Assistant Professor of Sociology, Washington State University, Pullman.

CHILD ABUSE is an ugly fact of life that is difficult to understand. The dimensions of the problem are tremendous as seen in the following statistics. In 1972 alone, according to Nagi, approximately 600,000 children were reported to local protective service agencies for abuse, neglect, or both.[1] Cohen and Sussman estimate that each year an additional 325,000 cases are unreported.[2] Even though the various states use diverse reporting procedures and definitions so that the figures on which this estimate is based are somewhat inconsistent, the total is still staggering.[3]

A recurring statement in the literature is the notion that "child abuse is not committed just by them"—that is, people of the lower classes.[4] As Hopkins has indicated, "an observer would find these people to be very much like any other group of parents."[5] In one of the first and most significant studies on child abuse, Gil surveyed the attitudes and opinions of a national random sample. Nearly 23 percent of the respondents thought they could at some time injure a child.[6]

Many professionals have argued that not age, sex, race, occupation, education, or income has any direct and significant correlation with child abuse.[7] According to this position, the abuse of children and the potential for such abuse are representative characteristics of parents in the United States. Although this may be a legitimate statement, it is not substantiated by empirical evidence; furthermore, it is debated in the literature. Gil, for example, points out that "physical abuse of children . . . was found to be over-concentrated among the poor and among non-white minorities."[8] Galdston, Gelles, and Paulson and Blake have reported similar findings.[9] Others claim that these findings involve reporting biases and institutional racism.[10]

The relationship of ethnic background to child abuse is pointed up in the following statement by Blanchard: "In my nine years with the Bureau of Indian Affairs, I am not aware of a single case of child abuse among Pueblo Indians."[11] Although this statement does not indicate that child abuse is nonexistent among Pueblo Indians, it raises critical questions about the definition of abuse and about the imposition of sociocultural values and norms on different ethnic groups.

Variance in definition and in cultural values are phenomena that are little explained and researched in child abuse. Philosophically, Gil is probably right in stating that the root cause of the problem lies in the social class structure of this society and that the solution lies in the elimination of poverty and degradation.[12] Unfortunately, even those who agree with Gil's view admit that the revolutionary changes he proposes are unlikely to occur for a long time. It is perhaps, then, practicality that has led the majority of clinical workers to concentrate their interventive efforts on the psychosocial phenomena related to child abuse. Most of the writings in the area pertain to the psychological makeup of the abusing parent, and their authors probably subscribe to Steele's proposition:

> Basic and constant in the instigation of abuse is the psychologic set of the parent which creates a recognizable style or pattern of parent-child interaction in which abuse is likely to happen.[13]

Although this proposition sounds reasonable enough, the total picture of child abuse is much more complex and bewildering. For example, as Steele and Pollock note:

> Child abusers have been described as "immature," "impulse ridden," "dependent." . . . Such adjectives are essentially appropriate to those who abuse children, yet these qualities are so prevalent among people in general that they add little to specific understanding.[14]

In a sense, this is a contradictory statement, but a significant one nonetheless. The literature is replete with these and other such terms describing abusing parents, and it is an arduous task to search for their origin.

The intent of this article is to analyze the two most common sociocultural statements about abusing parents in terms of their empirical and clinical validity. The author is not concerned with the myriad definitions

Reprinted from SOCIAL WORK, 22 (January 1977), pp. 5–9.

of abuse, but rather will review the literature and systematically evaluate the data base of the notions (1) that child abusers are inadequate parents and (2) that child abusers experienced abuse themselves as children.

PARENTAL INADEQUACY

It is an unfortunate social reality that parenting is primarily a generational art. Schools and institutions in the United States provide information on family planning and birth control, but offer little assistance with the care and upbringing of progeny. It is therefore not surprising to find that most people rely on their "parental instincts," personal experiences, and self-selected readings and observations when it comes to child rearing.

In essence, all of us are inadequately socialized to the role of parent. Inadequacy as used in the literature is a generic term that encompasses all facets of parental incapacity. The first question, then, that emerges is this: Why do only some parents abuse their children? The generational hypothesis —that abuse leads to abuse—has been the primary answer. This is not to say that there are no other causal factors, but rather that this one is the most prominently mentioned in the literature. In pursuing this proposition two related questons emerge: Are the abusing parents more inadequate in their parenting than the nonabusing parents? If they are, how do the abusing and the nonabusing differ?

De Lissovoy studied a group of nonabusing teenage parents over a period of three years. He reported that in general his subjects tended to be impatient, irritable, and prone to use punishment in their interactions with their children. Furthermore, they were unfamiliar with developmental norms, and followed their own parents' advice of "doing what comes naturally." [15] Abusing parents have been systematically described as interacting in similar ways. This then raises the basic question of stylistic differences between abusing and nonabusing parents.

Some agencies and organizations recognize that parental inadequacy is the norm and have attempted to rec-

"Schools and institutions in the United States provide information on family planning and birth control, but offer little assistance with the care and upbringing of progeny."

tify the situation by launching educational programs. In Pittsburgh, an experimental project begins parent education before the child is born; in Oklahoma City, mental health authorities distribute booklets to new parents describing the needs of the newborn.[16] These are examples of preventive efforts being directed to average parents, regardless of the potential for abuse. Such programs are particularly valuable since the basic philosophy of the laws of the United States gives parents broad freedom in child-rearing.[17] Unusual circumstances must arise before the child's rights receive attention.

Given the natural risk of inadequate parenting and the probability that among child abusers other interacting variables will compound the problems even further, those concerned with the welfare of children may well agree with Hammell that the "responsibility to assess parental capacity is inescapable and is the core of professional knowledge." [18] On the other hand, the following statements that are presented as a sine qua non in the clinical arena seem open to question:

1. "The distinguishing features of the abusing parents were their attitudes toward discipline and child-rearing." [19]

2. "Parenting is learned, and battering parents have usually been taught some very potent lessons by their own parents." [20]

In the opinion of this author, there is little or no empirical evidence to substantiate the idea that abusing parents follow parenting practices that are significantly different from those of nonabusing parents. This statement is made in view of the lack of comparison group studies to test that assumption.

Consider the following reviews of the literature or of clinical case studies of child abuse. Kaufman, reviewing the

work of Steele and his colleagues in Denver, reported that "the common denominator of all their patients who abused children was a pattern of child-rearing characterized by premature demand for high performance." [21] This is, however, an empirical question requiring the presence of a nonabusing comparison group. Similarly, Paulson and Blake, in considering studies of child abuse, point out that "inappropriate and distorted concepts of the nature and limits of discipline in child rearing are generally noted in the literature." [22] Here again, the conclusions were drawn from studies of abusing parents only, not from comparison of the abusing and the nonabusing. Nonetheless, the need for retraining in the parenting styles of abusers has been expressed vehemently by many authors.[23]

Roth presented clinical procedures for intervention with abusing parents and suggested that the teaching of parenting be a central part of the treatment regimen.[24] Burland, Andrews, and Headsten—in reviewing the record of 28 abused or severely neglected children—pointed out that inadequate parenting was expressed in a wide variety of behaviors.[25] Steele and Pollock studied 60 abusing families intensively for a period of five years and concluded that these parents made inappropriate demands and had unrealistic expectations regarding the capabilities of their children.[26] In the one control group study that the author encountered, Melnick and Hurley found that the abusing parents exhibited general difficulties with parenting, especially with regard to empathy toward their children.[27] However, the validity of this study is minimized by the small sample size.

REPARENTING

It is perhaps fair to say that the literature of child abuse agrees virtually unanimously that an educational program in reparenting is a critical factor in the treatment regimen. The two major reviews of the literature in the area by Lystad and Spinetta and Rigler essentially came to that conclusion.[28] However, three critical questions need to be answered prior to proceeding with intervention:

1. If all parents are potential abusers, how different are the child-rearing practices of the abusers and the nonabusers? Here the issues of definition and culture seem to transcend the problem. Blumenthal, Chadiha, Cole, and Jayaratne, reporting on a national study of attitudes toward violence, state that 48 percent of all respondents and 66 percent of black respondents indicated that under certain circumstances they would punish their children by hitting them with a belt or paddle.[29] Is this child abuse? If it is, does this mean that a massive national program of parent education is needed?

2. Are those involved in reparenting aware of and sensitive to cultural differences in child-rearing practices, or are they applying the middle-class yardstick as the criterion? Little is known about child-rearing practices in general, and even less is known about those of cultural and ethnic minorities. The work of Hoffman and Salzstein, among others, provides evidence that class differences exist in child rearing.[30] Similarly, Blumenthal et al note that "it is clear from the data that black respondents have very different norms about the use of physical punishment than do whites in the sample."[31] Given Gil's findings about the prevalence of abuse among the lower classes and the inherent probability of biased reporting, is a problem being created when it does not exist or a different value system being imposed when it should not be?[32]

3. What or whose child-rearing practices are being transmitted in parenting classes? Perhaps one could argue that socioemotional and affective aspects of parent-child interaction are sufficiently universal that they transcend class and culture. Also it is quite feasible to teach parents developmental norms without imposing values. What about discipline and parental expectations? Are these not affected by class and culture? Can values be dissociated from convictions in this sensitive area? Tracy and Clark maintain that, in the treatment of child abusers, similarity in racial (and possibly socioeconomic) background will engender a better therapeutic relationship.[33] Training in clinical procedures, however, should play a critical and significant role in the entire process. In the long run, the training of those conducting parent education classes, their background, and the ideas they are transmitting must be systematically evaluated.

GENERATIONAL HYPOTHESIS

The generational phenomenon of child abuse is one of the most commonly held conceptions (or misconceptions) about abusing parents. The essence of this proposition is that the victim of abuse incorporates patterns of aggression, which are then repeated from generation to generation. This position is illustrated in the works of numerous authors.[34]

Even a superficial survey of the literature reveals that many subscribe to the premise that "out of the ranks of today's maltreated children . . . will emerge tomorrow's maltreating parents."[35] In a review article, for example, Wasserman argued that battering parents felt that their own parents were punishing them when they were rejected.[36] Burland et al. in their review of 28 case records indicated that "parents who abuse their children usually themselves were abused as children."[37] Helfer, discussing the etiology of child abuse, said that abusing parents "invariably have had some kind of disastrous rearing experience when they were small."[38]

Despite the formidable array of authors and studies, Kadushin, in reviewing the literature, concluded: "There is little valid evidence to support the theory that abusive parents were themselves abused as children."[39] The need for validity in the evidence reported in the literature is an important point. A major and continuing problem with respect to validity is the lack of a normative comparison group. Also, the findings in a significant national study by Gil show that only 14.1 percent of the mothers and 7 percent of the fathers in the abusing sample had been victims of abuse in their childhood.[40]

EMOTIONAL ABUSE

It appears, then, that Lystad's review article, concluding that the generational phenomenon is "particularly well documented in the study of child abuse," is questionable, even from a purely definitional perspective.[41] For example, Steele and Pollock found that "several" of their subjects had experienced severe abuse but "a few reported never having a hand laid on them."[42] The primary causal factor appeared to be emotional stress rather than physical abuse per se. What explanation, then, can be offered for the presence of nonabused parents in this abusing sample? Similarly, Fontana concluded that abusing parents were emotionally crippled because of unfortunate childhood experiences.[43] Young reported that approximately 51 percent of the abusing parents in her study came from homes where they were physically abused or neglected—"more from neglecting"—but that no direct attempt was made to evaluate these circumstances.[44] In both these studies, the evidence seems tangential at best.

Silver, Dublin, and Lourie studied the case records of 34 suspected and proved battered children over a period of four years. They concluded that "the child who experiences violence as a child has the potential of becoming a violent member of society in the future."[45] These authors, however, were referring to generalized violence rather than to child abuse. Similar conclusions were reached via case-record analysis by Morris, Gould, and Matthews and by McHenry, Girdnay, and Elmer.[46] All these studies are fraught with the inherent weaknesses of the analytic procedures involved, such as differential recording and differences in interpretation.

In addition to the methodological weaknesses, there appears to be confusion of definitions between the generations. Whereas the vast majority of

> *"In the opinion of this author there is little or no empirical evidence to substantiate the idea that abusing parents follow parenting practices that are significantly different from those of nonabusing parents."*

child abuse studies deal with physical injury to the child, the etiological descriptions of parental experiences is not as clear-cut. As an illustration, consider the study by Tuteur and Glotzer, which looked at ten mothers who murdered their children. Not even a hint of physical abuse is evident in the mothers' backgrounds. "All of them grew up in emotionally cold, and often directly rejecting family environments." [47] Could it not be said, then, that "emotional abuse" and "physical abuse" are being considered as a single phenomenon? If they are a single phenomenon, then the sample is biased when only hospital cases, or other cases in which physical damage was done, are being evaluated. If they are different phenomena, then equating the two in etiological analyses will result in inaccurate and unreliable data. Whether they should be considered together or separately is an issue for discussion in the literature. [48]

When variance and inconsistency in definition exist and when the validity of evidence is questionable, important clinical questions such as these are likely to arise:

■ If abuse is a generational phenomenon, what happened to the adult siblings of the abusing parents? Although physical violence could conceivably be directed at only one child in a family, some studies suggest generalized abuse of all the brothers and sisters as the norm. [49] In addition, it is known that aggressive behavior is learned through observation and modeling. This theoretical perspective, then, leads to the need to study the adult siblings of abusing parents. Could it be that these siblings also are abusing their children but have escaped detection? If the generational phenomenon is viable, such a study might lead to the detection and prevention of further child abuse. If the generational hypothesis is not valid,

significant clinical data could be gathered as to why these siblings did not grow up to be abusing parents.

■ How different are the childhood experiences of abusing parents from their nonabusing counterparts? This obviously requires experimental studies utilizing comparison groups. [50] Furthermore, if such studies are to be truly productive, they must differentiate between the concepts of emotional and physical abuse.

■ Can it really be said that childhood experience is a valid predictor of adult behavior? This is purely a methodological issue, and pertains to the temporal aspects of the generational phenomenon. Furthermore, available data do not substantiate the direct and significant correlation that —according to the generational hypothesis—exists between abuse experience and abusing behavior. It is perhaps too simplistic to argue that innumerable events occurred during the period under consideration (from the time the parents allegedly were abused until the time they were abusing their own children) and that some of these happenings might explain much of the variance. This is nonetheless true, and the simplicity of the explanation belies the complexity of the picture.

CONCLUSION

In general, the literature suggests that parental inadequacy and misinformation are major contributing factors to child abuse. Where the studies in the literature fail is in the examination and delineation of different parenting styles between abusing and nonabusing family systems. This qualitative difference should be investigated from different cultural perspectives before parent training programs are implemented. The failure to base clinical intervention on empirical data is likely to result in redundant effort and little

success. As Oettinger points out, it is imperative to discover "the factors which contribute to parental inability to provide proper care for their young." [51]

With regard to the generational hypothesis of child abuse, the author is somewhat skeptical. Although, as Zalba maintains, "the epidemiological implications are rather serious," the literature is spotted with definitional confusion, poor methodology, clinical assumptions, and a definite "Rosenthal Effect"—that is, fulfilling a priori expectations of the research. [52] Virtually every clinical study encountered in carrying out the research on which this article is based delved into the notion that abuse leads to abuse and virtually all emerged successful—that is, emerged proving the notion. There is little doubt that experiential and observational learning play a significant role in parenting practices, but the available data on the generational hypothesis do not stand the test of empiricism. If this perspective is to be clinically legitimate, it must be empirically validated.

NOTES AND REFERENCES

1. Saad Z. Nagi, "Child Abuse and Neglect Programs: A National Overview," *Children Today*, 4 (May–June 1975), pp. 13–17.

2. Stephen J. Cohen and Alan Sussman, "The Incidence of Child Abuse in the United States," *Child Welfare*, 54 (June 1975), pp. 432–443.

3. Ibid, p. 16.

4. Richard G. Farrow, "Violence," *The National Humane Review* (September 1972), p. 13.

5. Joan Hopkins, "The Nurse and the Abused Child," *Nursing Clinics of North America*, 5 (December 1970), p. 590.

6. David G. Gil, *Violence Against Children* (Massachusetts: Harvard University Press, 1970), p. 138.

7. Brandt F. Steele, "Working With Abusive Parents: A Psychiatrist's View," *Children Today*, 4 (May–June 1975), pp. 3–5; and Sidney Wasserman, "The Abused Parent of the Abused Child," *Children*, 4 (1967), pp. 175–179.

8. David G. Gil, "A Socio-Cultural Perspective on Physical Child Abuse," *Child Welfare*, 50 (July 1971), p. 392.

9. Richard Galdston, "Observations on Children Who Have Been Physically Abused and Their Parents," *American*

Journal of Psychiatry, 122 (April 1965), pp. 440–443; Richard Gelles, "Child Abuse As Psychopathology: A Sociological Critique and Reformulation," *American Journal of Orthopsychiatry,* 43 (July 1973), pp. 611–621; and Morris J. Paulson and Phillip R. Blake, "The Physically Abused Child: A Focus On Prevention," *Child Welfare,* 48 (February 1969), pp. 86–95.

10. Richard J. Light, "Abused and Neglected Children in America: A Study of Alternative Policies," *Harvard Educational Review,* 43 (1975), pp. 556–596; and John J. Spinetta and David Rigler, "The Child Abusing Parent: A Psychological Review," *Psychological Bulletin,* 77 (April 1972), pp. 296–304.

11. Evelyn L. Blanchard, *The American Indian Perspective* (Albuquerque, N. M.: Bureau of Indian Affairs), p. 126. (Mimeographed.)

12. Gil, *Violence Against Children.*

13. Brandt F. Steele, "Parental Abuse of Parents and Small Children," in Elwyn J. Anthony and Therese Benedek, eds., *Parenthood* (Boston: Little, Brown & Co., 1970), p. 450.

14. Brandt F. Steele and Carl B. Pollock, "The Battered Child's Parents," in Arlene S. Skolnick and Jerome H. Skolnick, eds., *Family in Transition* (Boston: Little, Brown & Co., 1971), p. 360.

15. Vladimir De Lissovoy, "Child Care By Adolescent Parents," *Children Today,* 2 (July–August 1973), pp. 22–25.

16. *See* Stephanie Murphy, "Children's Programs: Meeting Some of the Needs," *Innovations,* 3 (Fall 1975), p. 24.

17. Michael G. Paulsen, "The Law and Abused Children," in Ray E. Helfer and C. Henry Kempe, eds., *The Battered Child* (Chicago: University of Chicago Press, 1968).

18. Charlotte L. Hammell, "Preserving Family Life for Children," *Child Welfare,* 10 (December 1969), p. 41.

19. Hopkins, op. cit., p. 590.

20. Elizabeth Davoren, "Working with Abusive Parents: A Social Worker's View," *Children Today,* 4 (May–June 1975), p. 87.

21. Irving Kaufman, "The Physically Abused Child," in Nancy B. Ebeling and Deborah A. Hill, eds., *Child Abuse Intervention and Treatment* (New York: Publishing Science, 1975), p. 81.

22. Paulson and Blake, op. cit., p. 87.

23. *See,* for example, J. Alexis Burland, Roberta G. Andrews, and Sally J. Headsten, "Child Abuse: One Tree In the Forest," *Child Welfare,* 52 (November 1973), pp. 585–592; Davoren, op. cit.;

Hammell, op. cit.; Joan C. Holter and Stanford B. Friedman, "Principles of Management In Child Abuse Cases," *American Journal of Orthopsychiatry,* 38 (January 1968), pp. 127–135; Hopkins, op. cit.; Alfred Kadushin, *Child Welfare Services* (New York: Macmillan Co., 1974); Barry Melnick and John R. Hurley, "Distinctive Personality Attributes of Child-Abusing Mothers," *Journal of Consulting and Clinical Psychology,* 33 (December 1969), pp. 746–749; Frederick Roth, "A Practice Regimen for Diagnosis and Treatment of Child Abuse," *Child Welfare,* 54 (April 1975), pp. 268–273; Steele, "Working with Abusive Parents: A Psychiatrist's View"; Steele and Pollock, op. cit.; and Wasserman, op. cit.

24. Roth, op. cit.

25. Burland, Andrews, and Headsten, op. cit.

26. Steele and Pollock, op. cit.

27. Melnick and Hurley, op. cit.

28. Mary H. Lystad, "Violence At Home: A Review of the Literature," *American Journal of Orthopsychiatry,* 45 (April 1975), pp. 328–344; and Spinetta and Rigler, op. cit., pp. 296–304.

29. *See* Monica D. Blumenthal, Letha B. Chadiha, Gerald A. Cole, and Toby E. Jayaratne, *More About Justifying Violence* (Ann Arbor: University of Michigan, Institute for Social Research, 1975).

30. *See* Martin L. Hoffman and Herbert D. Salzstein, "Parent Discipline and the Child's Moral Development," *Journal of Personality and Social Psychology,* 5 (January 1967), pp. 45–57.

31. Blumenthal et al., op. cit.

32. Gil, "A Socio-Cultural Perspective on Physical Child Abuse."

33. James J. Tracy and Elizabeth H. Clark, "Treatment for Child Abusers," *Social Work,* 19 (May 1974), p. 339.

34. *See,* for example, Burland, Andrews, and Headsten, op. cit.; James D. Delsordo, "Protective Casework for Abused Children," *Children,* 1 (November–December 1963), pp. 46–51; Vincent J. Fontana, "Further Reflections on Maltreatment of Children," *New York State Journal of Medicine,* 68 (1968), pp. 2214–2215; Galdston, op. cit.; Gil, *Violence Against Children;* Ray E. Helfer, *The Diagnostic Process and Treatment Programs* (Washington, D. C.: U.S. Department of Health, Education & Welfare, 1975); Paulson and Blake, op. cit.; Larry B. Silver, Christina C. Dublin, and Reginald S. Lourie, "Does Violence Breed Violence?" *American Journal of Psychiatry,* 126 (March 1969), pp. 404–407; Steele and Pollock, op. cit.; and Wasserman, op. cit.

35. Vincent J. Fontana, *Somewhere A Child Is Crying* (New York: Macmillan Co., 1964), p. 110.

36. Wasserman, op. cit.

37. Burland, Andrews, and Headsten, op. cit.

38. Ray E. Helfer, "The Etiology of Child Abuse," *Pediatrics,* 51 (1973), p. 777.

39. Kadushin, op. cit.

40. Gil, *Violence Against Children;* and Gil, "A Socio-Cultural Perspective on Physical Child Abuse."

41. Lystad, op. cit., p. 330.

42. Steele and Pollock, op. cit.

43. Fontana, *Somewhere a Child Is Crying;* and Fontana, "Further Reflections on Maltreatment of Children."

44. Leontine Young, *Wednesday's Children* (New York: McGraw-Hill Book Co., 1964).

45. Silver, Dublin, and Lourie, op. cit., p. 591.

46. Marian G. Morris, Robert W. Gould, and Patricia J. Matthews, "Toward Prevention of Child Abuse," *"Children,* 11 (1964), pp. 55–60; and Thomas McHenry, Bertram R. Girdnay, and Elizabeth Elmer, "Suspected Trauma with Multiple Skeletal Injuries During Infancy and Childhood," *Pediatrics,* 47 (June 1963), pp. 903–908.

47. Werner Tuteur and Jacob Glotzer, "Further Observations on Murdering Mothers," *Journal of Forensic Sciences,* 11 (1966), p. 375.

48. *See* Eustace Chesser, *Cruelty to Children* (New York: Philosophical Library, 1952); Irving Kaufman, "The Contributions of Protective Services," *Child Welfare,* 36 (1957), pp. 8–13; and Young, op. cit.

49. *See,* for example, Silver, Dublin, and Lourie, op. cit.; Helen E. Boardman, "A Project to Rescue Children from Inflicted Injuries," *Social Work,* 7 (January 1962), pp. 43–51; and Serapio Richard Zalba, "The Abused Child": I and II, *Social Work,* 11 and 12 (October 1966 and January 1967), pp. 3–16 and 70–79.

50. *See,* for example, Carol Schneider, Ray E. Helfer, and Carl Pollock, "The Predictive Questionnaire: A Preliminary Report," in C. Henry Kempe and Ray E. Helfer, eds., *Helping the Battered Child and His Family* (Philadelphia: J. B. Lippincott Co., 1972). These authors have begun to study abusing and nonabusing samples in order to establish differences in specific behavioral and psychological characteristics.

51. Katherine Oettinger, as quoted in Paulson and Blake, op. cit., p. 88.

52. Zalba, op. cit.

CHILD ABUSE AND NEGLECT:
The Myth of Classlessness

Leroy H. Pelton, Ph.D.

Bureau of Research, New Jersey Division of Youth and Family Services

Increasingly, professional and public media are promulgating the belief that the problems of child abuse and neglect are broadly distributed throughout society, suggesting that their frequency and severity are unrelated to socio-economic class. This paper argues that this belief is not supported by the evidence, and that its perpetuation serves to divert attention from the nature of the problems.

Child abuse is not a black problem, a brown problem, or a white problem. Child abusers are found in the ranks of the unemployed, the blue-collar worker, the white-collar worker and the professional. They are Protestant, Catholic, Jewish, Baptist and atheist.[7]

. . . [C]hild abuse and neglect occur among families from all socioeconomic levels, religious groups, races and nationalities.[16]

The problem of child abuse is not limited to any particular economic, social, or intellectual level, race or religion.[6]

 . . . [C]hild abuse and child neglect afflict all communities, regardless of race, religion or economic status.[4]

While such oft-repeated statements are true, they are only half-true. Child abuse and neglect have indeed been found among all socioeconomic classes, and within all of the other groupings mentioned. But these statements seem to imply that child abuse and neglect occur without regard to socioeconomic class, or are distributed proportionately among the total population. The impression that these problems are democratically distributed throughout society is increasingly being conveyed by professionals writing in academic journals, and to the public through the news media, despite clear evidence to the contrary.

This paper will be concerned primarily with three issues: 1) the extent and nature of the evidence associating child abuse and neglect with social class;

Reprinted from the AMERICAN JOURNAL OF ORTHOPSYCHIATRY, 48 (October 1978), pp. 608–617, by permission of the American Orthopsychiatric Association, Inc.

17

2) the reasons why the myth of class-lessness continues to be promulgated; and 3) the damaging effects of the myth on our ability to understand and deal with the problems.

WHAT THE STUDIES SHOW

Substantial evidence of a strong relationship between poverty and child abuse and neglect currently exists. Every national survey of officially reported child neglect and abuse incidents has indicated that the preponderance of the reports involves families from the lowest socioeconomic levels.

In the first of these studies, a nationwide survey of child abuse reports made to central registries, Gil[8] found that nearly 60% of the families involved in the abuse incidents had been on welfare during or prior to the study year of 1967, and 37.2% of the abusive families had been receiving public assistance at the time of the incident. Furthermore, 48.4% of the reported families had incomes below $5000 in 1967, as compared with 25.3% of all American families who had such low incomes. Only 52.5% of the fathers had been employed throughout the year, and at least 65% of the mothers and 55.5% of the fathers did not graduate from high school. On the other side of the coin, only three percent of the families had incomes of $10,000 or over (as compared with 34.4% of all American families for the same year), and only 0.4% of the mothers and 2.2% of the fathers had college degrees.

More recent data have been collected by the American Humane Association (AHA) through its national study of official child abuse and neglect reporting. For the year 1975,[2] family income information was provided by twenty states and territories on a total of 12,766 validated reports. For 53.2% of these reports, the yearly income was under $5000, and 69.2% of the families had incomes of less than $7000. In fact, less than eleven percent of the families had incomes of $11,000 or over.

The AHA 1976 data[1] on 19,923 validated reports, from a greater number of states and territories, show that 49.6% of the families had incomes under $5000, and 65.4% under $7000. Forty-two percent of the families were receiving public assistance, mostly Aid to Families with Dependent Children (AFDC). Only 14.9% of the reports indicated family incomes of $11,000 or over, and only nine percent of the families had incomes of $13,000 or above. The median family income was $5051 (which is at the 1976 poverty level for a family of four), as compared with about $13,900 for all American families in 1976. For reports of neglect only, the median income dipped slightly to $4250, and it rose slightly to $6882 for abuse only.

More geographically limited but in-depth studies substantiate this poverty picture. In her classic study of child abuse and neglect in the early 1960s, Young[20] examined the case records of 300 families, taken from the active files of child protection agencies in several different urban, suburban, and rural areas of the country. She found that: "Most of the families studied were poor, many of them very poor." Her data indicate that 42.7% of the families had been on public assistance at some time, and that only 10.7% of all of the families "were financially comfortable and able to meet their physical needs." In 58% of the families, the wage earner had not held one job continuously for as long as two years; in 71% of the families, the wage earner was an unskilled laborer. Furthermore, few of the families lived in adequate housing: "Poorly heated, vermin-ridden, in various states of disrepair, much of the housing was a hazard to health."

A recent study[14] in which a random sample of active cases from the state child protection agency caseload in Mercer County, New Jersey, was carefully screened for abuse and neglect, and the case records thoroughly analyzed, revealed that 81% of the families had received public welfare benefits at some time. Seventy-nine percent of the families had an income of $7000 or less at the time of case acceptance. Two-thirds of the mothers had left school by the end of the tenth grade.

Many more statistics are available that lead to the same unmistakable conclusion: The lower socioeconomic classes are disproportionately represented among all child abuse and neglect cases known to public agencies, to the extent that an overwhelming percentage —indeed, the vast majority—of the families in these cases live in poverty or near-poverty circumstances.

Those who uphold the myth of class-lessness do not generally dispute such findings. Rather, they offer several disclaimers. Poor people, it is suggested, are more available to public scrutiny, more likely to be known to social agencies and law enforcement agencies, whose workers have had the opportunity to enter their households. The family lives of middle-class and upper-class people, on the other hand, are less open to inspection by public officials; they are less likely than people in poor neighborhoods to turn to public agencies when help is needed. Thus,

injuries to children of the middle and upper classes are less likely to arouse outside suspicion of abuse and neglect; even when they do, the private physicians whom the parents consult, and with whom they may have a rather personal relationship, will be reluctant to report their suspicions to public authorities.

Therefore, it is claimed, the socioeconomic distribution of *reported* child abuse and neglect cases does not reflect that of *all* cases. It is further implied that there are proportionately more *unreported* cases among the middle and upper classes than among lower-class families, to such extent that child abuse and neglect are more or less proportionately distributed among all socioeconomic classes.

While the premises are valid—poor people *are* more subject to public scrutiny—the conclusions do not follow logically from them. We have no grounds for proclaiming that if middle-class and upper-class households were more open to public scrutiny, we would find proportionately as many abuse and neglect cases among them. Undiscovered evidence is no evidence at all.

Although poor people are more susceptible to public scrutiny, there is substantial evidence that the relationship between poverty and child abuse and neglect is not just an anomaly of reporting systems. The public scrutiny argument cannot explain away the real relationship that exists.

First, while it is generally acknowledged that greater public awareness and new reporting laws have led to a significant increase in reporting over the past few years, the socioeconomic pattern of these reports has not changed appreciably. The findings already reviewed here indicate that an expanded and more vigilant public watch has failed, over the years, to produce an increased proportion of reports from above the lower class.

Second, the public scrutiny argument cannot explain why child abuse and neglect are related to *degrees* of poverty, even *within* that same lower class that is acknowledged to be more open to public scrutiny. In studying only poor families, Giovannoni and Billingsley [9] found the highest incidence of child neglect to have occurred in families living in the most extreme poverty. A large, more recent study [19] in northern New Jersey compared AFDC recipient families known to the state child protection agency and identified as having abused or neglected their children, with AFDC families not known to that agency. The maltreating families were found to be living in more crowded and dilapidated households, to have been more likely to have gone hungry, and, in general, to be existing at a lower material level than the other AFDC families. The mothers in the maltreating families had fewer years of education than the mothers in the other families. The investigators concluded that the abusing and neglecting families are the poorest of the poor.

Third, the public scrutiny argument cannot explain why, among the reported cases, the most severe injuries have occurred within the poorest families. In his study of child abuse reports, cited earlier, Gil [8] found that injuries were more likely to be fatal or serious among families whose annual income was below $3500.

Severity certainly seems an important factor in this regard. If definitions of child abuse and neglect are viewed on a long continuum, and stretched to their most innocuous limits, it may indeed be concluded that, by "definition," child abuse and neglect are rampant throughout society. Moreover, the myth itself conveys the impression that severity, as well as frequency, of abuse is distributed proportionately among the classes. But, as Gil [8] has pointed out, officially reported incidents are more likely than unreported incidents to involve severe injury, since severity is an important criterion of reporting; as we have seen, the relationship between poverty and severity of injury obtains even among the reported incidents.

A British study [15] of 134 battered infants and children under five years of age, most of whom had been admitted to hospitals, found that the parents were predominantly from the lower social classes. The investigators concluded that "battering is mainly a lower class phenomenon." They further stated that

. . . as the criteria for referral of cases were medical we are reasonably confident that if more children from high social class families had been admitted with unexpected injuries then consultant paediatricians would have referred them.

The most severe and least easily hidden maltreatment of children is that which results in death. As a forensic pathologist associated with the Office of the Medical Examiner in Philadelphia, Weston [17] reviewed the mortality of all children under sixteen years of age in that city from 1961 through 1965. During this five-year period, 60 deaths due to child abuse and neglect were found. Among the 24 deaths due to neglect, Weston noted that more than 80% of the families had received some form of public assistance. The investigator divided the abuse victims into two categories, according to prior trauma. Of the thirteen children with no previous injury (36% of the abuse victims), he reported that "more than half" came from middle-class homes. As for the 23 children with a history of repetitive trauma (64% of the abuse victims), he noted that, with few exceptions, most came from "homes of extremely low socioeconomic level," and none came from upper-middle or upper-class families.

Kaplun and Reich [11] studied 112 of the 140 apparent homicides of children under fifteen years of age, recorded by New York City's Chief Medical Examiner, which occurred in that city during 1968 and 1969. Over two-thirds of the assailants in these homicides were parents or paramours. The authors found:

Most of the families of the murdered children (70%) lived in areas of severe poverty, and almost all were known to the city's public welfare agency.

Thus, we can conclude from these studies that the vast majority of the fatal victims of child abuse and neglect are from poor families.

Unlike certain other injuries to children, in only rare instances can death be hidden. Because of its greater severity and openness to public scrutiny than other injuries, its true causes, too, are less likely to go undetected. Death will prompt an investigation. However, it is probable that some child homicides have been successfully passed off as accidents by the parents, and some people will argue that investigative authorities have been more readily deceived by middle-class and upper-class parents than by lower-class parents.

Yet there is simply a massive amount of evidence, from our country and many others, that

. . . the overwhelming majority of homicides and other assaultive crimes are committed by persons from the lowest stratum of a social organization.[18]

As Magura [12] noted, the source of such evidence is not limited to official statistics and, moreover, any presumed bias in the detection of offenses cannot explain the fact that official crime rate differences between social classes are substantially greater for physically aggressive crimes than for property offenses. If anything, as Magura pointed out, since the seriousness of an offense is known to be related to the probability of police intervention, the role of a bias in police recognition of offenses would be expected to be least influential in the detection of the most serious offenses. The rate differentials can only mean that, in actuality, crimes of violence are far more prevalent among the lowest socioeconomic classes. There is little reason to believe that child abuse (leaving aside, for the moment, child neglect, which is an act of a different nature than most violent crimes) conforms to any different socioeconomic pattern than that of violent crimes in general. In fact, the available evidence, including that pertaining to fatal child abuse, indicates that it does not.

WHY THE MYTH PERSISTS

That belief in the classlessness of child abuse and neglect has taken hold with such tenacity among professionals and the public, despite evidence and logic to the contrary, suggests that it serves important functions for those who accept it. Maintenance of the myth permits many professionals to view child abuse and neglect as psychodynamic problems, in the context of a medical model of "disease," "treatment," and "cure," rather than as predominantly sociological and poverty-related problems. Moreover, like the popular conception of an epidemic disease, afflicting families without regard to social or economic standing, the myth allows the problems of abuse and neglect to be portrayed as broader than they actually are; indeed, as occurring in "epidemic" proportions.

Boehm [5] has pointed out that the strong psychodynamic orientation in the field of social work has led to the assumption that neglect is a classless phenomenon. Conversely, it can be said that the assumption of classlessness plays a key role in upholding the psychodynamic orientation, as well as the medical model of treatment.

The mystique of psychodynamic theories has captivated many helping professionals, who seem to view the espousal and practice of such theories as conferring status and prestige upon themselves. Unfortunately, the mundane problems of poverty and poverty-related hazards hold less fascination for them; direct, concrete approaches to these problems appear to be less glamorous professionally than psychologizing about the poor and prescribing the latest fashions in psychotherapy. Although concrete services are the ones most attractive to prospective lower-class consumers, they are the services that are least appealing to the middle-class helping professionals immersed in the "psychological society." [10]

Thus the myth serves several functions. It supports the prestigious and fascinating psychodynamic medical-model approach and, by disassociating

the problems from poverty, accords distinct and separate status to child abuse and neglect specialists. The myth holds that child abuse and neglect are not, for the most part, mere aspects of the poverty problem. Ultimately, by encouraging the view that abuse and neglect are widespread throughout society, the myth presumably aids in prying loose additional federal funds for dealing with these problems.

Politicians, for their part, have been amenable to the myth of classlessness because it serves certain functions for them. The questioning of David Gil by then-Senator Walter Mondale at the 1973 Senate hearings on the Child Abuse Prevention and Treatment Act was most revealing of this preference. Invoking the public scrutiny argument, Mondale pressed hard to establish that child abuse "is not a poverty problem." As Patti [13] noted,

. . . it seems that the Senator wished to avoid treating child abuse as another manifestation of poverty out of a concern that the poverty issue had lost its political appeal.

Berleman [3] commented on the same hearings:

Some legislators wished to be reassured that abuse was not disproportionately distributed according to socioeconomic class; they were particularly anxious not to have the problem become identified with the lower class. Many witnesses also gave the impression that the problem was not class-related.

Thus, both professional and politician, each for his own reasons, is disinclined to see the problems as poverty-related: the former to increase his chances of gaining funding for a medical-model approach, the latter to increase his own chances of getting a bill passed and thus being seen as aggressively dealing with the phenomenon of child "battering," which the public already perceives as a "sickness."

But the ends (obtaining increased funding) cannot justify the means (presenting a picture of child abuse and neglect not supported by the evidence) even on tactical grounds. When certain claims are made in order to secure funding, these claims will determine the disposition of the funds. If it is asserted that there are millions of undiscovered abuse and neglect cases among the middle classes, then legislators must reasonably conclude that money should be earmarked for finding them. And if it is claimed that the problems are unrelated to poverty, then money and attention will be diverted from poverty-oriented services.

Well-meaning mental health professionals may be drawn to the myth of classlessness, believing that the association of child abuse and neglect with poverty constitutes one more insulting and discriminatory act toward poor people, one more way to "stigmatize" them unjustly. In fact, the myth does a disservice to poor people and to the victims of child abuse and neglect; it undermines development of effective approaches to dealing with their real and difficult problems, and directs us toward remedies more oriented to the middle classes.

To say that child abuse and neglect are strongly related to poverty is not to say that poor people in general abuse and neglect their children. On the contrary, only a tiny minority of lower-class parents do so.[14] But the myth of classlessness diverts our attention from the "subculture of violence,"[18] the stresses of poverty that can provoke abuse and neglect, and the hazardous poverty environment that heightens the dangerousness of child neglect.

HOW THE MYTH SERVES AS A SMOKESCREEN

In the face of the evidence that child abuse and neglect, especially in their most severe forms, occur disproportionately among the lower socioeconomic classes, proponents of the myth of classlessness have provided little substance for their beliefs. Nonetheless, as suggested above, the myth is persistent and powerful enough to blind many of us to the real poverty-related problems of most abuse and neglect cases. For poverty is not merely "associated" with child abuse and neglect; there is good reason to believe that the problems of poverty are causative agents in parents' abusive and negligent behaviors and in the resultant harm to children.

As Gil[8] has pointed out, the living conditions of poverty generate stressful experiences that may become precipitating factors of child abuse, and the poor have little means by which to escape from such stress. Under these circumstances, even minor misbehaviors and annoyances presented by powerless children may trigger abuse. Such poverty-related factors as unemployment, dilapidated and overcrowded housing, and insufficient money, food, recreation, or hope can provide the stressful context for abuse. This is not to say that middle-class parents never experience stresses that might lead to child abuse, or that abuse is always contributed to by environmental stress. Nor does it mean that the additional stresses of poverty cause most impoverished families to maltreat their children. But, given the established fact that poverty is strongly

23

related to child maltreatment, we find that there are sensible explanations as to why poverty might be a partial determinant of it.

Child neglect is a far more pervasive social problem than is abuse, occurring in more than twice as many cases.[1, 14] Moreover, when harm to the child severe enough to have required hospitalization or medical attention has occurred, it is from one-and-a-half to two times as likely to have been due to neglect than to abuse. In addition, neglect is somewhat more strongly related to poverty than is abuse.[1, 14]

Like abuse, neglect may partially result from poverty-related stresses. In leading to neglect, these stresses may produce the mediating factor of despair rather than anger when, for example, a single parent attempts to raise a large family in cramped and unsafe living quarters with no help and little money. The relationship can be seen most clearly in those cases in which a terrible incident, such as a fire devastating the home, also destroys the mother's capacity to cope with poverty any longer.

However, no matter what the origins of neglectful behavior, there is a more immediate way in which poverty causes harm to neglected children. Poverty itself directly presents dangers for children, and very often neglect merely increases the likelihood that those dangers will result in harm.

Neglectful irresponsibility more readily leads to dire consequences when it occurs in the context of poverty than when that same behavior is engaged in by middle-class parents.[14] In middle-class families there is some *leeway* for irresponsibility, a luxury that poverty does not afford. A middle-class mother can be careless with her money and squander some of it, but still have enough so that her children will not be deprived of basic necessities. Identical lapses in responsibility on the part of an impoverished mother might cause her children to go hungry during the last few days of the month. The less money one has, the better manager of money one has to be.

Leaving a child alone or unattended is the most prevalent form of child neglect, occurring in 50% of all neglect cases.[14] A middle-class parent's inadequate supervision will not put the children in as great danger as will that of the impoverished parent, because the middle-class home is not as drastically beset with health and safety hazards. The context of poverty multiplies the hazards of a mother's neglect. Thus, poor people have very little margin for irresponsibility or mismanagement of either time or money.

In some cases, the mother does not have much choice but to leave her children alone. A welfare mother with many children cannot easily obtain or pay for a babysitter every time she must leave the house to do her chores; in addition, she may find it more difficult to do her shopping than would a middle-class mother. If she leaves her children alone, she is taking a gamble with their safety; if she stays with them, it may mean being unable to provide proper food or other immediate necessities. Thus, some mothers are caught up in difficult and dangerous situations that have less to do with their adequacy and responsibility as parents than with the hard circumstances of their lives.

The myth of classlessness diverts attention from the environmental problems of poor households that make neglect so much more dangerous to

24

children than it would be in middle-class homes. Recognition of the impoverished context of child neglect points us to the need for concrete services directed at the dangers of poverty, services such as house-finding, rat control, in-home babysitter services, installation of window guard-rails, and emergency cash for the repair of boilers or plumbing, the payment of gas and electric bills, a security deposit on a new apartment, or the purchase of food, crib, playpen, etc. Such measures will often directly prevent harm to children in protective services cases, and obviate the need for immediate child placement. In addition, reducing the immediate stresses of poverty may have a rapid and positive impact upon the parents' behavior.

Although the stresses of poverty certainly have psychological effects, the strong relationship between poverty and child abuse and neglect suggests that remediation of situational defects should take precedence over psychological treatments. These parents' behavior problems are less likely to be symptoms of unconscious or intrapsychic conflicts than of concrete antecedent environmental conditions, crises, and catastrophes. It is these root causes that must be addressed.

Child welfare agencies can neither enter the housing industry nor raise clients' welfare benefits. But they can seek to remedy many of the health and safety hazards that attend poverty and inadequate housing and that, in combination with parental factors produced in part by those very hazards, place children in danger of harm and abuse.

CONCLUSION

Both evidence and reason lead to the unmistakable conclusion that, contrary to the myth of classlessness, child abuse and neglect are strongly related to poverty, in terms of prevalence and of severity of consequences. This is not to say that abuse and neglect do not occur among other socioeconomic classes, or that, when they do occur, they never have severe consequences. However, widespread reports suggesting that abuse and neglect are classless phenomena are unfounded and misleading. The myth of classlessness persists not on the basis of evidence or logic, but because it serves certain professional and political interests. These interests do not further the task of dealing with the real problems underlying abuse and neglect; adherence to the myth diverts attention from the nature of the problems and diverts resources from their solution.

REFERENCES

1. AMERICAN HUMANE ASSOCIATION. 1978. National Analysis of Official Child Neglect and Abuse Reporting. American Humane Association, Denver.
2. AMERICAN HUMANE ASSOCIATION. Statistics for 1975. American Humane Association, Denver.
3. BERLEMAN, W. 1976. An analysis of issues related to child abuse and neglect as reflected in Congressional hearings prior to the enactment of the Child Abuse Prevention and Treatment Act of 1974. Center for Social Welfare Research, School of Social Work, University of Washington.
4. BESHAROV, D. AND BESHAROV, S. 1977. Why do parents harm their children? National Council of Jewish Women (Winter):6–8.
5. BOEHM, B. 1964. The community and the social agency define neglect. Child Welfare 43:453–464.
6. FONTANA, V. 1977. In statement printed in Senate hearings on extension of the Child Abuse Prevention and Treatment Act, April 6–7:505.
7. FRASER, B. 1976–77. Independent representation for the abused and neglected child: the guardian ad litem. Calif. Western Law Rev. 13.
8. GIL, D. 1970. Violence Against Children.

Harvard University Press, Cambridge, Mass.

9. GIOVANNONI, J. AND BILLINGSLEY, A. 1970. Child neglect among the poor: a study of parental inadequacy in families of three ethnic groups. Child Welfare 49:196–204.

10. GROSS, M. 1978. The Psychological Society. Random House, New York.

11. KAPLUN, D. AND REICH, R. 1976. The murdered child and his killers. Amer. J. Psychiat. 133:809–813.

12. MAGURA, S. 1975. Is there a subculture of violence? Amer. Sociol. Rev. 40:831–836.

13. PATTI, R. 1976. An analysis of issues related to child abuse and neglect as reflected in Congressional hearings prior to the enactment of the Child Abuse Prevention and Treatment Act of 1974. Center for Social Welfare Research, School of Social Work, University of Washington.

14. PELTON, L. 1977. Child abuse and neglect and protective intervention in Mercer County, New Jersey: a parent interview and case record study. Bureau of Research, New Jersey Division of Youth and Family Services.

15. SMITH, S., HANSON, R. AND NOBLE, S. 1975. Parents of battered children: a controlled study. *In* Concerning Child Abuse, A. Franklin, ed. Churchill Livingstone, Edinburgh.

16. STEELE, B. 1975. Working with abusive parents: a psychiatrist's view. Children Today 4:3.

17. WESTON, J. 1974. The pathology of child abuse. *In* The Battered Child (2nd ed.), R. Helfer and C. Kempe, eds. University of Chicago Press, Chicago.

18. WOLFGANG, M. 1967. Criminal homicide and the subculture of violence. *In* Studies in Homicide, M. Wolfgang, ed. Harper and Row, New York.

19. WOLOCK, I. AND HOROWITZ, B. 1977. Factors relating to levels of child care among families receiving public assistance in New Jersey. Final Report, Vol. 1, June 30, 1977 (grant No. 90-c-418). Submitted to the National Center on Child Abuse and Neglect, DHEW.

20. YOUNG, L. 1971. Wednesday's Children. McGraw-Hill, New York.

BY SERAPIO RICHARD ZALBA

The Abused Child: I. A Survey of the Problem

■ *This first part of a two-part paper reviews the literature on child abuse in an attempt to present a broader view of the problem than has been done previously. On the basis of this, the author will present in the next issue a proposed diagnostic-treatment typology.* ■

THE CLEVELAND, OHIO, *Plain Dealer* of February 4, 1965, carried a news story on page 25 which reported that a juvenile court hearing had been set

> . . . to determine the cause of injuries suffered by an eight-month-old baby hospitalized for a month . . . with two broken arms, a broken left leg, a fingernail missing from his left hand and body scars. . . . The child's mother said he fell forward from an upholstered chair and that his arms apparently caught in the sides of the chair, policewomen reported.

Dr. Henry C. Kempe and his associates reported on the "alarming number" of children being admitted to hospitals for traumatic injuries for which the parents could give no plausible explanations (28).[1] X-ray examination often disclosed that there had been earlier, sometimes numerous, serious injuries—e.g., fractures of the arms, legs,

ribs, or skull—that the parents were unable to account for, or would even deny outright. The children were generally in poor health, with unsatisfactory skin hygiene, multiple soft tissue injuries, subdural hematoma, and malnutrition. An indication of the problem's gravity was provided by Kempe's example of one day in November 1961 when there were four battered children in Colorado General Hospital alone—two died of central nervous system traumas and one was released to his home in satisfactory condition but subsequently died "suddenly" in an unexplained manner (a not unusual occurrence). A new term was coined to describe such situations: the "battered child syndrome."

Kempe and his associates may have intended to draw attention to the problem of severe child battering by their use of the dramatic, arresting label. If this is so, they seem to have succeeded.[2] The term itself, however, carries with it the implica-

SERAPIO RICHARD ZALBA, MSW, *is Lecturer, School of Applied Social Sciences, Western Reserve University, Cleveland, Ohio. The second part of this two-part paper on the abused child, "A Typology for Classification and Treatment," will appear in the January 1967 issue of this journal. The reference list at the end of this article—an exception to this journal's policy—is included because the paper depends on citations from the literature.*

[1] Numbers in parentheses refer to the numbered references that appear at the end of this paper. Actual figures were not indicated by Kempe, although Dodge (15) cites Kempe in reporting that 302 battered children were in 71 major hospitals in one year; of these 33 died and 85 suffered permanent brain damage.

[2] Even such popular television series as "Ben Casey" and "Slattery's People" have based episodes on battered child cases.

tion of a specific, identifiable sociomedical entity. This is a problematic assumption that will be considered in this paper, since it raises some important questions about the differential psychosocial meaning of the physical conditions described above.

The basic problem of serious child abuse by parents and parent substitutes is not new; indeed, as Elizabeth Elmer has pointed out, it is only comparatively recently in recorded history that there has been community consensus and sanction for recognizing and protecting the rights of children (17, pp. 100–101). In much of recorded history infanticide, child abandonment, maiming as an aid in begging, and the selling of children has been common rather than exceptional (4, chap. XXV). It was common to flog children without provocation in colonial times in America in order to "break them of their willfulness," and make them tractable, ostensibly for the good of their souls (4). It was not until the last half of the nineteenth century, precipitated by the infamous Mary Ellen case in New York City, that the first Society for the Prevention of Cruelty to Children was organized in the United States.[3] And it has only been since 1946 that articles have appeared in medical journals identifying traumatic injuries of children that could not be explained by the usual childhood accidents.[4]

A number of social work articles have been written about specific aspects of the problem (45). In this two-part paper, two approaches will be taken: Part I will attempt to provide a broader, although necessarily less intensive, view of the phenomenon of child-battering than has been true of earlier social work articles—in other words, a survey of the problem area. Part II, in contrast, will propose a diagnostic-treatment typology for child abuse cases

[3] For a brief description of the Mary Ellen case see DeFrancis (12).

[4] See the U. S. Children's Bureau bibliography (45), which includes a total of fifteen articles in medical journals from 1946 to 1959.

based primarily on earlier empirical studies.

HISTORY OF THE PROBLEM

Services and programs variously described as protective or preventive have existed since the New York Society for the Prevention of Cruelty to Children was created following the Mary Ellen case of 1866. In that case the American Society for the Prevention of Cruelty to *Animals* was the only agency that was willing and able to intervene in a case of extreme child abuse. The early protective services that developed after 1875 concerned themselves primarily with the prosecution and punishment of parents physically mistreating their children and inflicting bodily injury on them.

As Norris Class points out, the primary focus on *physical* abuse and neglect was associated with poverty, slums, ignorance, industrial exploitation, and immigration (9). Physical mistreatment was visible, and it was not difficult to introduce admissible and dramatic evidence into the courts in the prosecution of abusive and neglectful parents. But as the conditions associated with physical neglect and abuse abated, so did its visibility.

During social work's intensive romance with psychoanalysis and dynamic psychiatry in the 1920's and 1930's, it became concerned more with emotional factors and treatment and greater emphasis was given to permissive, voluntarily sought services (9, 10). There was confusion about the role of authority and legal sanctions in social work treatment. Acceptable legal evidence of *emotional* neglect or abuse was and still is more difficult to define or produce (9). The interest in protective services (and in corrections) declined. The close working relationship between the protective agency and the court deteriorated. On the positive side, however, social work became increasingly aware that prosecution of abusive and neglectful parents did not solve the problems of the victimized children or of the family itself. As the family system came to be seen as the diagnostic and even the treatment unit of reference, attention began to be paid to the efficacy of treating the parents and attempting to maintain the structural integrity of the family. The basic problem is still with us, and it has general relevance in child welfare—i.e., at what point does the harm of leaving a child in a poor home override the harm of splintering the family by use of foster home or other placement outside the parental home? (The pros and cons of strategies for placement or leaving children in the parental home will be discussed later in this paper.) An important factor in providing protective services, and an important value in American society, has been the tradition of parental rights regarding the rearing of their children. The intervention of the state in parent-child matters is for the most part invoked reluctantly and carefully. When there is a reasonable question as to parental adequacy, the propensity has been to be conservative and rule in favor of the parent. Maas and Engler furnish examples of the differential propensities in the various communities they studied (29). This may reflect a "folk wisdom" about the child's need for enduring family ties; on the other hand, children are sometimes left in homes that are neglectful and even dangerous (3, 9, 17).

The relatively recent interest in more aggressive (i.e., reaching-out) approaches in social work (9, 36, 47), greater clarification of the role of authority (43), and accumulated experience and knowledge in work with those persons psychiatrically categorized as character disordered have brought us to the place where we can meaningfully consider what we can and/or should do in the problem area of abused children (3, 6, 14, 18, 26, 36, 38, 41, 47).

DEFINITION OF CASES

Can we define more precisely those cases subsumed under the terms "battered" or "abused" children? In the Pittsburgh study by Elizabeth Elmer abused children were specifically defined as those physically assaulted by adults; neglect was defined as the chronic failure of adults to protect children from obvious physical danger. Both groups of children were later described as abused, in its more generic sense (i.e., badly treated), but the subjects in the study seemed to consist primarily of cases of inflicted physical injury (18); this was true for all of the cases studied in Los Angeles by Helen Boardman (3). Irving Kaufman considers protective cases to be basically the same, whether they are neglect or abuse cases; he assumes there is some of both kinds of mistreatment in every protective case (26). Eustace Chesser and Leontine Young, however, see a qualitative difference in the cases.

Chesser states: "There is a radical difference in character between cases of neglect and cases of cruelty to children," and then goes on to elaborate that while neglect may be a form of cruelty, it is more often caused or exaggerated by extreme poverty or ignorance. Cruelty, on the other hand, is more likely to be related to deep-seated characterological or psychological causes rooted in the childhood experiences of the abusing parent or parents, such as physical or mental cruelty inflicted upon *them* by *their* parents (8).

Young cites the general willingness of neglectful parents to allow social workers to come into their homes, form relationships with their children, and even remove the children to foster care. In contrast, abusive parents tend to resist efforts at intervention, whether it comes in the form of casework services in the home, taking a child on an outing, or removing him for protective placement (48).

This paper will address itself primarily to those cases in which physical injury is inflicted on a child by a parent or parent-substitute to the extent that the child's health or life are endangered. Admittedly there is no clear demarcation between severe punishment and abuse. The extreme positions on the continuum are, however, fairly clear. A mild spanking on the buttocks of a 2-year-old child is quite different from the case of abuse found in a protective agency, where a child may have had scalding water poured on his genitals by a cruel, disturbed parent.

The most extreme cases are probably seen in the hospital setting, especially since the younger children typically seen there are unable to defend themselves by running away from battering or abuse. Yet some of the nonhospital studies yielded cases of equally serious abuse.[5] Some examples of typical abuse cases have been provided by Merrill in reporting on the study of the Massachusetts SPCC (32):

> A five year old girl went onto her porch though told not to do so; she was kicked into the house, thrown across the room, and hit on the face and head with a frying pan.
> A nine months old boy's eyes were blackened, his fingers, face, and neck burned, and his skull fractured by his father.
> A thirteen months old girl was X-rayed at the hospital; revealed were multiple skull fractures—some old, some new—and marked subdural hematoma.
> X-rays on a seven months old boy showed healed fractures of one arm, the other one currently broken, healed fractures on both legs, and multiple skull fractures.

NATURE OF THE PROBLEM

As Kempe's seminal paper indicated, the physical abuse of a child does not generally occur only once (28). (In most of the twenty cases studied by Nurse there had been abuse of from one to three years' duration (35).) Indeed, one of the medical indicators that physical injuries may have

been inflicted rather than accidental is X-ray evidence of prior, often multiple, injuries (18, 28). The parents tend to deny that they inflicted the injuries (3, 14, 18, 26, 28, 35). In many cases one specific child is singled out of the several in the family as the object of repeated abuse (3, 6, 14, 28, 35).

In the hospital studies of Elmer (18) and Boardman (3) the children were very young, with over half of the combined sample of 64 cases under 1 year of age. In addition, they reported a high mortality rate: 12 children dead out of 56 cases followed up (21 percent). Of the 46 homicides of infants and preadolescents studied by Adelson in Cleveland, 21 were under 3 years old (1). In contrast, in the private agency protective services studies reported by Bryant and Merrill in Massachusetts (6, 32) and Delsordo in Philadelphia (14) the children were older, with half the children (combined sample of over 260 children) under 7 years old, and no report made of deaths.

Abusers of the children. These were usually their own parents with whom they were currently living—mothers and fathers were identified as the abusers in equal numbers of cases (6, 8, 14, 35). While there was a great deal of marital and family conflict found in the cases studied, the nonabusive parent tended to protect the abusive one, although supporting his denial of having abused the child (3, 35). As a way of hiding the effects of their abusive behavior, many parents shopped around for medical care—e.g., one child under 1 year of age had been hospitalized three times in three different hospitals (3). To quote Adelson:

> It is relatively simple to destroy the life of a child in almost absolute secrecy without the necessity of taking any elaborate precautions to ensure that secrecy (1).

Characteristics of parents. The parents in the cases reported on were not necessarily from the lower socioeconomic classes.

---

[5] Ten of Nurse's twenty New York County Family Court cases had been hospitalized, and hospitalization would have been warranted for an additional four (35).

Many were middle class and self-supporting, with well-kept homes. However, they were characterized as impulse-ridden, socially isolated, and having serious social problems, including marital conflict, difficulties in financial management, and faulty community relations (6, 28, 32). Kaufman indicates that the physical abuse of children implies a distortion of reality—the child as a target is perceived by the parent in a symbolic or delusional way (e.g., the psychotic portion of himself he wishes to destroy, his own abusive parent, or the like). The vast majority of abusive parents are probably character disordered, but the most violent and abusive ones may have schizophrenic personality cores (27). This latter group may be those whose children are seen most often in hospitals; they predominate in Kempe's category of Battered Child Syndrome. In Adelson's study, 17 of the 41 murderers of children were patently mentally ill (i.e., had been hospitalized or had shown profound mental disturbance for some time before the eruption of violence) (1).[6] The Massachusetts group reported that in 50 percent of their 115 study families there was premarital conception (6). Reports also point out the typicality of youthful marriages, unwanted pregnancies, illegitimacies, and "forced" marriages, all of which are consistent with the described impulsiveness of the abusive parents (14, 18, 28, 35). Many of the parents had themselves experienced abuse and neglect as children (6, 28, 39, 41). The epidemiological implications are, consequently, rather serious (5). While the 180 children in the Massachusetts study were generally normal physically, *all* of them were found to have seriously impaired relationships with the abusive parent. These children tended to overreact to hostility, were de-

pressive, hyperactive, destructive, and fearful. They were usually the victims rather than the provokers of parental abuse (6). The Philadelphia study characterized the children in their cases as bed-wetting, truanting, fire-setting, and withdrawing (14).

Referrals for protective services. Referrals for help from the Massachusetts SPCC came almost equally from relatives (24 percent); legal agencies, i.e., probation and police (23 percent); and neighbors (22 percent). Only 9 percent came from doctors or hospitals, even though 30 percent of the cases had been treated medically, a situation that new child abuse laws are seeking to correct by *requiring* medical authorities to report such cases to law enforcement agencies. A number of states have passed such laws (45).

Numbers. It is difficult to assess the number of children being physically abused or battered. For one thing, the proportion of abuse cases actually being reported is not known. For another, figures given by individual protective agencies or hospitals may be typical only for their geographic locality. Reported statistics on referrals to protective agencies generally include cases of both neglect *and* abuse; no definitive statement of how many of each are involved can be made.

Chesser, in reporting on the work of England's National Society for the Prevention of Cruelty to Children, concluded that between 6 and 7 percent of all children are at some time during their life "so neglected or ill-treated or become so maladjusted as to require the help of the N.S.P.C.C." (8). On the basis of a 1964 study in California, it would appear that a minimum of approximately 20,000 children were in need of protective services in that state alone (39). The American Public Welfare Association reported that in 1958 approximately 100 cases were referred monthly to the public welfare department in Denver, Colorado, for protective services (40). Elizabeth Barry Philbrook cited the figure of 250,000 children living

---

[6] The current state of the art of behavior-prediction is such that it would be difficult to justify, even if it were legally permissible, the commitment or incarceration of persons believed to be capable of serious violence *before* such acts have actually been committed and legally verified.

outside their own homes in 1960. She indicated that one-third of the children had been moved to at least two or three different foster homes and that protective services were needed in those cases, implying that this would serve a preventive as well as restorative function (38).

Extrapolation on the basis of the data from California and Colorado gives a conservative estimate that there are between 200,000 and 250,000 children in the United States needing protective services each year. If, in addition, the ratio of neglected to abused children holds true for this country as Chesser (8) reported for England, approximately 15 percent—30,000 to 37,500 children—need protection against serious physical abuse.

TYPOLOGIES

Earlier efforts have been made to develop typologies of abusing parents (6, 14, 41). As might be expected, there are both similarities and differences in the classifications used.

One of the major values in devising typological systems is that they can provide guidance for making intervention decisions. Ideally the categories utilized should be descriptively rich, precise, and mutually exclusive enough to permit reliable classification and, in addition, they should give valid information as to the relative danger to the client and others, the most efficacious treatment, and the prognosis for change. It is in this respect that the formulations of Delsordo (14) may have greater utility, despite the lack of logical consistency in the abstract dimensions in which his categories are ordered. He attempts to assess the physical danger to the children if they remain in the parental home and also gives his estimate as to the prognosis for treatment of the parents. For example, he advises that separation of child and parent is imperative in cases falling into his categories of "Mentally Ill," "Overflow Abuse," and "Battered Child."

A cautionary note should be sounded,

however; his generalized prescriptions for child removal were made on the basis of experience with a total of only twenty-five cases in the three categories mentioned. Still, the possibility that he has accurately identified those cases in which child removal is imperative begs for further investigation and test. His thesis is supported by Chesser's diagnostic categorization of "Consistent Active Cruelty—in such instances where cruelty is the expression of a mode of existence it is unlikely that the person concerned can ever be taught the error of his ways" (8).

Here, as in other specific areas of social work practice, there is need for more refined, sophisticated, and precise classifications that carry empirically validated specific implications for choice of social work interventions. It is this consideration that led the author to attempt the development of the typology that will be developed later in this paper. Such formulations are of maximum value when they are followed by field studies that use them and test the hypotheses implied in them. For example, it would appear to be important to test the danger-predictive value of Delsordo's prognostic formulations.

TREATMENT

There seems to be agreement about the general strategy in protective service with cases of child abuse. The first step is to verify the actual existence of abuse, then determine the imminent danger of harm to the children if they remain in the home. These are extremely difficult tasks for a variety of reasons.

Identification. As Kempe and others have pointed out, a number of factors militate against the recognition and reporting or referral of cases of child abuse. Medical personnel do not always recognize that traumatic injuries may be inflicted rather than accidental or owing to physiological factors. When they do recognize that injury was inflicted, they are reluctant to risk involving themselves in court appearances and the like by reporting the incidents to the authorities (3, 16, 17, 28).

Inadequacies exist as well in case-finding and referral for protective services from other social welfare institutions in the community. While this is partly owing to the factors mentioned above, it is also related to the general lack of communication and co-ordination of community welfare services (9, 38, 39, 40, 41).[7] Law enforcement personnel tell of having identified cases in need of protective treatment, but not having local resources to which to refer them.[8] Developing a community program of protective services requires a balance of both community co-operation in case-finding and the provision of adequate resources for treatment once cases are identified.

Evidence. In cases where abuse or neglect are suspected it is difficult to get conclusive evidence for the following reasons: the abusers tend to deny their actions, marital partners tend to protect the abusing ones, the children are often too young to give credible testimony, often there are no witnesses. Consequently the task of establishing the fact of serious child abuse is difficult, especially since time is of the essence in the protection against further, sometimes fatal, injury (3, 18). When imminent danger is believed to exist, it may be necessary to petition the courts for removal of the child or children, or the abusive adult, from the home. Protection against unwarranted infringement of the adult's rights requires that sufficient evidence be presented to the court that danger of serious abuse does exist. The dual demands of sufficient and immediate evidence thus contribute to the difficulty of the protective worker's task.

Diagnosis. The next step in providing protective services is to determine in greater depth and detail the dynamics of the case and the diagnosis and prognosis. When it is consistent with the safety of the children,

it is considered preferable to keep the children in the home and proceed with treatment on that basis (6, 14, 38, 41). When removal becomes necessary, care must be exercised to avoid returning the child home until there is some assurance that significant and stable change has been accomplished that makes it safe to return him. The hospital studies and the Philadelphia study are very careful to make this point (3, 14, 18, 28).

Removal. While the physical safety of the children must be the primary criterion in deciding whether their removal is absolutely necessary, there are other important considerations. Despite or perhaps because of the disturbed relationship with the abusing parent, the victimized child may not be able to tolerate losing the only security he knows, namely, his home, his other parent, and his siblings (7, 21, 26, 38). Because of the abuse he has experienced he may also have emotional and behavioral disorders (e.g., bed-wetting, truanting, firesetting, or withdrawing) that make him extremely hard to place in foster home care (14, 26). Keeping him in placement may require moving him as he aborts a number of placements. Such a pattern is very trying for the agency and worker and devastating for the child (38, 49).

Yet if children remain in homes where there is repeated abuse they are likely to internalize the behavioral models to which they are exposed. As Reiner and Kaufman say:

> Having experienced loss of love or inconsistent care themselves, they are unable as adults to provide a mature and consistent type of parental care for their children, but pass on these elements to them. . . . Such parents have a tendency to subject their own children to similar losses and to experiences that will engender the same attitudes. (41)

There are other considerations when removal of an abused child is contemplated. What about the children who remain behind? It may be that removal of the abused

---

[7] For a study on the difficulties in the co-ordination and co-operation of services for a similar clientele *see* Zalba (49).

[8] Personal communications to the writer.

child will result in the choice of a new scapegoat. Also, while in some cases one specific child is the target of abuse, this is by no means always true. Often two, three, or all of the children are abused, and this happens in some of the most serious and dangerous cases (14).

Casework treatment. Perhaps the issue to be faced is that we are dealing with disturbed families—that even in cases when all the children are removed from the home a seriously disturbed individual (the abusing parent), who may need treatment or supervision, remains behind. The parents we are considering are among the core group of the "hard-to-reach" families, well known to all social welfare agencies. Reiner and Kaufman state, "It is probably safe to say that families with members suffering from severe character disorders represent the most serious social problem in our country" (41). They are a difficult group of clients to work with because of their demanding, hostile, inconsistent behavior (41). When treatment is provided, a long-term, consistent, relationship-oriented approach is indicated; there appears to be general consensus on the inadvisability of short-term, emergency-oriented treatment (6, 14, 38, 41).

The specifics of casework treatment with child-abusing parents cannot be dealt with adequately in a paper of this length. The reader should refer to the Reiner and Kaufman book, which deals with the treatment of character-disordered parents, who make up the majority of child-battering parents (41). There are, however, a number of treatment problems indigenous to protective treatment that it might be useful to enumerate here:

1. Massive denial of abusive behavior or other personal problems.

2. Provocative behavior toward the worker, such as demandingness, rage, hostility, and acting out.

3. Fear of closeness in relationships; preference for authority-based relationships.

4. Little guilt over abusive or other hostile behavior.

The basic treatment objectives are to work closely with the clients and perform certain ego functions for them, such as setting limits on behavior, making realistic judgments for and with them, and helping them develop their own reality perception by pointing out distorted perceptions and consequences of their choices and acts. In effect the worker is lending his ego abilities to his client in the hope that his positive relationship with the client and the effectiveness of his ego behavior will lead the client to incorporate some of the worker's "ego strengths." As a consequence he would then be able to face the depressive nucleus of his personality and express his underlying feelings of fear and hurt, instead of defending against depression and anxiety through flight and denial. In this way he would come to realize and accept the finality of his childhood losses, begin to incorporate the attitudes of the worker, and evolve a new ego ideal and sense of identity. The foregoing description of Reiner and Kaufman's formulation of the treatment process provides some sense of why the client in such cases is so fearful of investing in a positive meaningful relationship with the worker; he needs to assure himself that he will not suffer another significant interpersonal loss, which he is so poorly equipped to handle. Part of his basic malady is an uncertain sense of identity.[9] Thus he is also handicapped in dealing with changes in workers or referrals from one agency to another.[10]

Group methods. There is some indication that group methods of treatment are desirable, perhaps even preferable, in the treatment of many abusive parents. Such parents have been described earlier as typically isolated and socially unskilled.

---

[9] Bernard L. Diamond provides a succinct statement of this problem (15).

[10] Those who have worked with correctional clients will recognize many of the client attributes described here. Character-disordered people make up the bulk of correctional case loads. This is true for county jail and probation clients as well as prison inmates and parolees.

They tend to deny their difficulties, have problems of control over impulses, and have difficulties with authority. These characteristics make them prime candidates for ego-oriented group treatment. Reiner and Kaufman do, in fact, say that group techniques may be indicated with parents who have character disorders (41). McFerran reports on a successful program of group counseling with parents in child neglect cases in Kentucky (31). There has been extensive correctional experience with group treatment methods in New Jersey (30), California (25), and with county jail clientele similar to the abusive parents under consideration.[11]

The children. The discussion of treatment up to this point has dealt primarily with the parents. The child-battering literature has little to say on treatment of the children. When the children are very young and remain in the home, it is likely that the main course of treatment *for* (rather than *of*) children is change of the malignant environment, either by removal from it or by changing it through treatment of the parents or removal of the abusive one. When the children are old enough and disturbed enough to need direct treatment, some guidance is provided by Kaufman, who outlines three phases of treatment:

1. Management of the reality situation and achievement of environmental stability (preferably in the child's own home).

2. With regression and expression of direct hostility by the child (i.e., testing) the worker needs to be firm and consistent; it is helpful to use activity programs such as trips, ball games, and so on.

3. Psychotherapy when needed.

Another possible treatment approach would be to treat the whole family conjointly. This has been done successfully with schizophrenics by Don D. Jackson and Virginia Satir (24). Both probation officers and parole officers with training in the conjoint family therapy method have treated juvenile delinquents and their families.[12]

Treatment personnel. In discussing the question of who should provide the protective treatment services, Kaufman has stated repeatedly that relationship therapy is indicated—i.e., the presentation of a reality situation—and that social workers are good at this kind of treatment (26, 27, 41). He feels that some social workers perceive relationship therapy as having low status; they would prefer doing "psychotherapy." This is an unfortunate assessment, in his view, because of the efficacy of the treatment; the choice of technique should be in terms of its efficacy, not its status (26). An important qualification for effective work with this client group is the proper temperament. There are tremendous emotional, as well as technical and intellectual, demands in the work (41). The worker must communicate on both a verbal *and* nonverbal level with clients whose behavior is bizarre, asocial, aggressive, childish, and provocative. The clients are extremely sensitive to artificiality or insincerity. The worker must therefore be alert to his own feelings and honest and forthright, yet in control of his hostility.

The problem, as Reiner and Kaufman point out, is not so much one of cross-cultural conflict between worker and client, but of psychosexual developmental conflict; it is difficult to be tolerant of an oral or anal character who is messy, demanding, or who cannot hold onto money or a job (41). Such demands on a worker necessitate that he receive support and assistance from his peers, supervisor, and agency, and the agency must make provision to meet those needs.

---

[11] The writer has visited group-oriented programs in the California county jail systems of San Diego and Santa Clara counties, and conducted group counseling programs in San Francisco and San Mateo counties.

[12] The writer was acquainted with a number of probation officers in San Mateo County's family-centered unit who used conjoint family therapy. Some of the Youth Authority parole officers in California's Community Treatment Project have also used this technique (22).

In addition to the difficulties and demands that inhere in relationships with such clients, the worker must cope with the complexity of the medical and legal matters involved. He will need consultation—medical, legal, and psychological (22)—and, as any correctional or protective worker can testify, he will need tact and patience in dealing with the courts.

TREATMENT PROGNOSES AND RESULTS

Little can be said about the efficacy of treatment efforts reported by the studies reviewed in this paper. The Massachusetts group indicated that 66 percent of the 115 families included in their study were structurally intact at the time of their report, children had been placed outside the home in 27 percent of the cases, and the family structure had been changed (i.e., removal of an adult) in 12 percent (14). It does not seem wise to infer that the figures given are indices of treatment outcomes. If the structurally intact homes are taken to be indicative of successful treatment, what must be said about the splintered homes? Common sense tells us that the removal of a seriously battered child from a dangerous situation at home in time to avoid his destruction or permanent injury must be counted as successful intervention.

Delsordo, by specifying categories of parents with poor prognoses for treatment, implied that favorable results were achieved (or could have been achieved) with the other categories. He gives the following prognostic assessments of treatability (14):

1. *Battered child.* "I know of no case of classical child battering in which the child has been able to remain safely with the abusive parent." Even after separation and treatment, extreme care should be taken not to reunite the abused child and the abusive parent precipitously. (Delsordo reports on one case of precipitous reunion in which the child was killed.)

2. *Disciplinary abuse.* While the parents may comply temporarily with the worker's standards, he should continue his services until real progress is made (implied treatability).

3. *Misplaced abuse.* Prognosis is good. Children are rarely in danger of death, and parents manifest some guilt and are able to control their behavior. While this group is amenable to casework treatment, they are not easy to treat.

4. *Mentally ill* (this category is the same as the "psychotic attitudes" category of Reiner and Kaufman). Prognosis is poor. These parents need psychiatric treatment; they should be separated from the children until substantially improved through treatment.

McFerran and Reiner and Kaufman indicate that favorable results are achieved by use of group techniques, but they do not specify *which* parents would be most amenable to *which* group techniques. In a report on the treatment of delinquents in the community, a California group indicated that conjoint family therapy was most successful with the families of high maturity delinquents, and family re-education (counseling and discussion) with the families of middle maturity cases (22).[13]

COMMUNITY CONSIDERATIONS

Because of the extremely serious consequences of child battering it is imperative that it be recognized and reported when it is encountered. Physicians are an especially crucial group in this respect, yet, as Kempe (28), Dodge (16), and others have pointed out, many of them are not aware of the phenomenon and some prefer to do nothing when they do recognize it. This points to the need for educational efforts directed to the medical profession and to other groups that are likely to have frequent contact with serious cases of child abuse, e.g., law enforcement personnel, schools, public health nurses, social agen-

---

[13] The Community Treatment Project of the California Youth Authority uses a typology of delinquents based on interpersonal maturity levels (1 through 4) and delinquent subtypes associated with specific levels (e.g., middle maturity, I_3; Subtype: Manipulator, M_p) (22).

cies, and the like. Some states have specific laws that make it mandatory to report cases of verified or suspected child battering.[14] Even in states where protection against physical injury derives from the more general statutes pertaining to mayhem, assault and battery, and so on, the physician, as Schoepfer (42) points out, may make himself an accessory to a crime by accepting a fee from the offender (abusive parent) for treating the victim (abused child) and then not reporting the crime. Some writers recommend the passage of specific anti-child-battering laws (in all states) as a way of clarifying the societal sanction for reporting cases of child abuse (16, 32).

Resources. Part of the dilemma in protective services is that the resources for dealing with the cases identified and reported are rather limited. The study of protective service needs and resources in California makes this clear (39). Moreover, while authorities in the field point out the specialized nature of the technical and emotional demands inherent in protective work (26, 38), Reiner and Kaufman (41) report that during the past few years case loads in a variety of social work agencies appear to contain more and more character disorder cases. If this is true, then the techniques and problems associated with protective cases will become the same as those found in the other agencies, and protective *services,* rather than protective *agencies,* should be the goal.

It was noted earlier that there is a polarization of private agency auspices for protective services in the East and public agency auspices in the West. Nevertheless, it has been pointed out that in *all* states it is a public responsibility to assure the provision of such services (40). Arguments can be made for both patterns of auspices— the *right to services* is associated with public

programs, and *flexibility to experiment* is associated with private programs—but if private agencies are to prosper, the financial realities of increasing difficulty in private fund-raising would seem to indicate a pattern of public purchase of the private service (38). Ultimately, however, there is public responsibility for the availability and provision of protective services.

While public welfare programs are generally organized along state lines (sometimes with county administration), a number of federally financed projects to demonstrate the efficacy of protective services have been conducted on the local level. But despite the general agreement that the utility and effectiveness of such programs has been satisfactorily demonstrated, once the project funds have been exhausted the services tend to be dropped (39). What seems necessary is a federally supported ongoing program of such services, and it appears that the efforts continually being made to strengthen the AFDC and child welfare programs under the Social Security Act have this objective partly in mind. A major requirement in accomplishing this is the upgrading of the skills of the public assistance worker, which involves vastly improved and intensified in-service training of personnel. It is crucial that graduate schools of social work participate and provide some leadership in this important task.

Agencies attempting to give increased emphasis to protection or prevention-focused services are faced with the need to modify some of the typical features of social agency practice. Protective case needs cannot generally be met by a worker during prescribed office hours at the agency. A great deal of field work and investigation are required, often in the evening. Accommodations must be made to the availability of the clients and ancillary resources. Stereotypes about law enforcement and correctional personnel must be discarded, and contacts must be individualized. Community organization is every worker's job, and in protective cases this will become especially apparent.

---

[14] Fontana cites the following states as having such laws as of 1964: California, Colorado, Florida, Minnesota, Ohio, Pennsylvania, Tennessee, Wisconsin, and Wyoming (20). De Francis adds Idaho and Oregon to the list of states with such laws in 1963, but omits Tennessee (13).

Descriptions of other hard-to-reach clients (36, 47, 49) give an indication of their essential similarity to the clients in protective cases. Consideration thus might be given to following the pattern set by the Family-centered Project in St. Paul, where an interagency pool of skilled, well-trained workers was created to provide treatment for the most critical cases identified in the community (37).

DISCUSSION AND CONCLUSIONS

Child-battering and serious child abuse are inflicted by parents with a variety of problems ranging from violent and episodic schizophrenia to immature and impulse-ridden character disorder, who displace and act out their anger over marital conflicts onto their children. The common element among them is that children are used as targets of abuse and injury in the process of projecting, displacing, and denying intrapsychic and other-object-oriented hostility and aggression.

The children are the injured parties, and the term "battered child syndrome" may be of use in hospitals where it is important to identify the external source of the injuries. But insofar as the term does not identify the etiological problems involved —i.e., the psychosocial dynamics and problems of the parents and the family that result in the battering of the child—it is of little use to those involved in providing protective services. A more appropriate label would be "families with child-battering adults"—without the term "syndrome," since there is no *clearly defined entity* that can be identified.

The family environment plays a crucial role in the development of the child's personality, character, and social style of life. Life in an unfavorable family environment can result in a dependent, unstable, impulse-ridden, delinquent adult who will, in turn, be a poor parent, generating in this way an epidemiological chain of inadequate, destructive parenting. Many of the studies cited in this paper have reported on the histories of childhood abuse, neglect, and deprivation typical of the abusive parent.

Early identification and intervention are thus indicated. While the schools are good at identification, it would be preferable to identify the still earlier, preschool instances of neglect and abuse. The National Study Service's report on California observes that many of the protective cases coming to the attention of the authorities had histories of prior mistreatment; thus the difficulties had continued without identification or remedy for some time (39). Class comments on the more recent tendency in this country to "play it safe," to not get involved in the personal affairs of others (9). He cites a case in which three children had been chained to a bed for days, yet neighbors were not aware that the children lived in the house, although they had been there for six months! In the past few years a number of incidents have been reported prominently in the national press in which citizens stood by without taking action while some innocent person was beaten or stabbed. (This is, perhaps, another of the unfortunate consequences of industrialization and the movement from rural openness and co-operation to urban privacy and isolation.) Hopefully, help will come to the abused child and his family before it is too late. Abuse, like other behavior, becomes habitual; children learn from the behavior they witness and they internalize conceptions of themselves communicated to them by others.

Beginning attempts have been made at a typology of child abuse. Typological systems have been hypothesized and given preliminary tests. Treatment models have been proposed. What is needed now is a more precisely formulated typological system, replete with predictive indicators of the danger to the children and the probabilities of various outcomes for specifically prescribed treatment.

An American Public Welfare Association report calls for the statutory assignment of responsibility for protective services in each state (40). Only then is there any accountability and ultimate assurance of at least a minimum acceptable level of service. In the report of the National Study Service the recommendation is made that protective services in California be a function of public child welfare services in a new division to be called "Child Care and Protection" (39). Class argues that probation departments are already overloaded and that public welfare agencies are identified with public assistance; he proposes that protective services be located in "child welfare agencies" (9). (Many public welfare departments would resent the implication that they are not, at least partly, child welfare agencies, but Class seems to be referring to the private "family" agencies.)

As the APWA report states, ultimately there is public responsibility to see that protective services are available when needed (40). The problems of many public assistance families require treatment similar to that considered efficacious for protective service cases. There appears to be a significant similarity of purpose, technique, and public responsibility that makes public welfare auspices a natural environment for protective services.

Any agency carrying the responsibility for protective casework services will have to work out viable relationships with a number of agencies that share responsibility for aspects of protective work other than the primary casework with the parents. Law enforcement personnel are extremely important and crucial. They generally have responsibility for answering emergency calls, especially during evenings, weekends, and holidays. Often they have to make immediate decisions about whether to remove a child from his home. When there is no specified emergency child shelter care, the task of the juvenile police officer is even more difficult. Often juvenile detention homes, hospitals, and jails are utilized for emergency care. In some cases police officers will even take children to their own

---

[15] Personal communication to the writer.

homes, even though this may not be legally authorized.[15] It can be seen that the police officer is an extremely important ally and colleague in protective work. So are the probation officer, the doctor, the judge, and school personnel. The logical necessity for interagency co-operation belies the extreme difficulty of accomplishing it (49).

A number of ancillary services are required for an effective program of community protective services. Included are emergency shelter care, homemaker services, day care, foster homes, financial assistance, and psychiatric treatment.

Part I of this paper has attempted to bring some perspective to the extremely serious problem of child battering and abuse. The recent interest and concern with the problem is, it is hoped, a harbinger of increased services and research activity.

REFERENCES

1. Adelson, Lester. "Slaughter of the Innocents," *New England Journal of Medicine*, Vol. 264 (1961), pp. 1345–1349.
2. Allen, A., and Morton, A. *This is Your Child: The Story of the National Society for the Prevention of Cruelty to Children.* London, Eng.: Routledge & Kegan Paul, 1961.
3. Boardman, Helen E. "A Project to Rescue Children from Inflicted Injuries," *Social Work*, Vol. 7, No. 1 (January 1962), pp. 43–51.
4. Bossard, James H. S. *The Sociology of Child Development.* New York: Harper & Bros., 1948.
5. Bowlby, John. *Child Care and the Growth of Love.* London, Eng.: Whitefriars Press, 1953.
6. Bryant, Harold D., *et al.* "Physical Abuse of Children in an Agency Study," *Child Welfare*, Vol. 42, No. 3 (March 1963), pp. 125–130.
7. Burlingham, Dorothy, and Freud, Anna. *Infants Without Families.* New York: International Universities Press, 1944.
8. Chesser, Eustace. *Cruelty to Children.* New York: Philosophical Library, 1952.
9. Class, Norris E. "Neglect, Social Deviance, Community Action," *NPPA Journal*, Vol. 6, No. 1 (January 1960), pp. 17–23.
10. Cohen, Nathan E. *Social Work in the American Tradition.* New York: Dryden Press, 1958.
11. DeFrancis, Vincent. *Child Protective Services in the U.S.* Denver: Children's Division, American Humane Association, 1956.
12. ———. *The Fundamentals of Child Protection.* Denver: Children's Division, American Humane Association, 1955.

13. ———. *Review of Legislation to Protect the Battered Child*. Denver: American Humane Association, undated.

14. Delsordo, James D. "Protective Casework for Abused Children," *Children*, Vol. 10, No. 6 (November-December 1963), pp. 213–218.

15. Diamond, Bernard L. "Newsletter of the Northern California Service League." San Francisco, January 1959. Mimeographed.

16. Dodge, Philip R. "Medical Implications of Physical Abuse of Children," in *Protecting the Battered Child*. Denver: American Humane Association, 1962. Pp. 23–25.

17. Elmer, Elizabeth. "Abused Young Children Seen in Hospitals," *Social Work*, Vol. 5, No. 4 (October 1960), pp. 98–102.

18. ———. "Identification of Abused Children," *Children*, Vol. 10, No. 5 (September-October 1963), pp. 180–184.

19. Erikson, Erik H. *Childhood and Society*. New York: W. W. Norton & Co., 1950.

20. Fontana, Vincent J. *The Maltreated Child*. Springfield, Ill.: Charles C Thomas, 1964.

21. Freud, Anna. "Special Experiences of Children—Especially in Times of Social Disturbance," in Kenneth Soddy, ed., *Mental Health and Infant Development*. New York: Basic Books, 1956.

22. Grant, Marguerite Q., Warren, Martin, and Turner, James K. "Community Treatment Project Report No. 3." Sacramento: California Youth Authority, 1963.

23. Housden, Leslie G. *The Prevention of Cruelty to Children*. London, Eng.: Cape, 1955.

24. Jackson, Don D., and Weakland, J. H. "Conjoint Family Therapy: Some Considerations in Theory, Technique, and Results," *Psychiatry*, Vol. 24 (1961), pp. 30–45.

25. Kassebaum, Gene G., Ward, David A., and Wilner, Daniel M. *Group Treatment by Correctional Personnel*. Sacramento: California Department of Corrections, 1963.

26. Kaufman, Irving. "The Contribution of Protective Services," *Child Welfare*, Vol. 36, No. 2 (February 1957).

27. ———. "Psychiatric Implications of Physical Abuse of Children," in *Protecting the Battered Child*. Denver: American Humane Association, 1962. Pp. 17–22.

28. Kempe, Henry C., *et al*. "The Battered Child Syndrome," *Journal of the American Medical Association*, Vol. 181, No. 1 (July 7, 1962), p. 17.

29. Maas, Henry S., *et al*. *Children in Need of Parents*. New York: Columbia University Press, 1959.

30. McCorkle, L. W., Elias, A., and Bixby, F. L. *The Highfields Story: A Unique Experiment in the Treatment of Juvenile Delinquents*. New York: Henry Holt & Co., 1958.

31. McFerran, Jane. "Parents' Groups in Protective Services," *Children*, Vol. 5, No. 6 (November-December 1958), pp. 223–228.

32. Merrill, Edgar J. "Physical Abuse of Children—An Agency Study," in *Protecting the Battered Child*. Denver: American Humane Association, 1962. Pp. 1–16.

33. Morris, Marian G., and Gould, Robert W. "Role Reversal: A Concept in Dealing with the Neglected/Battered-Child Syndrome," in *The Neglected Battered-Child Syndrome*. New York: Child Welfare League of America, 1963.

34. ———, Gould, Robert W., and Matthews, Patricia J. "Toward Prevention of Child Abuse," *Children*, Vol. 11, No. 2 (March-April 1964).

35. Nurse, Shirley M. "Parents Who Abuse Their Children," *Smith College Studies in Social Work*, Vol. 35, No. 4 (October 1964), pp. 11–25.

36. Overton, Alice. "Aggressive Casework," *Social Work Journal*, Vol. 33, No. 3 (July 1952), pp. 149–151.

37. ———, and Tinker, Katherine H. *Casework Notebook*. St. Paul: Family-centered Project, 1957.

38. Philbrick, Elizabeth Barry. *Treating Parental Pathology Through Child Protective Services*. Denver: Children's Division, American Humane Association, 1960.

39. *Planning for the Protection and Care of Neglected Children in California*. Sacramento: National Study Service, 1964.

40. *Preventive and Protective Services to Children, A Responsibility of the Public Welfare Agency*. Chicago: American Public Welfare Association, 1958.

41. Reiner, Beatrice Simcox, and Kaufman, Irving. *Character Disorders in Parents of Delinquents*. New York: Family Service Association of America, 1959.

42. Schoepfer, Arthur E. "Legal Implications in Connection with Physical Abuse of Children," in *Protecting the Battered Child*. Denver: American Humane Association, 1962. P. 26.

43. Studt, Elliot. "Worker-Client Authority Relationships in Social Work," *Social Work*, Vol. 4, No. 1 (January 1959), pp. 18–28.

44. U.S. Bureau of the Census, *Statistical Abstract of the United States 1964*. Washington, D. C.: U.S. Government Printing Office, 1964.

45. U.S. Children's Bureau, "Bibliography on the Battered Child." Washington, D.C.: U.S. Government Printing Office, October 1963. Mimeographed.

46. U.S. Department of Health, Education, and Welfare. *The Abused Child: Principles and Suggested Language by Legislation on Reporting of the Physically Abused Child*. Washington, D.C.: U.S. Government Printing Office, 1963.

47. Wiltse, Kermit T. "Social Casework Services in the ADC Program," *Social Service Review*, Vol. 28, No. 2 (June 1954).

48. Young, Leontine. *Wednesday's Children*. New York: McGraw-Hill Book Co., 1964.

49. Zalba, Serapio R. *Women Prisoners and Their Families*. Los Angeles: Delmar Publishing Co., 1964.

PART 2
Developing Strategies
for Practice

BY SERAPIO RICHARD ZALBA

The Abused Child: II. A Typology for Classification and Treatment

■ A problem/treatment typology is presented for families in which there has been physical abuse (i.e., injury) of children by parents. Each of the categories specifies (1) the immediate danger to the child, (2) the locus of the dysfunction in the child-parent relationship, and (3) the immediate reason for the aggression/abuse. In addition, treatment objectives are outlined and treatment strategy is linked, point by point, with the objectives. ■

IN PART I of this paper the writer reviewed the recent literature on child abuse, attempting to provide a perspective on the dynamics of this system of problem behavior and the parameters of its occurrence.[1] There is little question that the abuse of children, sometimes unto death, is and must be of serious concern to social work, and indeed to the larger society itself.

Admittedly there is no clear demarcation between severe punishment and abuse. The extreme positions on the continuum are, however, fairly clear. A mild spanking on the buttocks of a 2-year-old child is quite different from the case of abuse found by a protective agency, where a child may have had scalding water poured on his genitals by a cruel, disturbed parent, or may have been beaten until unconscious.[2]

Attempts to identify cases of child abuse (sometimes called the "battered child syndrome") encounter formidable obstacles.[3] Once the worker has identified a case, he has the difficult task of deciding what to do about it. The removal of the abused child from his home may be one solution, but not necessarily the best one. Other possible interventions must be considered, especially when there are a number of chil-

SERAPIO RICHARD ZALBA, MSW, is Lecturer, School of Applied Social Sciences, Western Reserve University, Cleveland, Ohio. The first part of this paper, "A Survey of the Problem," appeared in the October 1966 issue.

[1] Serapio Richard Zalba, "The Abused Child: I. A Survey of the Problem," Social Work, Vol. 11, No. 4 (October 1966), pp. 3–16. The concept "behavior system" involves the consideration of recurrent, patterned behavior as consisting of a multiplicity of specific behaviors that are interrelated with one another, are functional within the system, and take into consideration cultural values, social roles, personality, and environmental reality factors. This concept is related to Merton's conception of deviant behavior as being determined by and being a function of social structure—i.e., of social systems. See Robert K. Merton, Social Theory and Social Structure (New York: Free Press of Glencoe, 1962). Greater emphasis, however, must be placed on the influence of the personality as it develops first in childhood within the family system and subsequently during adult life experiences. Thus Freudian personality theory is relevant and will be utilized as part of the theoretical framework for this paper. However, the writer agrees with Merton's objection that the psychoanalytic point of view tends to explain deviant behavior almost exclusively on the basis of intrapsychic factors. Consequently, role theory and systems theory will also be utilized as part of the theoretical frame of reference. The author is indebted to Dr. Elizabeth Meier for encouragement and advice in the development of this typology and in the writing of this paper.

[2] See Edgar J. Merrill, "Physical Abuse of Children—An Agency Study," in Protecting the Battered Child (Denver: American Humane Association, 1962), pp. 1–16; Harold D. Bryant et al., "Physical Abuse of Children in an Agency Study," Child Welfare, Vol. 42, No. 3 (March 1963), pp. 125–130.

[3] The term "battered child syndrome" was coined by Dr. Henry C. Kempe and his associates. See Kempe et al., "The Battered Child Syndrome," Journal of the American Medical Association, Vol. 181, No. 1 (July 7, 1962), p. 17. For a discussion of the obstacles to recognition of cases of child abuse see Zalba, op. cit., pp. 8–9.

Reprinted from SOCIAL WORK, 12 (January 1967), pp. 70–79.

dren in the home, some of whom may not have been abused (as is often the case). The relatively limited literature on the abused child has not yet provided us with a systematic problem/treatment typology that might serve as a guide in the formulation of intervention strategy in child abuse cases. It is the intent of this paper to make a beginning attempt at outlining such a typology in the hope of providing the rudiments of a guide, however crude, for planning intervention strategy. It would further serve as a take-off point for the development of increasingly sophisticated and viable typologies validated empirically by field studies.[4]

ANALYSIS OF HUMAN BEHAVIOR

A prescriptive typology requires the *systematic* identification of (1) where the basic problem lies, (2) what causes and maintains the problem behavior despite pressures toward social conformity, and (3) what can be done to eliminate or ameliorate the problem and its consequences.[5] The salient organizing principles in constructing a classification scheme in a *specified* behavior system—i.e., child abuse—have some relevance in a more general frame of reference in that the determinants of human behavior in the variety of behavior systems that society labels "problem behavior" (e.g., juvenile delinquency, mental illness, financial dependency) consist of elements along the same general dimensions. Thus, a typology for problem/treatment classification in a specific behavior system will reflect an underlying approach to the explanation of

human behavior in general. In addition, however, the typology should account for the typical and recurring features of cases in the specific problem area under consideration. Logically or theoretically possible categories for which cases do not occur empirically may help to provide theoretical closure to a classification scheme, but they are of little practical value; consequently they will not be dealt with in this paper.

In social work, human behavior is typically seen as being determined by the following factors:

1. The individual's personality system (e.g., his basic pattern of id/ego/superego functioning).

2. His significant interpersonal relationships—especially the nuclear family of which he is a current member, but also extended kinship and important friendship and work (and other activity-oriented) relationships.

3. His values, which reflect cultural and subcultural influences.

4. The number, complexity, and congruence of—and his relative mastery over—the social roles he performs.

5. His physical makeup and condition—i.e., physical assets, liabilities, disabilities, chronic or acute illness, and so on.

6. The amount of stress or support provided by the external environment, in physical-social-cultural-political-economic resource terms (e.g., depression, discrimination, opportunity, rapid social change, barren terrain, and natural catastrophes).

The identification of the primary or crucial factor precipitating or maintaining a specific case of child-abusing behavior should be made by considering the data about the case from the perspective afforded by the analytic framework described above. A determination then must be made of what aspect of the case is most relevant in classifying it in such a way as to indicate the most efficacious intervention. The point made here is that the basis for typological classification does not necessarily follow the logic of causation categories. On the contrary—when the major purpose of the ty-

---

[4] The pioneering classification efforts of Delsordo and the team of investigators at the Massachusetts SPCC must be acknowledged appreciatively by subsequent venturers in this field. *See* James D. Delsordo, "Protective Casework for Abused Children," *Children*, Vol. 10, No. 6 (November-December 1963), pp. 213–218; Bryant, *op. cit.;* and Merrill, *op. cit.*

[5] *See* the discussion of the requirements of typologies in Samuel Finestone, "Issues Involved in Developing Diagnostic Classifications for Casework," in *Casework Papers 1960* (New York: Family Service Association of America, 1960).

pological system is to organize cases according to similarities in their intervention strategies, other principles of classification may be followed. Such is the case in the typological system to be outlined here, where classification will be made along the dimensions of locus of the problem (e.g., personal system, family system, social system, and so forth), ability of the abusive person to control such behavior, and the psychosocial source of abusive behavior.[6]

UNIT OF CLASSIFICATION

The unit of classification in the typology to be developed here will be the family. In arriving at the diagnostic/treatment classification of a specific family, attention must be paid to the way in which the various members of the family system impinge on one another, and how factors external to the family system (e.g., the external environment) affect transactions within the family system.[7]

First, however, let us consider what the literature says about the behavior system of child abuse—facts for which a typology must account. In summary:

1. In many cases only *one* of a number of children in the family is chosen as the target of abuse, and frequently that child was conceived or born extra-maritally or premaritally.[8]

2. Marital partners tend to protect the abusive parent from disclosure or prosecution through patent denial of obvious facts.[9]

3. Occasionally an abusing father also

abuses his wife, but more frequently he restricts his serious abuse to his children.[10]

4. Some abusive parents are *generally* abusive, getting into altercations with the spouse, casual drinking acquaintances, and so on.[11]

5. The parents in child abuse cases tend to resist the interventions of social agencies even when these are directed toward the children alone (in contradistinction to neglectful parents, who do not seem to mind interventions, even when these include removal of or attention to the children).[12]

6. Many of the homes involved meet or exceed middle-class standards for furnishings and cleanliness; the parents in them may be generally perceived as "upstanding citizens," although cold and rigid.[13]

7. In over half the cases in which child abuse results in hospitalization there is precedent or subsequent abuse of equal severity.[14]

8. Not infrequently the battered child requiring multiple hospitalizations is taken to a series of different hospitals in order to conceal the recurrence of injuries, which might arouse suspicion as to their causation.[15]

9. The abusive parent is most often impulse-ridden, with a great deal of marital and family conflict and faulty community relations.[16]

10. Many abusive parents had experienced abuse as children.[17]

---

[6] *Ibid.*

[7] *See* Marian G. Morris, Robert W. Gould, and Patricia J. Matthews, "Toward Prevention of Child Abuse," *Children*, Vol. 11, No. 2 (March-April 1964), who suggest taking into account many of the same factors.

[8] Helen E. Boardman, "A Project to Rescue Children from Inflicted Injury," *Social Work*, Vol. 7, No. 1 (January 1962), pp. 43–51; Bryant *et al., op. cit.;* Delsordo, *op. cit.;* Henry C. Kempe *et al., op. cit.;* Shirley M. Nurse, "Parents Who Abuse Their Children," *Smith College Studies in Social Work*, Vol. 35, No. 4 (October 1964), pp. 11–25.

[9] Boardman, *op. cit.;* Nurse, *op. cit.*

[10] Delsordo, *op. cit.;* Merrill, *op. cit.*

[11] *Ibid.*

[12] Leontine Young, *Wednesday's Children* (New York: McGraw-Hill Book Co., 1964).

[13] Merrill, *op. cit.*

[14] Elizabeth Elmer, "Identification of Abused Children," *Children*, Vol. 10, No. 5 (September-October 1963), pp. 180–184; Kempe *et al., op. cit.*

[15] Boardman, *op. cit.*

[16] Bryant *et al., op. cit.;* Kempe *et al., op. cit.;* Merrill, *op. cit.*

[17] Bryant *et al., op. cit.;* Kempe *et al., op. cit.;* Morris *et al., op. cit.; Planning for the Protection and Care of Neglected Children in California* (Sacramento: National Study Service, 1964); Beatrice Simcox Reiner and Irving Kaufman, *Character Disorders in Parents of Delinquents* (New York: Family Service Association of America, 1959).

11. Children tend to have impaired relationships with the abusive parent.

12. Abused children tend to be depressive, hyperactive, destructive, fearful, withdrawn, bed-wetters, truants, and fire-setters; they overreact to hostility.[18]

These data seem to provide a clear justification for using the family as the unit of classification. The demands made on the individual in his role as parent and as spouse seem clearly related to the frustrations, hostility, and subsequent violent actions of many of the abusive parents. Indeed, Morris and Gould conceptualize some child abuse as being an outcome of "role reversal," wherein the parents had expectations that children would meet their needs rather than require need-meeting services on the part of the parents.[19] In other cases one gets the impression that the complicity of the other parent in not disclosing the actions of the abusive one and the resistance of both to removal of the ostensibly unvalued child are related to a desire to keep the scapegoat who acts as the object of displaced or reflected hostility arising out of marital conflict, disappointments, and inadequacies. In any case of child abuse by a parent or parent substitute the abuse is an intrafamilial transaction and, consequently, a family matter.

TREATMENT PRESCRIPTIONS

An attempt will be made to identify the most efficacious treatment specifics that correspond to the various classifications that are constructed. Perhaps the term "treatment specifics" is misleading in view of the writer's conviction that only broad interventive strategies—e.g., removal of a child from his home—can be prescribed for a case away from the actual treatment situation. However, the term *is* useful in this discussion because unless even broad interventive strategies can be shown to be specific for a particular problem classification, the problem typology will be useless as a guide for formulating intervention strategies.

There is a balancing consideration that limits the specificity with which interventive prescription can be made: discrete acts of intervention tend to be made on a tactical basis—in response to a concrete, "here-and-now" issue that arises during an interview or group meeting (or other social work practice circumstance) when the issue could not necessarily have been predicted in advance.[20] The differentiation being made is between broad strategies of interventive entry in a case, which *can* be determined in a diagnostic staffing, and the "on-the-scene" tactics and techniques of the practitioner. The latter decisions can be made only "on site."[21] This is part of the reason social work practice is referred to as an art.

The relevant literature provides some principles that should be kept in mind in developing treatment prescriptions in child abuse cases:

1. Emergency treatment alone is useless and dangerous.[22]

2. An attempt should be made to keep the child in the home; often he falls apart when removed, even from an extremely poor (historically) environment.[23]

[18] Bryant *et al., op. cit.;* Delsordo, *op. cit.*

[19] Marian G. Morris and Robert W. Gould, "Role Reversal: A Concept in Dealing with the Neglected/ Battered-Child Syndrome," in *The Neglected/Battered-Child Syndrome* (New York: Child Welfare League of America, 1963).

[20] *See* Martin Bloom, "Connecting Formal Behavioral Science Theory to Individual Social Work Practice," *Social Service Review,* Vol. 39, No. 1 (March 1965), who differentiates between strategies and tactics. Roy Grinker, on the other hand, takes the more extreme view that *all* decisions are tactical. *See* "A Transactional Model for Psychotherapy," in Morris I. Stein, ed., *Contemporary Psychotherapies* (New York: Free Press of Glencoe, 1961), pp. 190–213.

[21] The tactical skills of practitioners can be *fostered* through review and analysis of what has been done in a case, and the consequent outcomes of the tactics used.

[22] Bryant *et al., op. cit.;* Delsordo, *op. cit.;* Elizabeth Barry Philbrick, *Treating Parental Pathology Through Child Protective Services* (Denver: Children's Division, American Humane Association, 1960); Reiner and Kaufman, *op. cit.*

[23] Irving Kaufman, "Psychiatric Implications of

3. Clients in child abuse cases tend to respond positively to authority.[24]

4. Prognosis is best when parents show guilt, anxiety, and concern over the children, rather than being mainly concerned with what will be done to them as abusers.[25]

5. Protective service workers must beware of *surface compliance*, which is designed primarily to get the agency personnel out of the picture.[26]

6. Continuity of treatment, despite client rebuffs, acting-out, and testing, is extremely important in view of typical histories of perceived rejection, unlovability, and the like.[27]

7. Removal of parent or child from the home is an event of great stress for the family, requiring casework services to minimize the psychological and social traumata.

8. Group treatment may be the method of choice for the abusive parent, the marital couple, or even the whole family.[28]

Physical Abuse of Children," in *Protecting the Battered Child* (Denver: American Humane Association, 1962), pp. 17–22.

[24] Reiner and Kaufman, *op. cit.*

[25] Delsordo, *op. cit.*

[26] *Ibid.*

[27] Reiner and Kaufman, *op. cit.*

[28] J. E. Neighbor *et al.*, "An Approach to the Selection of Patients for Group Therapy," in Max Rosenbaum and Milton Berger, eds., *Group Psychotherapy and Group Function* (New York: Basic Books, 1963).

CONSTRUCTION OF TYPOLOGY

The problem typology will be constructed along three dimensions (see Table 1 for a schematic of case classifications):

1. The immediate danger of further harm to the child within the family structure as currently composed, despite interventive efforts short of removal of child or parent from the home (i.e., the ability of the abusive parent to control his abusive behavior).

2. The locus of the dysfunction that eventuates in child abuse (e.g., psychosis in the individual, the individual's general inability to control aggressive and hostile impulses, marital conflict, or resentment toward an extra-maritally conceived child; problems located in the family system; problems located in the person-environment or family-environment system).

3. The immediate reason for the hostility that is vented on the abused child.[29]

The treatment prescriptions that are linked to specific problem categories will be made with regard to treatment objectives and treatment strategy for (1) the abused child or children, (2) the abusive parent, and (3) other members of the family unit. It should be noted that the lower case letters representing treatment strategies are linked to the corresponding upper case letters representing treatment objectives.

---

[29] Finestone, *op. cit. See also* Merrill, *op. cit.*

TABLE 1. SCHEMATIC OF CASE CLASSIFICATIONS

Locus of problem	Control over abuse	
	Uncontrollable abuse	Controllable abuse
Personality system	I. Psychotic parent	
	II. Pervasively angry and abusive parent	IV. Cold, compulsive, disciplinarian parent
	III. Depressive, passive-aggressive parent	
Family system		V. Impulsive but generally adequate parent with marital conflict
Person-environment or family-environment system		VI. Parent with identity/role crisis

TYPOLOGY: UNCONTROLLABLE ABUSE

Classification I. Psychotic parent.

Abuse is unpredictable, ritualistic, sometimes violent; it has idiosyncratic meaning related to the fantasies of the abuser. Infanticide and child homicide most often fall into this category.[30] The children are in grave danger.

Treatment Objectives	*Treatment Strategy*
A. Separation of abuser and children.	a. Use of aggressive casework with legal sanctions, including court wardship and law enforcement intervention when needed; commitment of abusive parent to a psychiatric institution; provision of homemaker services or foster home placement when needed.
B. Stabilization of family environment through the provision of psychological and material support and realistic, viable plans for the short and long run.	b. Supportive casework, co-ordinating, and referral services; assistance in reality planning for the family for the present and the future; assistance in obtaining needed material resources; homemaker services when needed.
C. Resolution of residual psychosocial problems of children and parents.	c. Children are often fearful, anxious, withdrawn, and require reassurance and stable, nurturing relationships that can be provided by a caseworker, a Big Brother or Big Sister, a community center group worker, and so on.
	cc. The remaining parent may need a supportive relationship with a caseworker.
	ccc. The psychotic parent requires psychiatric treatment. Treatment prognosis is poor.
D. Maintenance of separation until significant change in the abuser makes reunion safe.	d. Supervision over the family situation to insure that precipitous reunion is avoided.[31]

Classification II. Pervasively angry and abusive parent.[32]

Abuse is an impulsive and unfettered expression of general rage and hostility, which is part of the person's childhood-determined personality and character. Personal inadequacy, alcoholism, evictions, poor housekeeping and financial management, and irresponsibility are typical, as is illegitimacy. There is a preponderance of women in this category—there is no father in the home in over half these families; when the father is present, there is severe and open marital conflict. There is no pattern of abuse; *all* children in the family are abused. Most often the abused children are over 5 years old and are rebelling against parental values; however, these homes are very dangerous for infants.[33]

---

[30] Lester Adelson, "Slaughter of the Innocents," *New England Journal of Medicine*, Vol. 264 (1961), pp. 1345–1349; Delsordo, *op. cit.*; Kaufman, *op. cit.*; Kempe *et al.*, *op. cit.*

[31] Delsordo, *op. cit.*

[32] This term was suggested by Elizabeth Meier, professor, School of Applied Social Sciences, Western Reserve University, Cleveland, Ohio.

[33] Delsordo, *op. cit.*; Eustace Chesser, *Cruelty to Children* (New York: Philosophical Library, 1952).

Classification II. Pervasively angry and abusive parent (Continued)

Treatment Objectives

Same as for Classification I.

Treatment Strategy

a. Same as for Classification I, except that jail or prison is a more appropriate facility for custody and control.

b. Same as for Classification I.

c. Same as for Classification I.

cc. Authority and relationship-based treatment for the abusive parent, with consistent and appropriate limit-setting and supervision (e.g., probation); group treatment aimed at socialization (i.e., awareness of effect of self on others, interpersonal satisfactions, and group-sanctioned support for social control).[34] Prognosis is generally poor.

d. Same as for Classification I.

Classification III. Depressive, passive-aggressive parent.[35]

Abuse represents resentment and anger at having to meet the needs of others[36] and at inability to meet the role expectations of a nurturing parent (the parent's personality feature—dependency—limits his ability to meet societal role demands). Children are seen as competitors for resources and attention. The abuser often seems unassuming and reticent about expressing feelings and desires, depressed, unhappy, and unresponsive; he is not sure he wants a marriage, home, or children. Usually only one child is abused, but sometimes all of them are. The children are in grave danger.[37]

Treatment Objectives

Same as for Classification I.

Treatment Strategy

a. Use of aggressive casework with legal sanctions, including court wardship and law enforcement intervention when needed; removal of abusive parent; provision of homemaker services or foster home placement when needed.

aa. It may be that only one child was abused. If others seem safe, it may be best to remove only the abused child and consider long-term foster care or relinquishment for eventual adoption. Leaving the nonabused children in the home should be contingent on treatment of the abusive parent and supervision of the home by a protective agency.

b. Same as for Classification I.

c. Same as for Classification I.

cc. Relationship-based therapy for the abusive parent (as described by Reiner and Kaufman for character-disordered adults).[38] Prognosis is poor.

d. Same as for Classification I.

---

[34] *See,* for example, Neighbor *et al., op. cit.*

[35] This is the group of cases generally discussed in hospital studies under the term "Battered Child Syndrome." *See,* for example, Kempe *et al., op. cit.;* Boardman, *op. cit.;* and Elizabeth Elmer, "Abused Children Seen in Hospitals," *Social Work,* Vol. 5, No. 4 (October 1960), pp. 98–102.

[36] This is the role-reversal dynamic described by Morris and Gould, *op. cit.*

[37] Delsordo, *op. cit.;* Merrill, *op. cit.*

[38] *Op. cit.*

TYPOLOGY: CONTROLLABLE ABUSE

Classification IV. Cold, compulsive, disciplinarian parent.

Abuse is in reaction to the children's need for closeness and affection, interest in body and sex (the parent's personality feature—compulsiveness—limits his ability to meet societal role demands). Such parents have compulsively clean homes, avoid dirt and sex, cannot relax or talk well; they are cold, rigid, not friendly or warm; often they are upstanding citizens. Their main concern is with their own pleasures; they are unable to feel love or protectiveness toward their children. They defend their right to discipline (i.e., abuse) their children, who are usually over 7 years old and are generally abused with implements (e.g., belts, sticks, pokers, and the like) rather than by direct contact with hands or fists; abuse may be coldly sadistic. When confronted with societal intervention, these parents will appear to conform (at least temporarily) in order to effect termination of the service (i.e., surveillance).[39]

Treatment Objectives	*Treatment Strategy*
A. Control over parents' abusive behavior.	a. Home supervision (i.e., surveillance), with legal child protection sanctions (e.g., probation), until alterations in intrafamily dynamics indicate that the children are no longer in danger.
B. Development of greater parental self-awareness of own feelings and ways of expressing them; trust in self and others, and consequent improvement in marital and parental role performances.	b. Group therapy for both parents in order to explicate fears of warmth, intimacy, feelings, and loss; learning to express, give, and receive emotionally oriented communication and behavior in more direct (i.e., not displaced) and socially acceptable ways; get realistic feedback (i.e., reality confrontation) of own role behavior and alternative behaviors utilized by others, in a protected environment (i.e., the group).[40]
C. Resolution of residual problems, mainly of the children.	c. Same as for Classification I.

Classification V. Impulsive, but generally adequate, parent with marital conflict.[41]

Abuse is the result of marital conflict displaced onto a child. In many of these cases there was premarital conception or birth and abuse was limited to the child involved (who was usually over 5 years old). The abuser (usually the father) can control his behavior and manifests anxiety over it; homes are generally neat and adequate; the children in the family tend to be bed-wetters, truants, fire-setters, and withdrawn; there is rarely danger of the death of a child through abuse.

Treatment Objectives	*Treatment Strategy*
A. Control over abusive behavior.	a. Same as for Classification IV.
B. Development of awareness that abuse represents a displacement of frustration and aggression toward the spouse; the establishment of more direct and satisfying communication among all members of the family system (vis-à-vis child abuse, marital satisfaction, and child behavior problems such as bed-wetting and fire-setting).	b. Group therapy for the parents or conjoint family therapy for the whole family.[42] When one parent dominates completely, individual treatment may be preferable; but since treatment should be aimed at exposing the marital conflict, its bases, and its part in the child abuse, and helping the family communicate more directly and less destructively, a group approach would seem to be the treatment of choice.
	bb. Psychotherapy for the abused child or children when residual personality effects of abuse warrant intensive treatment.

---

[39] Delsordo, *op. cit.*; Merrill, *op. cit.*

[40] *See,* for example, Neighbor *et al., op. cit.*

[41] This classification takes in approximately one-half of Delsordo's child abuse cases.

[42] *See,* for example, Don D. Jackson and J. H. Weakland, "Conjoint Family Therapy: Some Considerations in Theory, Technique, and Results," *Psychiatry,* Vol. 24 (1961), pp. 30–45.

Classification VI. Parent with identity/role crisis.

Abuse represents displaced anger at loss of capability for role performance, such as following bodily damage. Such parents are angry, controlled, rigid, disciplinarian; the women in this category are often alcoholics, promiscuous, arrested as vagrants (i.e., "lewd and lascivious"). This classification is similar to Classification IV, except that the abuse in this classification is a result of the stress of external factors (physical disability and change in role abilities and expectation—e.g., the disabled man who stays home while his wife now becomes the wage-earner), or a personality not resilient enough to make the required role changes without threat or loss of identity. The locus of the problem in this classification is thus the person-environment system (rather than the person system, as in Classification IV).[43]

Treatment Objectives	*Treatment Strategy*
A. Control over abusive behavior.	a. Same as for Classification IV.
B. Development of awareness that abuse is a displacement of frustration and aggression felt because of inability to meet old role demands and resultant identity crisis. Opportunity for direct expression of frustration and development of new and realistic conception of self, including development of new role skills.	b. Casework for expression of feelings, clarifications of self-image and others' expectations; elaboration of a realistic self-image; development of restorative social role skills. bb. Physical and vocational retraining when applicable.
C. Resolution of residual problems of other family members.	c. Same as for Classification I. cc. Same as for Classification I.

SUMMARY

It can be seen that in the first three classifications of the typology it is *not* expected that abuse can be controlled without separation of the abusive parent from the children. The locus of the problem in each of those classes is the personal system of the abuser, the basic determinant being personality structure (or lack of adequate development in certain personality functions). For Classification IV, the cold, compulsive parent, the problem is also centered in the basic personality or character of the abusive parent, but here the abuser has control over such behavior (i.e., can respond to social environmental pressures), and hidden marital conflict is a contributing factor. For Classification V, the problem is located primarily in the marital system —i.e., the family system—and for Classification VI, in the person-environment system. In each of these classes the abuse of the children is generally amenable to control by methods other than separation of children and parent(s).

When the problem is located in the individual system primarily (i.e., Classifications I, II, and III) the treatment prescribed tends to be individually based.[44] When the problem is located primarily in the individual but marital or intrafamilial interaction is an important contributory factor (i.e., Classification IV), individual, group, or both treatment approaches may be indicated. When the problem is primarily located in the family system (i.e., Classification V), conjoint family therapy or some equivalent may be indicated. When the problem is located in the person-environment system, treatment may be addressed toward that system (e.g., increasing personal capability, as with vocational rehabilitation, or reduced environmental demands, as in sheltered workshops).

From Classification I to Classification VI there is also a progression in improved prognosis for change in the abusive parent and prospects for the improved functioning of the total family as a system.

---

[43] Merrill, *op. cit.*

[44] For Classification II (pervasively angry and abusive parents), group treatment may be efficacious in view of the experiences of correctional agencies in group treatment of similar clients.

The treatment strategies specified are primarily differentiated in terms of (1) authority-based control and environmental manipulation (e.g., institutional commitment of parent or removal of child), (2) reality-based planning and use of community resources for child care, financial assistance, and so on, (3) relationship-based casework (as described by Reiner and Kaufman),[45] (4) traditional psychoanalytically oriented psychotherapy, (5) psychiatric treatment (for psychotics), (6) activity/relationship treatment, as in Big Brothers, youth development services (e.g., scouts, community centers, and the like), (7) group therapy (when social performance and relationship dynamics are confronted and awareness and skills in interpersonal relations are developed), (8) conjoint family therapy, and (9) ego-supportive surveillance (as is typical in correctional treatment). Specific descriptions of each kind of treatment are not provided herein, since they are readily available in the literature.

[45] *Op. cit.*

As was pointed out by Shumway regarding his own effort to develop a problem/treatment typology for school attendance problems, the principles underlying the construction of the classification system developed in *this* paper are not new to social work.[46] Consequently, the classifications and the treatment prescriptions linked to them are likewise not novel. It is the hope of the writer, however, that this paper has brought together a number of elements that heretofore have been scattered throughout the literature. If this aim has been accomplished, the effort will have been of value. In addition, while the problem characteristics and classifications are taken directly from the empirically based literature (i.e., Merrill, Delsordo, Reiner and Kaufman, Elmer, Boardman, and Nurse), the treatment strategy linkages are not. Thus, they represent problems in validation and refinement—an action-research task.

[46] E. Gene Shumway, "A Diagnostic and Treatment Typology for School Attendance Problems." Unpublished manuscript, Cleveland, Ohio, 1965.

Effective treatment of child abuse and neglect

Anne Harris Cohn

The aim of the federally funded National Demonstration Program in Child Abuse and Neglect was to develop and test alternative treatment strategies. This article reports on an evaluation of treatment services in the eleven projects in the program. Implications of the findings for social policy are presented.

Anne Harris Cohn, DPH, was, until September 1979, Congressional Science Fellow (sponsored by the American Association for the Advancement of Science), Office of Rep. Albert Gore, Jr., Washington, D.C. She is now a White House Fellow, serving as a Special Assistant to the Secretary of the Department of Health, Education, and Welfare. Portions of this article were delivered at the Second International Conference on Child Abuse, London, England, September 1978. Research on which this article is based was supported by Contracts HRA 106-74-120 and HRA 230-76-0075 from the National Center for Health Services Research to Berkeley Planning Associates, Berkeley, California—a former employer of Dr. Cohn.

THE INCREASED PUBLIC AWARENESS of and concern about child abuse and neglect in the 1970s have stimulated efforts to determine the most effective means of alleviating the problem. Research activities, demonstration treatment programs, evaluation studies, and technical assistance projects, sponsored by public and private institutions, have sought to identify the causes and effects of child abuse and neglect, the range of intervention strategies, and the most efficacious methods of intervening. This article presents findings from one such effort —a three-year evaluation of the first National Demonstration Program in Child Abuse and Neglect. Although the findings are not conclusive, they prompt policy recommendations for more effective intervention.

BACKGROUND

In May 1974, the Office of Child Development and the Social and Rehabilitation Service, U.S. Department of Health, Education, and Welfare (HEW) jointly funded eleven three-year child abuse and neglect service projects under a program entitled the National Demonstration Program on Child Abuse and Neglect. The thirteen projects in the program were Arkansas Child Abuse and Neglect Program, Little Rock; Child Abuse and Neglect Demonstration Project, Bayamon, Puerto Rico; Child Development Center, Neah Bay, Washington; Child Protection Center, Baton Rouge, Louisiana; Family Care Center, Los Angeles, California; Family Center, Adams County, Colorado; Family Resource Center, St. Louis, Missouri; Panel for Family Living, Tacoma, Washington; Parent and Child Effectiveness Relations Project, St. Petersburg, Florida; Pro-Child, Arlington, Virginia; and Union County Protective Services Demonstration Project, Union County, New Jersey. This article discusses findings related to the effectiveness of treatment, based on the studies of parents and children served by the projects.

The aim of the program was to develop and test alternative strategies for treating abusive and neglectful parents and their children and alternative models for coordinating community-wide child abuse and neglect treatment systems before spending funds appropriated to the Child Abuse and Neglect Prevention and Treatment Act, P.L. 93-247. The projects, spread throughout the country and in Puerto Rico, differed in size, the types of agencies in which they were housed, the kinds of staff they employed, and the variety of services they offered.

The National Center for Health Services Research and Development, Health Resources Administration, HEW, awarded a contract in 1974 to Berkeley Planning Associates, Berkeley, California, to conduct a three-year evaluation of the projects. The overall purpose of the evaluation was to provide guidance to the federal government and local communities on how to develop systematic and coordinated community-wide programs to deal with problems of child abuse and neglect. The study, which combined both formative (or descriptive) and summative (or outcome/impact-related) evaluation concerns, documented the content of the different treatment services tested by the projects and sought to determine the relative effectiveness and cost effectiveness of these strategies.

Specifically, the evaluation included the following in relation to child abuse and neglect projects:

1. Identification of the essential elements of a well-functioning community-wide interdisciplinary service system.

2. Identification of the problems inherent in establishing a treatment program.

3. Specification of the elements of organizational structures and management styles that contribute to a project's success and help avoid burnout in workers.

4. Suggested standards of high-quality case management.

5. Identification of the range of services that can be offered and their cost.

6. Assessment of the effectiveness and cost-effectiveness of alternative service strategies.[1]

7. Preliminary specification of the

Reprinted from SOCIAL WORK, 24 (November 1979), pp. 513–519.

53

range of problems exhibited by children who have been maltreated and their subsequent treatment needs.[2]

TREATING PARENTS

Until recently, public and professional response to parents who maltreated their children was punitive ("throw the parent in jail"). However, in the past ten years or so, the general sentiment has become more supportive. There is a growing belief that many, if not all, abusive and neglectful parents can be helped through treatment and that society has a responsibility to ensure that parents identified as abusive or neglectful are provided with treatment.

Although many professionals accept the notion that treatment "works," few agree on what kind of treatment works. Theories range from an emphasis on therapeutically oriented intervention (such as psychiatric counseling), to concrete services (such as homemaking and employment of financial assistance), to education (such as parenting classes).[3]

A primary concern in evaluating the eleven child abuse and neglect projects was to determine the relative effectiveness of different strategies for treating abusive and neglectful parents, since such treatment is central to these projects. Since the study was the first major effort in the field, it was not anticipated that conclusive findings about treatment outcomes could be obtained; rather, suggestions about the effectiveness of short-term treatment were sought.

To study the effects of treatment, all adults receiving treatment services from the demonstration projects for at least one month (from January 1975 to December 1976) were included in the study population. Data were recorded by case managers, trained to complete forms developed by the evaluators. Data included information on (1) basic demography and case histories, including the nature and severity of maltreatment, (2) the types and amount of services received by the parent from the project and on a referral basis, and (3) outcome, including recurrence of abuse

or neglect during treatment and workers' judgments of a parent's propensity or lack of propensity for future abuse or neglect by the end of treatment.

A variety of bivariate and multivariate analyses were performed on the data. Although results from multivariate analyses (notably multiple-regression analysis and discriminate-function analysis) generally paralleled findings from less complex bivariate analyses, only statistically significant findings from bivariate analyses are reported here.

The 1,724 parents included in the study's client population formed a heterogeneous group. Some had come to treatment voluntarily, while others had been forced to do so by court order; some had, without question, maltreated their children, while others were recorded as being at high risk or potential cases. They differed most notably from those cases routinely handled by departments of public protective services (as reported by the American Humane Association) in that a somewhat greater proportion were cases involving physical abuse (as opposed to neglect).[4] In the majority of cases, more than one adult lived in the household (69 percent), no adult in the household held a high school degree (61 percent), at least one adult was employed (70 percent), the reported annual family income was less than $5,500 (56 percent), at least two children were present in the family (70 percent), and at least one of the children was a preschooler (73 percent).

On the average, clients were in treatment six to seven months and had contact with a service provider about once a week. Approximately 30 percent of the clients received a service package that included lay services (lay or parent aide counseling and/or Parents Anonymous) plus individual counseling or case management and other services. Only 12 percent received a group treatment service package (including group therapy or parent education classes) along with other services. Over half (54 percent) received individual counseling without lay or group services. No general patterns emerged to suggest that the re-

ceipt of a specific service was related to clients' characteristics that were measured.

In discussing findings, a number of methodological constraints that limit the conclusiveness of findings must be taken into account. First, the study included no control or nontreatment groups. Thus, although it was possible to compare outcomes for clients receiving different mixes of services, taking into account differences among clients, it was not possible to determine the effects of treatment versus no treatment. Second, the projects were selected for study because of the different treatment strategies they proposed to demonstrate; they were not necessarily representative of child abuse and neglect projects in general. Third, all data were collected from those working with families rather than directly from the clients themselves; thus, the data may contain clinical biases. Fourth, data were collected from the time clients entered treatment through termination. Therefore, the findings reflect "outcome" at the time treatment was completed and do not necessarily indicate any longer term effects of treatment. It is with these limitations in mind that the implications of the study must be considered.

FINDINGS ABOUT RECURRENCE

That abuse or neglect does not occur or recur during treatment cannot be regarded as a measure of the outcome or effect of treatment. Incidents of abuse may go undetected; children may have been removed from the home, thus eliminating the possibility of recurrence; or the supportive environment of treatment may serve to deflect temporarily a parent's inclination to abuse or neglect. However, the recurrence of abuse or neglect during treatment may be a good indication of how well a program is, in general, protecting the children in clients' families.

Of the 1,724 parents studied, 30 percent were reported to have severely abused or neglected their children while in treatment. "Severe reincidence"—the term used in the study—was operationally defined to include severe or moderate physical injuries (such as fractures, serious bruises, burns, or lacerations, severe or moderate physical neglect (including serious malnourishment and lack of supervision for long periods), and sexual abuse. Severe reincidence, which varied from 13 percent in one project to 51 percent in another, excluded reports of emotional abuse, mild physical injuries, emotional neglect, or mild physical neglect. Although no benchmarks exist against which one could compare the experience of the demonstration projects studied, the 30 percent figure seems high and raises serious questions about how well these projects, and perhaps child abuse and neglect treatment programs in general, help to maintain a safe environment for abused or neglected children.

Were particular characteristics of clients related to the reported severe reincidence during treatment? Of all the variables used to measure differences among clients, the single best predictor of reincidence appeared to be the severity of the case at intake. In other words, clients with a previous history of abuse or neglect, clients who had severely abused or neglected their children immediately prior to treatment regardless of their previous history, and clients whose households contained a wide range of stress factors that apparently triggered the maltreatment were more likely again to abuse or neglect their children severely while in treatment.

Were specific service delivery practices related to reported reincidence during treatment? Of the variety of service delivery and case management practices measured, reincidence was lowest in those projects that utilized highly trained workers to handle the intake, initial diagnosis, and planning of treatment. Higher reincidence rates were found in projects that relied on less well-trained workers to conduct intake and handle case management.

These findings suggest some important policy considerations for service programs. First, the findings suggest that it should not be taken for granted that children are in a protected environment simply because their parents are in treatment. The provision of treatment alone is not necessarily sufficient to deter an episode of abuse or neglect.

Second, it can be predicted that the more serious the case at intake, the more likely it is that the child could again be abused or neglected. Certainly, intake on all cases should be handled by skilled workers whose knowledge and experience can be used to differentiate the serious from the less serious cases and to assess what it will take to make the home environment safe for the child. Once a serious case is identified, a professionally trained worker should be assigned to it, all identified needed resources for the family should be made available, and, at least initially, supportive intervention with the family should be intense. If "children's protective services" is to merit its name, its foremost concern must be for a safe environment for the children in care. Leaving a child at home often may be in the best long-term interests of the child and the family. For that long-term interest to manifest itself, however, enough supports must be given in the short term for the entire family to survive the crisis.

POTENTIAL FOR FUTURE ABUSE OR NEGLECT

One method of measuring the effectiveness of treatment is to ask workers if a client has improved sufficiently in a number of problem areas during treatment to suggest that the client's potential for abusive or neglectful behavior has been reduced. Although such a judgment, when made at the time services are terminated, does not directly measure the outcome (or long-term effects) of treatment, it does provide insights into how much a worker believes that intervention has been of value.

In one of several approaches to gauging the success of treatment, workers were asked to report, for each client served, whether the client's propensity for future maltreatment had been reduced during treatment. "Reduced propensity" was determined by comparing workers' recorded judgments about a client's potential for abuse or neglect at the time the parent came into treatment and at the time treatment services were terminated. Although there was no validation by workers outside the project of these judgments, they were recorded concurrently with clinical ratings on thirteen indicators of parental functioning that were developed to tap the parents' potential for abuse or neglect.

Indicators of Parental Functioning The development of these measures began with a search for possible indicators of parental functioning that are indicative of the potential for abuse or neglect. Over fifty such indicators were culled from a careful study of the literature, which contains many different but not empirically tested perspectives on abuse and neglect, and from interviews with abusive and neglectful parents and certain professionals working in the field.

The list of indicators was evaluated by others working in the field and was reduced to twenty-eight indicators that reflected parental situations, attitudes, and behavior. At the same time, a sample of fifty parents was identified and used to study how these indicators applied in practice.

In developing the final list of indicators, those who were working most closely with the parents in the study sample were the primary source of data. After being trained in the use of data collection instruments, the workers recorded judgments about the parents' functioning on the twenty-eight indicators. To assess the reliability of the information collected, data on each parent's functioning was also recorded by a worker who knew the parent but worked outside the treatment program and by the researcher through direct interviews with the parent.

Analysis of data collected focused on sorting out which of the original twenty-eight indicators were reliable, valid, and nonredundant and, as such, would have utility in future studies of child abuse programs. Reliability was determined by comparing the responses of the two workers and the responses of the primary worker and the parent. The Tau c statistic was used for this purpose. Validity was explored by asking all clinician-respondents to which indicators they thought they could most accurately respond. Redundancy was determined by looking at which indicators varied together over time, suggesting that they were all indicative of the same phenomena of change in the parents' functioning. Factor analysis was used here.

As a result of these reliability, validity, and redundancy tests, the original list of twenty-eight indicators was reduced to thirteen. The thirteen indicators were general health, control over personal habits, stress created by living situation, sense of the child as person, behavior toward child, assessment of child development, extent of isolation, ability to talk out problems, reactions to crisis situations, the way anger is expressed, sense of independence, understanding of self, and self-esteem. The ratings on the indicators of parental functioning were shown to be powerful as a group in predicting the overall judgments of propensity for future abuse or neglect.

Among the 1,190 parents from eight projects in which substantial data on propensity were available, workers reported that only 42 percent had a reduced potential for future abuse or neglect (with a range of 25 percent at one project to 58 percent at another). In other words, workers judged they had been successful with less than half their cases. Few of the parental characteristics, such as age, race, or employment status, appeared to be related to this outcome.

Workers also reported that those who do not abuse alcohol or drugs were more likely than substance abusers to have a reduced propensity for child abuse or neglect, and physical abusers were somewhat more likely than neglecters to have a reduced propensity for such future behavior. It was also found that there was no significant relationship between severe reincidence during treatment and a lack of reduced propensity by the end of treatment.

Given the paucity of comparable studies on other child abuse and neglect treatment programs, it is not

known if the experiences of the demonstration projects represent a norm for the field. However, the demonstration projects had an advantage over public protective service programs across the country. They received special resources, which resulted in lower caseloads than is the norm in public agencies, and special attention, including ongoing feedback from the evaluators. Thus, it may be fair to assume that the projects studied did at least as well in working with clients as most other programs across the country. If this is the case, the systematic judgments obtained from professionals in these programs suggest that child abuse and neglect treatment programs are not nearly as successful as society has been led to expect. And it must be remembered that since the workers were to some extent judging the potential outcomes of their own efforts, the 42 percent reduced propensity for future maltreatment may reflect an optimistic estimate of success. Theoretically, it may be argued that for this complex problem, a "success" rate of about 40 percent is not bad and, indeed, all that can be expected. But when one considers what the 60 percent failure represents in terms of human suffering and thwarted development, it is clear that better ways are needed to help abusive and neglectful parents.

RELATIVE SUCCESS OF LAY SERVICES

Although the demonstration projects as a group exhibited only limited success with clients, it was still of interest to know whether clients receiving one type of service or service package seemed to fare better in treatment than clients receiving other types of services. The experience of the demonstration projects did not point to a single best method of service delivery. No one service or service package was related to success with substantially more than half the clients receiving the service.

However, clients receiving lay services (lay or parent aide counseling and/or Parents Anonymous) as part of a service package were more fre-

quently reported to have reduced propensity than clients not receiving these services. As shown in Table 1, in the entire study population, 53 percent of those provided with lay services were judged to have improved during treatment; fewer than 40 percent of the clients receiving any other mix of services were reported as improved. As is also shown in Table 1, the relationship between improvement and lay services was true also for clients in individual projects.

The lay-service package generally included case management carried out by a full-time trained worker. It also included the services of a lay person (an individual, usually volunteer, trained on the job and under ongoing supervision) who was assigned to the client to serve as a friend, support, and social contact. This lay counselor or parent aide met with the client once or several times a week and was generally available to help the family in a variety of daily needs. The lay service package also may have included participation in Parents Anonymous, a self-help group of abusive and neglectful parents.

There are many reasons why the lay-service model may have been somewhat more effective than other treatment models. The lay counselor or parent aide carries a small caseload (from one to three clients) and thus has more energy and time to give to each client. (Most full-time workers in the demonstration projects carried twenty to twenty-five cases.) The lay counselor's job is to become the client's friend and to help the client break down some of the social isolation he or she is experiencing. Workers with large caseloads do not have the time to do this; paid workers generally carry the stigma of authority that does not enable them to do this.

A service such as Parents Anonymous encourages parents to help themselves and help others in comparable situations. Interaction with others struggling with similar problems (and sometimes seemingly worse problems) helps to put problems and solutions into perspective and seems to foster independence as well as greater self-esteem. (It is interesting to note that,

56

in general, clients receiving professionally sponsored group services, such as group therapy, were not as frequently reported with reduced propensity as those receiving client-sponsored Parents Anonymous.)

A treatment service model that includes lay services is, as might be expected, less costly than other service models. (The annual expense per case for the lay-service model is about $1,400, compared to $1,700 for a service model based on individual counseling by paid workers only.) Given the somewhat greater effectiveness of the lay-service model (the success rate is approximately 53 percent), it also appears as a more cost-effective service strategy. (It costs the program approximately $2,600 a year for each successful case versus $4,700 a year for each successful case for the individual counseling model.) More cost effective than the individual counseling model is a service package that includes professionally provided group services (at a cost of $4,000 a year per successful case). This professionally provided group-service model was found to be particularly beneficial for physical abusers, as opposed to neglecters or emotional maltreators. Moreover, although it clearly costs a program money to keep a client in treatment for any length of time, this study found that the likelihood of reduced propensity is significantly increased and it is more cost effective if a client is in treatment for six months to a year.

Once again, although no particular service or service mix appeared to be dramatically effective, a service model that included lay or parent aide counseling and Parents Anonymous was somewhat more effective and certainly less costly than other alternatives. These findings suggest that this service model ought to be more widely tested and studied.

TREATING CHILDREN

Although public concern about child abuse certainly has been prompted by outrage at what happens to the children, almost all resources have been directed to treating the parents. Public and private agencies working with abuse or neglect rarely provide direct therapeutic treatment to children. Only three of the eleven demonstration projects studied—Family Care Center, Family Center, and Family Resource Center—provided child-specific treatment services.

There are many explanations for this focus on parents. Some professionals maintain that by helping the parent, one is in turn helping the family and thus the child. Other professionals find working with the parent easier; parents are more accessible, generally more verbal, and certainly more mobile. Working with parents is also less expensive and less time consuming. And agencies are often mandated to work with the parent, not the child.

Little research has been done on abused or neglected children. The few studies done to date indicate that these children sustain a number of developmental and emotional problems.[5] It is further theorized that these problems may lead to abusive or neglectful behavior in adulthood. This theory suggests the desirability of early and effective intervention with the victims of abuse and neglect. Thus the evaluation of the demonstration programs also focused on the characteristics and types of developmental, emotional, and psychosocial problems of abused children and the effects of therapeutic intervention on these problems.

The children receiving direct therapeutic treatment services at three demonstration projects were followed from

TABLE 1. CLIENTS SHOWING REDUCED PROPENSITY TOWARD CHILD ABUSE OR NEGLECT, BY SERVICE MODEL [a]

Project	Lay Model [b]		Group Model [c]		Social Work Model [d]		Other		Total	
	Number	Percentage	Number	Percentage	Number	Percentage	Number	Percentage	Number	Percentage
Family Center	36	56	14	29	59	54	12	25	121	49
Pro-Child	10	30	22	41	143	43	11	18	186	41
Child Protection Center	3	67	6	67	84	46	3	35	96	48
Child Abuse and Neglect Demonstration Project	2	100	18	78	99	36	4	25	123	43
Arkansas Child Abuse and Neglect Demonstration Project	165	56	—	—	3	33	1	100	169	36
Family Resource Center	20	35	54	20	6	17	1	100	81	25
Panel for Family Living	27	74	55	49	9	67	2	50	93	58
Union County Protective Services Demonstration Project	62	44	13	15	226	27	20	20 [e]	321	29
Total	325	53	182	39	629	38	54	26 [e]	1,190	42

[a] Number refers to the total number of clients receiving this service model; percentage refers to the percentage of clients receiving this service model who showed a reduced propensity toward child abuse or neglect.
[b] The lay model includes lay counseling and/or Parents Anonymous as well as other services.
[c] The group model includes group therapy and/or parent education classes as well as other services except lay services.
[d] The social work model includes individual counseling as well as other services except lay or group services.
[e] Chi-square significant at less than or equal to 0.05.

intake through termination. Problem-oriented records were maintained by workers on seventy children served by these projects. The data set included case history information, information on services received, and descriptions of the range and severity of the children's problems and the degree to which these problems appeared to be resolved during treatment.

The seventy children studied ranged in age from birth to 12 years; 44 percent were 3–5 years old and almost three-quarters were between the ages of 2 and 7. Most of the children, who were not representative of all children whose parents received treatment from the projects, were victims of emotional abuse or neglect or were high-risk children, although 16 percent had sustained a severe injury. Although the key demographic characteristics of the children's families were similar to those of other abusive and neglecting families served by the demonstration projects, it is not known how similar the children served are to all the abused and neglected children whose parents received treatment from the projects.

Problems Exhibited At the time they entered treatment, the children exhibited a wide range of problems. There was no single area of functioning in which they were all deficient nor any specific behaviors that stood out as universal problems. All children, however, exhibited some dysfunctional behavior. In the area of socialization skills, 70 percent of the children did not relate well with their peers and 57 percent had problems in their interactions with adults. Over half the children had difficulty in dealing with frustration, and their attention span was poor; they exhibited problems in their development of a healthy sense of self, their ability to give and receive affection, and other characteristics of general happiness. Family interaction problems were equally prevalent; over half the parents had inappropriate expectations of their children's behavior and development and inappropriate perceptions of their children's needs. Although specific growth or physical problems were not common, deficits in the children's cognitive, language, and motor skills appeared widespread, as revealed through standardized tests of development.

Progress during Treatment Analysis of workers' reports of the children's progress in overcoming their problems during treatment indicated uneven success. Some children improved a great deal, but others seemed to make little or no progress. Some made consistent gains across a variety of problem areas; others made major improvements in some areas but regressed or stayed the same in others. Although patterns of success were not evident, it is significant that many of the children's problems were partially or totally resolved and at higher rates than were seen for parents.

Twenty-four socialization and family-interaction problem areas were reported at intake; in all but five areas, over half the children identified as having the problem were said to have improved. Approximately two-thirds of those children with problems in the following areas improved: apathy, giving and receiving affection, general happiness, hypermonitoring one's environment, ability to protect oneself, and general interaction with adults. The number of children reported to have physical problems was small, and most of the physical problems were at least partially corrected by the end of treatment. At the time of termination, most children had significantly higher scores on standardized tests for cognitive, language, and motor skills, although they were still at the low end of the "normal" range.

The study population was too small to identify the characteristics of clients and the factors of service that might explain variations in improvement. However, the number and variety of problems these children exhibited indicate a need for therapeutic intervention; the improvements seen suggest that although the most effective means of working with maltreated children are not as yet completely understood, treatment can be beneficial. Clearly there is a need for additional research and demonstration treatment in this area.

POLICY IMPLICATIONS

The evaluation of the first National Demonstration Program in Child Abuse and Neglect sought to identify the essential elements of a well-functioning program of treatment for child abuse and neglect. Although the study included concerns about the organization and management of such service programs and their roles in the larger community child abuse system, this article has dealt specifically with the provision of treatment services to abusive and neglectful parents and their children.

Three critical findings stand out. First, reincidence of abuse or neglect during treatment occurred with alarming frequency; cases of severe reincidence were reported for 30 percent of the parents studied while they were in treatment. Second, systematic professional judgments revealed that in most cases the efficacy of treatment was questionable: in only 42 percent of the cases did workers judge that propensity for future abuse had been reduced at the time services were terminated. Third, the findings indicated that a substantial number of problems were exhibited by maltreated children; the children were as much in need of treatment as the parents.

Other findings from the study address the problems just noted and offer some tentative policy guidelines for the design of treatment programs in child abuse. Whatever the long-term outcome of these treatment programs, at the very least, society has the right to expect that they will protect the child at risk during treatment. Findings from the study suggest that this protection is most strongly associated with the utilization of highly trained professionals in intake and treatment planning. At these two sensitive points, skillful diagnosis is required to assess the seriousness of the case, the degree of risk of reincidence, and the resources needed for treatment. It is clearly also important for programs to explore what protection and treatment can be provided for the abused child as treatment for parents begins. With regard to the treatment outcomes, the study did not reveal a service mix that promises a high degree of success. However, the findings showed that, of the treatment packages studied, those which included lay counseling and Parents Anonymous had the highest rates of success in reducing the parents' propensity for future abuse. Finally, the findings from the projects that offered therapeutic services to children indicated that the services had beneficial results in relation to many of the problems exhibited by the children when they entered treatment.

In sum, treatment programs should seek to mesh the use of professionals and lay persons in providing services. And these programs should include services for all family members—the parents and the children. To do so would appear to be cost effective. But, at the same time, those who operate treatment programs in child abuse and those who study such programs must recognize the limitations of the current approaches to treatment. Designs for treatment programs that can be predicted to benefit the majority of abusive or neglectful families in need of treatment have not yet been developed. The challenge of identifying truly effective approaches to treating child abuse and neglect remains.

NOTES AND REFERENCES

1. Anne H. Cohn, *Final Adult Client Impact Report,* prepared by Berkeley Planning Associates, 1977 (Washington, D.C., U.S. Technical Information Service, 1978).

2. Mary Kay Miller, *Final Child Impact Report,* prepared by Berkeley Planning Associates, 1977 (Washington, D.C.: U.S. Technical Information Service, 1978).

3. Susan L. Klaus, *Innovative Treatment Approaches for Child Abuse and Neglect,* a symposium report prepared for the National Center on Child Abuse and Neglect (Washington, D.C.: U.S. Department of Health, Education & Welfare, 1977).

4. *National Statistical Analysis of Child Neglect and Abuse Reporting* (Denver, Colo.: American Humane Association, 1977).

5. Harold P. Martin, ed., *The Abused Child: A Multidisciplinary Approach to Developmental Issues and Treatment* (Cambridge, Mass.: Ballinger Publishing Co., 1976). ◄

Clayton T. Shorkey

A Review of Methods Used in the Treatment of Abusing Parents

Individual psychotherapy, group psychotherapy, transactional analysis, behavior therapy, humanistic-behavioral group therapy, and multiple family therapy can all be used in the treatment of child-abusing parents. A review of these approaches, their similarities and differences, provides treatment guidelines.

Clayton T. Shorkey is an Associate Professor, School of Social Work, The University of Texas at Austin, Austin, Texas.

PHYSICAL INJURY OF CHILDREN by parents has now generated national attention, and a wide range of human service agencies concerned with this phenomenon have dramatically increased their interest in obtaining information and training materials to help combat the problem. Despite recent vigorous efforts to increase knowledge in this area, many important questions have not, however, been fully addressed—such as the influence of life crises as precipitating factors in abuse and characteristics of children that increase the probability of their abuse.[1] Additional information is especially needed concerning sociological and contextual variables and psychological variables contributing to child abuse, as well as knowledge regarding effective strategies for primary and secondary prevention and treatment.[2]

The purpose of this article is to summarize and critique current information available regarding treatment procedures used with abusing parents.[3] Treatment procedures will be reviewed according to their philosophical view of the client, major theoretical assumptions, major treatment techniques used, client prerequisites, time limits, and preliminary information related to outcome.

The Psychotherapeutic Perspective

From the "medical model" perspective of psychotherapy, parents who abuse their children suffer from underlying personality disorders. Inability to tolerate frustrations in interaction with their children, hostility, aggression, rigidity, depression, self-depreciation, and anxiety are all seen as symptoms of the underlying personality disorder. From this perspective, abusing parents are viewed as requiring treatment and supportive services to help them overcome their emotional

1. Clayton T. Shorkey and Josleen Lackhart, *Indexed Bibliography and Summaries of Child Abuse and Neglect Journal Literature* (Austin, Tex.: Center for Social Work Research, Region IV Resource Center on Child Abuse and Neglect, 1976); Blair Justice and David F. Duncan, "Life Crisis as a Precursor to Child Abuse," *Public Health Reports* 91 (March/April 1976): 110-15; and William N. Friedrich and Jerry A. Broiskin, "The Role of the Child in Abuse: A Review of the Literature," *American Journal of Orthopsychiatry* 46 (October 1976): 580-90.

2. Richard J. Gelles, "Child Abuse as Psychopathology: A Sociological Critique and Reformulation," *American*

Journal of Orthopsychiatry 43 (July 1973): 611-21; Richard J. Gelles, "The Social Construction of Child Abuse," *American Journal of Orthopsychiatry* 45 (April 1975): 363-71; Clayton T. Shorkey, "Psychological Characteristics of Child Abusers: Speculation and the Need for Research," *International Journal of Child Abuse and Neglect* 2 (Spring 1978): 69-76; and Kerby T. Alvy, "Preventing Child Abuse," *American Psychologist* 30 (September 1975): 921-28.

3. This article does not review reports regarding treatment of abusing parents that do not include clear information related to the theoretical basis of the treatment procedure, dynamics of abuse, and treatment techniques.

Reprinted from SOCIAL CASEWORK, 60 (June 1979), pp. 360–367, by permission of the Family Service Association of America.

disturbances. Children of these abusing parents are often transferred to out-of-home placements until treatment improves the psychological health of the parents in areas that pose dangers to their children.

Treatment Process

The psychoanalytic model specifies the major sources of underlying disorders of abusing parents as inadequate mothering or nurturance in early developmental stages, and lack of adaptive development of ego and superego functions because of inadequate resolution of phases of psychosexual development. Successful individual psychotherapy generally requires from one to two years of contact between the abusing parent and therapist. Changes in ego functions, such as impulse control, object relations, and problem solving, and appropriate uses of psychological mechanisms of defense are major indicators of client improvement in therapy.

Successful treatment requires voluntary and continuous participation by the clients, and parents who refuse treatment are viewed as resisting awareness of their condition and avoiding painful aspects of therapeutic resolution of their problems.

The treatment process includes engaging the client in the process; reviewing the client's developmental history and current functioning, uncovering and working through repressed conflicts, and improving aspects of the client's ego functions—including appropriate uses of defense mechanisms. Major therapy techniques include support, catharsis, ventilation, anxiety reduction, uncovering, insight facilitation, interpretation, clarification, use of the transference relationship, and reassurance.

Case Reports

A number of reports illustrate the use of psychotherapy in individual treatment of abusing parents. Harvey L. Schloesser and Patricia T. Schloesser illustrate the dynamics and treatment of two abusing mothers who had physically harmed their preschool boys.[4]

One client discussed was a thirty-nine-year-old mother, diagnosed as severely depressed, who attacked her five-year-old son with her husband's hunting knife. Her history revealed that this woman's own strict and demanding mother contributed to the development of her harsh superego, and that her father, who was in the home irregularly, frequently displayed violent outbursts of temper and physically abused members of the family. The Schloessers interpret the client's attack on her child as an attempt to deal with poorly repressed Oedipal conflicts, triggered by her own husband's absences and the child's beginning of kindergarten: "Again an ambivalently held male—the last one—was leaving the patient."[5] Treatment focused on decreasing the client's fears and anxieties related to stressful childhood experiences by reducing her "unconscious alliance and identification with the fearsome figures of her past," strengthening her ego functions, and reestablishing effective use of defense mechanisms.[6] Following two years of treatment, the authors report, the client was functioning satisfactorily.

William R. Flynn reviews two case studies that illustrate the clients' "extraordinary reliance on ego-defense mechanisms of repression, denial, and projection, causing an incapacity to learn from experience and to appreciate realistically the possible consequences of their actions."[7] Flynn attributes the core of one client's disorder to unresolved sibling rivalry and early abuse of the client by her sister. The second client's vicious beatings of her three-year-old daughter reflect repression and denial of the client's dislike for little girls because of her own early rejection by her father. The author considered both clients improved after their having a year of individual therapy.

Finally, Charles A. David discusses the importance of confrontation as a technique in psychotherapy with abusing parents, using as a case example the treatment of a twenty-two-year-old mother who had been abusing

4. Harvey L. Schloesser and Patricia T. Schloesser, "Psychiatric Treatment of Abusing Mothers: Two Case Studies," *International Journal of Child Abuse and Neglect* 1 (Spring 1977): 31-37.

5. Ibid., p. 33.

6. Ibid., p. 34.

7. William R. Flynn, "Frontier Justice: A Contribution to the Theory of Child Battery," *American Journal of Psychiatry* 127 (September 1970): 151.

her four-year-old daughter.[8] The major symptoms reported were anxiety and depression reflected in futile efforts to attain self-control. David describes important aspects of the client's history as revealing a pathological relationship with her mother, in which deficits of caring and understanding resulted in the client's lack of self-esteem and a conception of herself as a nonperson, an object or thing. This pain-producing relationship with her own mother was introjected and resulted in punitive superego operations related to herself and her four-year-old daughter. The poor behavior of her child, says David, precipitated abuse due to the "release of old memory tracers": the client sees the child behaving as she did and uses drastic punitive measures to control her.[9]

Treatment included relieving anxiety and depression, controlling aggressive drives, reducing critical aspects and increasing approval aspects of the superego, and reducing the fusion between the client and her child. David used confrontation to provide the client with a degree of needed social control by telling the client to stop punishing the child for anything. Following eight months of therapy, the client was reported to be improved with no evidence of further abuse.

The use of the confrontation technique to assist in the psychotherapy process is recommended as an effective technique with these clients after the establishment of an adequate treatment relationship. The technique and the working through of feelings related to confrontations is suggested to help clients control drives, impulses, and desires that are causing conflicts.

Significantly, in all available cases related to the use of individual psychotherapy, marital and family therapy is recommended following improvement in the individual functioning of the client.

Group Psychotherapy

Little material related to the use of group psychotherapy techniques specifically with

abusing parents is currently available. However, information about one program has been presented by Morris J. Paulson and Anne Chaleff, and Paulson et al.[10] This group approach attempts to provide a positive "reparenting" experience for abusing parents who suffered severe emotional deprivation during infancy and childhood. Group psychotherapy tries to resolve problems related to early developmental phases through allowing regression, and "reliving of early experiences . . . in the light of more mature insights and more realistic emotions."[11] Both a male and a female therapist work with the abusing parents to allow for more effective identification of parent surrogate roles by the group members. The groups each meet for one and one-half hours per week for traditional group psychotherapy sessions and for an additional half hour each week for instructions on child care and infant development.

Traditional psychotherapeutic techniques used include reassurance, abreaction, catharsis, confrontation, and stimulation of group process. Following three years of work with fifty-four abusing parents, the authors report that the treatment procedure successfully deals with intrapsychic problems. The clients' improved social and emotional behavior in group therapy and in their homes demonstrates positive results. Although the actual number of weekly sessions attended by parents in the groups varies, the average number of sessions attended by most parents is between twenty and forty.[12]

Transactional Analysis

The use of transactional analysis in groups with abusing parents has also been reported

8. Charles A. David, "The Use of Confrontation Technique in the Battered Child Syndrome," *American Journal of Psychotherapy* 24 (October 1974): 543-52.

9. Ibid., p. 547.

10. Morris J. Paulson and Anne Chaleff, "Parent Surrogate Roles: A Dynamic Concept in Understanding and Treating Abusive Parents," *Journal of Clinical Child Psychology* 2 (Fall 1973): 38-40; Maurice J. Paulson et al., "Parents of the Battered Child: A Multidisciplinary Group Therapy Approach to Life-Threatening Behavior," *Life-Threatening Behavior* 4 (Spring 1974): 18-31.

11. S. R. Slavson, "Types of Group Psychotherapy and Their Clinical Applications," in *The Challenge for Group Psycho-Therapy,* ed. Stefano de Schill (New York: International Universities Press, 1974), p. 53.

12. Morris J. Paulson, 19 July 1978: personal communication.

as achieving positive outcomes.[13] Three ego states (parent, child, and adult) reflected in the overt behavior patterns of individuals provide the behavioral referent for assessment and treatment in transactional analysis. Drawing heavily on the psychoanalytic concept of symbiosis related to disturbed parent-child relationships, the major focus of treatment with abusing parents is to break up destructive symbiotic relationships and to realign the relationships in more constructive ways.

According to this approach, symbiosis occurs in at least two forms in abusive families: Symbiosis between parent and child may result in abuse when the parent's demands for caring and nurturing from the child are frustrated, causing anger, resentment, and abuse by the parent. Passive abuse, which occurs when one parent allows abuse of the child by the other parent, reflects a symbiotic relationship between the two parents as they compete for the child ego state.

An important aspect of treatment using transactional analysis is strengthening the separateness of ego states by confronting discounts, "the thought process that underlies symbiotic behavior, consisting of devaluing (1) the existence of the problem, (2) its significance, (3) its solvability, or (4) the person's ability to handle it."[14] Other aspects of the treatment process include contracting with clients to achieve desired change, using script questionnaires, and correcting information related to effective parenting. Thirty couples, in groups of four or five, participated in the treatment program of one and one-half hours per week over an average time of five to six months. Twenty-two couples had successfully completed therapy at the time that the report was drawn up; four couples dropped out of therapy and lost permanent custody of their children, and the remainder were continuing therapy.[15]

13. Rita Justice and Blair Justice, "TA Work with Child Abuse," *Transactional Analysis Journal* 5 (January 1975): 38-41; and Blair Justice and Rita Justice, *The Abusing Family* (New York: Human Sciences Press, 1976).

14. Justice and Justice, *Abusing Family,* p. 146.

15. Blair Justice and Rita Justice, "Evaluating Outcome of Group Therapy for Abusing Parents," *Corrective and Social Psychiatry* 24 (January 1978): 48.

Behavior Therapy

Behavior therapy with abusing parents focuses on increasing the knowledge and skill needed for positive and effective parenting, correcting misinformation, and reducing the frequency of undesirable behavior. Abusing parents are often deficient in knowledge of the social, psychological, and environmental needs of their infants and children, as well as in knowledge and skill related to effective and humane methods of child management. Other deficiencies may be in knowledge and skills related to effective methods of anxiety reduction, problem solving, decision making, conflict resolution, and communication. The presence of irrational beliefs, ideas, and expectations related to their children's behaviors, as well as inappropriate methods of discipline, contribute to abuse according to this perspective.

In contrast with the psychoanalytic approach, behavior therapy views the identified behavioral deficits and surfeits as the core of the problem rather than as a symptom of an underlying personality disorder. Assessment and treatment focus on the identifiable and observable behavior of parents in their current interactions with their children. Treatment time varies from one month to one year.

According to social learning theory, there are several possible historical antecedents for inappropriate behavior or deficits in current behavioral repertoires, including lack of exposure to required knowledge, inappropriate modeling, lack of corrective feedback related to adaptive behavior patterns, insufficient and inconsistent social reinforcement, and deficits in discrimination training.

Individual Assessment in Treatment

Techniques used in behavior therapy with individual clients are selected according to individual assessment of treatment goals. These techniques may include social reinforcement, extinction, response shaping, behavioral rehearsal, modeling, discrimination training, relaxation training, desensitization, corrective feedback, cognitive restructuring, homework assignments, and instructions. Supportive services are used in conjunction with therapy to reduce environmental and social stresses that make effective family performance difficult for the client. Engaging clients in treatment may be a major problem in behavior therapy as well as in other approaches. Abusing parents may need both numerous opportunities for entrance into treatment and the provision of supportive services.

A range of different behavioral methods in the treatment of abusive parents is presented in the current literature. William Reavley and Marie-Therese Gilbert report on work with individual clients in their home setting.[16] Here treatment includes identification of goals by the client and worker, development of a detailed record-keeping system maintained by the client, and development and implementation of a behavior modification plan. Techniques used include instructions, modeling, prompting, fading, behavioral rehearsal, anxiety management, and social reinforcement.

Case Report

A case from Reavley and Gilbert involves a thirty-three-year-old mother who was afraid of losing control and harming her child. This mother experienced extreme anxiety in attempting to touch and care for her daughter. Treatment included the use of cognitive restructuring of irrational ideas and beliefs related to playing with, dressing, diapering, feeding, and bathing the baby, as well as comforting her when she cried. The client also learned necessary additional skills for the care of her child through modeling, reinforcement, and behavioral rehearsal. The therapists first saw the client on a weekly basis for three months, followed by biweekly sessions for three and one-half months until she was interacting with her child comfortably and reporting satisfaction in caring for her child. The authors report very effective results with individualized use of behavioral techniques involving extensive assessment and treatment planning, including the clients' preferences and limitations; but they caution

that "by merely applying 'techniques' one can achieve very disappointing results."[17]

Child Abuse Prevention Programs

Specific behavioral goals and individualized intervention strategies characterize the child abuse project at the Presbyterian University Medical Center at the University of Pennsylvania in Philadelphia, which provides service to the black community near the hospital.[18] According to the major assumptions guiding this project, abusive parents (1) have few skills to help them function as competent adults, (2) lack adequate knowledge related to healthy child development, (3) frequently use punishment in child discipline and lack knowledge of alternative means of child management, and (4) respond best to workers of similar socioeconomic and racial backgrounds as themselves.

One black and two white social workers conducted behavioral assessment interviews with individual parents and formulated goals and plans for treatment. Four black family health workers, who lived in the clients' neighborhood, carried out treatment through teaching, demonstration, and monitoring; thus, they provided a role model for clients and functioned as advocates for the families to obtain needed social services. Behavior change was monitored according to individual intervention goals, using data supplied by the clients. The authors report good progress in increasing the positive parenting skills of clients participating in the program. Forty-one families were provided services related to 129 specific treatment goals over a one-year period. The authors report success in achieving 84 percent of the treatment goals.

Child abuse is viewed by John B. Reid and Paul S. Taplin[19] as the outcome of parents'

16. William Reavley and Marie-Therese Gilbert, "The Behavioral Treatment Approach to Potential Child Abuse—Two Case Reports," *Social Work Today* 7 (June 1976): 166-68; and Marie-Therese Gilbert, "Behavioral Approach to the Treatment of Child Abuse," *Nursing Times* 72 (29 January 1976): 140-43.

17. Reavley and Gilbert, "Behavioral Treatment Approach," p. 168.

18. James J. Tracy and Elizabeth H. Clark, "Treatment for Child Abusers," *Social Work* 19 (May 1974): 338-42; and James J. Tracy, Carolyn M. Ballard, and Elizabeth H. Clark, "Child Abuse Project: A Follow Up," *Social Work* 20 (September 1975): 398-400.

19. John B. Reid and Paul S. Taplin, "A Social Interactional Approach to the Treatment of Abusive Families," mimeographed (Eugene, Oreg.: Oregon Research Institute, 1976).

feeling that they have lost control of their children and that they are dominated by them. These authors report that a treatment program to restore family equilibrium is successful in developing parents' skills in "using consistent, effective and positive techniques in teaching their children prosocial skills and in handling discipline situations." Their approach is based on earlier work by Gerald R. Patterson et al. for work with families with aggressive children.[20] Essential aspects of the program include observations of family interactions at home, instruction in child management using a programmed text, films, and videotapes, the use of modeling, and contingency contracts. The authors report improvement in parenting skills and reduction in overall levels of hostile behavior for those mothers in the twenty-four families who received at least four weeks of treatment. No significant changes from baseline were observed, however, for total aversive behavior of the fifteen fathers involved in the program.

A unique program developed by the Catholic Children's Service in Tacoma, Washington, combines operant and respondent conditioning techniques, parent effectiveness training, cognitive restructuring, assertiveness training, values clarification techniques, and fair-fighting and crisis intervention techniques.[21] Six full-time therapists work for six weeks with families whose children would otherwise be removed from the home. Families receive as much of the therapist's time as necessary in their homes during the six weeks, and workers have no more than three families on a caseload at one time. When problems cannot be resolved by the end of the six-week period, therapists recommend out-of-home placement of the children. A therapist works with the family as a group, and also with individual family members, to develop intervention goals and carry through appropriate behavior change strategies. Therapists also work closely with staff members from other agencies involved with the family and make use of a broad

range of community resources to assist the family. During the first years of this project, 207 families were provided services. Out-of-home placement has been avoided as a result of treatment in 87 percent of the cases.

Finally, a behavioral-educational treatment program for adjudicated abusive and high-risk families has been recently developed as a joint effort of four child service agencies in Pittsburgh.[22] Each of the clients in the program—mostly mothers with babies between eight and eighteen months of age—spends three days per week in a converted apartment with her child and a teacher (surrogate, model mother). Six to eight parents and children are served at any one time for periods of about six months each. Each teacher becomes familiar with the families assigned to his or her care, and develops a therapeutic program involving formal and informal teaching, modeling, and practice in effective methods of dealing with typical activities in the home. Parents are trained to set goals for themselves and their children, plan methods for goal achievement, and maintain records of related behavior. In addition to individualized training, clients also participate in workshops on child rearing, family living, and so on, and participate in group discussions.

After clients have participated in the program for six months, cases are reviewed and recommendations are made to the local child welfare department and juvenile court. Parents may either be released from the program with no further commitment, required to participate in the program for an additional six months, or have their child removed from their home. Although no statistical data related to the project are currently available, the authors report positive changes in all parents who have thus far participated in the project.

Humanistic-Behavioral Group Therapy

Supported by a grant from a local foundation, Foothill Family Service agency in Pasadena, California, implemented a 120-

20. Gerald R. Patterson et al., *A Social Learning Approach to Family Intervention: Families with Aggressive Children* (Eugene, Oreg.: Castalia Publishing Co., 1975).

21. Jill Kinney, "Homebuilders: An In-home Crisis Intervention Program," *Children Today* 7 (January-February 1978): 15-35.

22. A. Hardman, C. Lammers, and S. Stiffler, "FACT: Families and Children Together," *International Journal of Child Abuse and Neglect* 1 (1977): 391-95.

hour treatment program for abusing parents.[23] Nine families were recruited through local human service agencies for the program. Parents met for a therapeutic camping experience for four weekends, and later received sixteen hours of postcamp follow-up counseling. Four Saturday morning sessions were devoted to discussions of common human concerns; self-esteem, self-gratification, mutual sharing, responsibility for one's own life, and so on. Children and parents spent Saturday afternoons in dance and drama therapy. On Sunday mornings, parents attended a four-session program on family life education that introduced them to behavioral methods of child management and helped them develop individual programs of behavior management for their children. The parents used a book, *Living with Children* by Gerald Patterson,[24] to guide them for the four sessions. Early results of the program are presented as very positive. The author of the report, Audrey Oppeheimer, provides brief vignettes describing the nature and amount of immediate improvement in specific clients. She stated that "an immediate decrease in shouting, screaming, or hitting as a form of discipline by the parents was noted, and no further abusive behavior has been reported with these families."[25]

Multiple Family Therapy

Two major assumptions regarding child abuse provide the rationale for the use of multiple family therapy with abusing parents described by L. R. McKamy.[26] The first assumption relates to the social isolation, anomie, mobility, and loss of extended family as important contributing factors in child abuse. The second is that child abuse by one family member is a symptom of family pathology.

Problem solving in individual family interaction patterns is combined with network therapy in which four to six families meet for two hours in large treatment groups to provide a mutual support system. In this setting, problems of individual families may be shared and solved. Three or more therapists work with each group, guiding members in dealing with interactional problems rather than with problems of individual family members. Therapeutic techniques used include listening skills, support, interpretation, and facilitation of problem-solving efforts. Group processes may include problem specification, bargaining, conflict resolution, and contracting between family members. Although no specific outcome data are currently available, McKamy reports that initial observations indicate that the approach provides an effective method for work with abusing parents.

Summary

Although the reports reviewed differ markedly with regard to their theoretical frame of reference and techniques and procedures used, they also offer many similarities. Each model of treatment views historical factors as contributing to present behavior patterns. Each approach makes use of behavioral referents of clients in assessment, treatment planning, and evaluation. Each approach emphasizes vigorous activity by the workers involved, who engage the clients in a consistent process aimed at changing their individual functioning. Each approach combines therapy with other supportive social services to reduce stress and improve clients' satisfaction with their daily lives. Each approach requires a considerable investment of time, resources, and effort to maintain clients in the treatment process. Finally, each approach is reported as achieving positive changes in most participants.

None of the studies available for review has made use of either single-case experimental designs or of control groups to evaluate absolute or relative effectiveness of the methods used. None of the approaches reported on has provided services to a large number of clients relative to the actual client population.

A much greater realization of the need for

23. Audrey Oppenheimer, "Triumph over Trauma in the Treatment of Child Abuse," *Social Casework* 59 (June 1978): 352-58.

24. Gerald Patterson, *Living with Children: New Methods for Parents and Teachers* (Champaign, Ill.: Research Press, 1976).

25. Oppenheimer, "Triumph over Trauma," p. 358.

26. L. R. McKamy, "Multiple Family Therapy: A Treatment Modality for Child Abuse Cases," *International Journal of Child Abuse and Neglect* 1 (1977): 339-45.

resources and efforts to make treatment programs available to abusing parents is currently required. It is not surprising that empirical research in connection with relative effectiveness of promising approaches is almost nonexistent, because most communities do not have systematic or extensive treatment programs in operation. As P. J. Breezley of the National Center for the Prevention and Treatment of Child Abuse states, "a family gets whatever services a community has, regardless of the family's special problems."[27]

The reports reviewed in this article provide a broad array of potentially useful approaches to treatment of abusing parents, to guide the development of additional services for families with this special need. Research on the relative effectiveness of different approaches to treatment, based on client characteristics and need, will also be facilitated by this information.

27. P. J. Breezley, "Critical Factors for the Long Term Management of Child Abuse," *International Journal of Child Abuse and Neglect* 1 (1977): 321.

Staff of a child abuse program in a Philadelphia hospital worked with parents in their own homes to help them develop greater competence as adults and as parents. This article describes the use of social learning theory, with some techniques of behavior therapy, as the basis for treatment.

Treatment for child abusers

by James J. Tracy and Elizabeth H. Clark

James J. Tracy, Ph.D., is Acting Assistant Professor of Psychiatry and Behavioral Sciences, University of Washington, and Director of Entry and Assessment Service, Harborview Community Mental Health Center, University of Washington School of Medicine, Seattle, Washington. Elizabeth Hughes Clark, MA, is Director, Social Service Department, Presbyterian–University of Pennsylvania Medical Center, Philadelphia, Pennsylvania.

For eleven years public attention has been focused on child abuse. In writing of the "battered child syndrome," Helfer and Kempe helped define the problem.[1] Explanatory theories and treatment programs for child abuse are emerging rapidly at the same time as adequate research is falling behind. Although reference is frequently made to emotional and psychological abuse, *child abuse* in this article refers to children who show evidence of physical injury or physical neglect by the parent.

The bulk of professional opinion, as summarized by Spinetta and Rigler, maintains that psychological factors within the parents are the primary causes of child abuse.[2] Because psychodynamic theorists have generated them, most theories of child abuse are concerned with the effects of mental and emotional forces that developed in early childhood. In *Helping the Battered Child and His Family*, Kempe and Helfer summarized several treatment strategies.[3] Participants in treatment programs too often end up discussing better relations between and within professional agencies without addressing themselves to the abused child or the adults who are abusing him. Hence, both professional opinion and treatment programs seem limited.

Social learning theory is so named because of its concern with society's effect on the individual. The theory attempts to identify the psychological processes and techniques used to help individuals participate socially. Bandura and Walters outlined social learning theory in a developmental context,[4] and psychologists, psychiatrists, and social workers have demonstrated how to apply learning theory to their fields.[5]

The child abuse project at Presbyterian–University of Pennsylvania Medical Center chose social learning theory as the basis for its treatment model.[6] This was done because the project was designed to change behavior through the use of social as opposed to primary reinforcement. The theory involved an identification of behavioral goals, followed by specific techniques of achieving them and by constant evaluation. Also the model seemed well suited to deal

Reprinted from SOCIAL WORK, 19 (May 1974), pp. 338–342.

with environmental factors that prevent a person from developing competence as a parent and an adult. The choice was appropriate for another reason. The project consultant, realizing the negative attitude many social agencies hold toward learning theory and behavior modification, was prompted to use less provocative words.

The program strives to move beyond diagnosis and etiological concerns to help abusive adults achieve competence in their roles as parents. In contrast to many popular theories that make assumptions about the pathology of abusing adults, a social learning analysis of child abuse makes the following observations:

- Abusive adults have few skills to help them function competently as adults. They gain little satisfaction from their role as parents.
- Abusive adults are frequently ignorant of child development. They expect behavior too advanced for young children.
- They control their children's behavior almost exclusively through punishment, because they lack knowledge of alternative means of controlling them.
- Abusive adults are more likely to respond to therapeutic personnel who are of similar socioeconomic and racial background and who will work with them in their own homes.
- Therapeutic personnel, both professional and paraprofessional, frequently overestimate the competence of abusive adults.

These assumptions were made after working with abusive adults in their own homes over a period of one year.

CHILD ABUSE PROJECT

The project described in this article took place in the area surrounding the Presbyterian–University of Pennsylvania Medical Center. Because this is a predominantly black neighborhood, the decision was made to have blacks work in the project.

Three full-time members of the social service department are available for suspected cases of child abuse. At present one of these social workers is black and lives in the community surrounding the hospital. The coordinator of the outreach program is a black registered nurse who is familiar with the community served by the hospital. All four of the family health workers are black women ranging in age from 35 to 50 who live in the nearby community. They were selected for their ability to listen sensitively in an interview and to respond in simple language. No specific educational level or prior training was required.

Outline of the program. The first step in the child abuse project is to identify the cause of injury. All children entering the emergency ward are screened. If the attending physician has any suspicion of child abuse, he is instructed to alert the staff pediatrician and the social service department. Two members of the social service department are on voluntary twenty-four-hour call, seven days a week. If the examination or evaluation by the staff pediatrician or social worker supports the suspicion of child abuse, the child is hospitalized, regardless of the extent of his injuries. Further assessment of the case continues for the next few days. If the suspicion of child abuse remains, a legal form is completed and sent to the city's department of public welfare with a statement that the child abuse project will be providing this family with continuing services in the home.

The second step in the child abuse project is to conduct a precise behavioral analysis of the parent's techniques of child management. The authors observed that the abusing adult was most often a single mother. The initial analysis is based primarily on a detailed interview. The staff member makes no attempt to get a description of the specific abuse, but rather asks the parent to discuss general punishment or techniques of controlling the child. From the everyday pattern it is not difficult to extrapolate the abusive behavior that caused the child's hospitalization. Often it becomes clear that punishment is the adult's only way of controlling the child. Subsequent interviews and observation identify the times and places when an adult is likely to be easily upset and short-tempered. Special attention is directed to the child's actions and to the adult's thoughts and feelings immediately before a confrontation with the child. The interview also focuses on the immediate consequences or what happened directly after the abusive action. What did the child do? What did other adults do? The parent is asked when the child is easier to cope with and when he is likely to trigger punishment. The hospital social worker conducts these assessment interviews with the goal of completing an analysis of abusive behavior—its antecedents and consequences.

The third step in the child abuse project is to decide whether the child can be returned to the family if the outreach program provides continued assistance. In all cases so far, there has been sufficient evidence to allow the child to return home. No parent has refused the treatment offered.

The fourth step involves formulating plans and goals for treatment. These are discussed by the social worker and the parent and are based on the behavioral analysis the social worker has prepared.

The fifth step is to introduce the family to the outreach staff, usually at the time the child is discharged from the hospital. Using the behavioral analysis and treatment plans as a starting point, the family health worker begins to work with the child's parents within a few days of his release from the hospital.

TREATMENT

If analysis reveals that severe turmoil at bedtime is likely to illicit strong punishment, specific plans can be developed by the family health worker and the parent. Together they will discuss the environmental obstacles that block a peaceful bedtime. For example, it may well be that the child has no bed—only a drawer or a bed he must share. If easing the stress at bedtime is a high priority, the worker can help the parent get a bed or can rearrange the sleeping facilities to lessen the aggrava-

tion. In this manner she can help the parent gain beginning competence. Too, it may be that the turmoil at bedtime is increased by constant verbal punishment. In this case, the worker can demonstrate the technique of "catching the child being good," a technique that involves teaching the parent to reinforce positively the child's good behavior. Frequently, the adult has developed the habit of ignoring good behavior and attending only to bad behavior.

The specific plans attempt to move the adult into a role of competent parenthood. The parent is encouraged to contribute ideas and to take part in making plans. As small gains are made, the family health worker reinforces them by explicitly pointing out the ways in which the parent was successful. The goal of these consultations is to demonstrate informally positive techniques of child management.

In working with a family, the worker is encouraged and helped to reformulate the behavioral analysis and plans for treatment. These revisions often serve as a valuable learning experience for the staff, including the social workers and medical personnel who identified the problem.

The family health worker frequently becomes an advocate for the family in housing projects or welfare offices. She tries, however, to avoid reinforcing dependent behavior. Instead, she serves as a role model for appropriate assertive behavior. The role of the family health worker is, then, an active one. She is not intended to be a lecturer, but someone who can articulate and demonstrate effective principles and techniques.

Continuity of service. An important goal of the child abuse project is to establish continuity between the child's hospitalization and the treatment within the family. Every precaution must be taken to insure that parents understand the connection between the treatment given in the hospital and at home. From previous experience it was found that partial or redundant interviews conducted by a variety of professionals only confuse the parents. Consequently, the physician and social worker are the only professionals to interview parents while the child is hospitalized. Only after the child is discharged does the social worker introduce the coordinator of the outreach program and the family health worker assigned to the case.

One specific objective in achieving continuity in the delivery of service was to teach all staff a common language for describing behavior, formulating treatment, and communicating with one another. A psychological consultant conducted two ninety-minute training sessions a week—one for the hospital staff and the other for the family health workers. The coordinator of the outreach program attended both sessions. After the first six weeks of the program the consultant conducted bimonthly sessions based on prepared materials and specific cases. The material was designed to teach the assessment of behavior through interviews and observation. Abusive behavior was defined together with its antecedents and consequences. Because the parent and child are caught in a reciprocal system, both the parent's abusive behavior and the child's actions that precipitated it must be analyzed carefully.

Evaluation. A high priority in the project is the development of objective instruments to evaluate behavioral change. The social learning model attempts to define specific behavior related to child abuse, and much of the data necessary in evaluating social change is provided by the analysis of behavior. Specific behavior is monitored by the use of frequency counts, which are usually charted on a weekly basis. Because these are based on the limited observation of family health workers or on the parents' verbal reports, additional evaluative procedures are necessary.

Several pediatricians involved in treating abused children constructed a form designed to assess and quantify the physical symptoms of a child they suspect of being abused. The "Trauma X" form, which is currently used by three Philadelphia hospitals, is the last of three such efforts. The attending physician fills out this form for any child suffering from unexplained trauma. The pediatrician completes it during the frequent interviews at the clinic after the child is discharged. This permits objective evaluation of the possibility of a recurrence of the abusive behavior. The coordinator of the outreach program can also add to the form if she visits the home.

The development of specific instruments of evaluation may allow direct comparison of different approaches to the treatment of child abuse. In this way empirical research can directly address the questions previously answered by theoretical speculation and clinical vignettes.

PROBLEMS AND LIMITATIONS

A recurring problem is staff discomfort created by accountability—in this case responsibility for a clear report of the problem behavior, the treatment and any progress made. Because the project employs the social learning model, the staff is continually confronted with the specifics of accountability.

An anticipated problem was the use by staff members (particularly the professional staff) of vague terminology in their descriptions. References to "a character-disordered" mother or to "hypothetical etiological processes" have decreased as the staff became familiar with terms that describe specific behaviors.

A related problem is the stereotype many professionals hold of theories of learning and behavior therapy. In the beginning this stereotype prevented a close examination of the social learning model, but gradually it has given way to a more inquiring view. Humanistic concern for the client's feelings, for example, appears compatible with the model and is dealt with explicitly. In fact, one social worker remarked that through the learning model she uncovered several middle-class values that had previously masqueraded as objective criteria.

The present pilot project needs to provide additional time for consultation. In the beginning, two full days each month were allowed for this. Although the consultant must ultimately teach skills that

71

will help the hospital staff to function independently, more extensive consultation is needed during the initial phases. At present, all consultation and evaluation have been funded through private donations or given without cost. The present project has been more successful in informal than in formal evaluation.

The child abuse project hopes to provide a model for delivering services that is flexible enough to be applied to areas other than child abuse. High-risk surgical patients, for example, need systematic help after they are discharged. Already the social learning model has been applied to elderly and terminally ill patients.

Although the project is making progress toward the ideals of a social learning model, problems and limitations are still evident. Future goals include attaining more comprehensive quantifiable data on each case, extending the model to problem behaviors other than child abuse, and comparing research with other treatment modalities.

NOTES AND REFERENCES

1. *See* Ray E. Helfer and C. Henry Kempe, eds., *The Battered Child* (Chicago: University of Chicago Press, 1968).

2. *See* J. J. Spinetta and D. Rigler, "The Child-Abusing Parent: A Psychological Review," *Psychological Bulletin*, 77 (1972), pp. 296–304.

3. C. Henry Kempe and Ray E. Helfer, eds., *Helping the Battered Child and His Family* (Philadelphia: J. B. Lippincott Co., 1972).

4. Albert Bandura and R. H. Walters, *Social Learning and Personality Development* (New York: Henry Holt & Co., 1963).

5. *See* Albert Bandura, *Principles of Behavior Modification* (New York: Holt, Rinehart & Winston, 1969); Arnold A. Lazarus, *Behavior Therapy and Beyond* (New York: McGraw-Hill Book Co., 1971); R. B. Stuart, "The Role of Social Work Education in Innovative Human Services," in Frank W. Clark, D. R. Evans, and L. A. Hamerlynck, eds., *Implementing Behavioral Programs for Schools and Clinics* (Champaign, Ill.: Research Press, 1972); and Joseph Wolpe, *The Practice of Behavior Therapy*, "General Psychology Series," Vol. 1 (New York: Pergamon Press, 1969).

6. This project is supported by the Haas Community Fund of Philadelphia and consultation is provided by private donations.

Lucile Cantoni

Clinical Issues in Domestic Violence

Characteristics of violence-prone clients and family patterns
that promote domestic violence are discussed. Treatment involves
the violence-prone family in a nurturing, therapeutic process
designed to help clients recognize interacting family dynamics
so that aspects of the system in need of change may be addressed.

Lucile Cantoni is Associate Executive Director for
Program, Family Service of Detroit and Wayne County,
Detroit, Michigan. This article is based on a paper
presented at the 1978 Workshop for Directors of
Professional Services, Zion, Illinois, 22–25 October,
1978.

DOMESTIC VIOLENCE HAS COME out of
hiding—it occurs in families of all races and
cultures, at all socioeconomic levels. Within
the past five years, social caseworkers have
learned to recognize various manifestations
of domestic violence and to treat the families
involved. Individual, group, and family
systems treatments have been utilized.

In 1975, when the staff of Family Service
of Detroit and Wayne County (FSDWC) first
studied casework treatment of parents who
abused their children, there was very little
casework literature on child abuse.[1] The
agency study group found that caseworkers
frequently minimized or ignored child abuse
problems in their clients. In studying the
abused wife problem in 1976, Beverly B.
Nichols said that ". . . caseworkers rarely
pick abusiveness as the focus of intervention;
rather, they tend to ignore this symptom."[2] In
1977, Kay M. Tooley found that sibling abuse

was rarely even recognized and reported,
much less treated by caseworkers.[3] And, in
the spring of 1979, Mary Ellen Elwell pointed
out that the sexual abuse of children was only
beginning to be recognized and treated by the
professional community.[4]

Even though many caseworkers are still
learning to deal with issues of domestic
violence, progress has been made in recognizing and treating violence-prone families.
Much work with abusive parents has been
reported in the past five years. Recently,
Clayton T. Shorkey reviewed various
methods used in the treatment of abusing
parents.[5] In 1977, Margaret Ball reported a
study conducted by Family Service of Detroit
and Wayne County in the treatment of adult-
adult violence.[6] Later, Margaret Elbow theorized about the dynamics of abusing husbands.[7]

1. See Sally A. Holmes et al., "Working with Parents in
Child-Abuse Cases," *Social Casework* 56 (January
1975): 3–12.

2. Beverly B. Nichols, "The Abused Wife Problem,"
Social Casework 57 (January 1976): 27–32.

3. Kay M. Tooley, "The Young Child as Victim of Sibling Attack," *Social Casework* 58 (January 1977): 25–28.

4. Mary Ellen Elwell, "Sexually Assaulted Children and
Their Families," *Social Casework: The Journal of
Contemporary Social Work* 60 (April 1979): 227–35.

5. Clayton T. Shorkey, "A Review of Methods Used in
the Treatment of Abusing Parents," *Social Casework:
The Journal of Contemporary Social Work* 60 (January
1979): 360–67.

6. Margaret Ball, "Issues of Violence in Family
Casework," *Social Casework* 58 (January 1977): 3–12.

7. Margaret Elbow, "Theoretical Considerations of
Violent Marriages," *Social Casework* 58 (November
1977): 515–26.

The dynamics are similar in violence-prone families, regardless of whether the victim is a child, spouse, parent, or sibling.[8] In a common pattern, the man assaults the woman, the woman assaults one or more of the children, the children attack siblings, other children, small animals, and so on. Young people seen in runaway shelters are often running from some form of domestic violence. Aged parents who are attacked by their adult offspring are frequently "getting back some of their own medicine." This article considers clinical issues in casework treatment of violence-prone families.

Common Characteristics

Domestic violence occurs when a person loses control of himself and injures a family member or intimate associate. The counselor addresses the issues of domestic violence whenever a family member (1) demonstrates that self-control has been lost, (2) fears that self-control may be lost, or (3) is preceived by others as out of control of his or her own behavior or in danger of becoming so. Certain characteristics that are generally present in members of violent families are described below.

Role Reversal and Role Confusion

When a parent has been inadequately nurtured he or she may turn to the child as a source of nurture.[9] The most dramatic example is the mother and the toddler. The toddler hurts himself but does not cry out. Instead, he looks with fear at his parent. His silence is deafening. But, when the parent begins to show signs of upset, the toddler rushes over to the mother, pats her and snuggles up to comfort her. The child is the parent and the parent is the child. The mother is repeating the experience of her infancy; she was once the caring infant, now her infant must care for her.

Inappropriate Sexual Expression

A high percentage of violent family members were sexually exploited as children.[10] Counselors may not be aware of this fact, because they traditionally avoid exploring this area of a client's case history, and clients often have such intense feelings of hostility, shame, and confusion about these experiences that he or she is only able to reveal these events in a fully accepting atmosphere.

Typically in such cases, the girl was sexually exploited by her father, grandfather, stepfather, or older brother. She was told directly or indirectly that something terrible would happen if the sexual experiences were revealed. Despite the implicit awareness of the activity by all members of the family, it was never mentioned. (Usually, revealing the secret means that something terrible *does* happen.) Although the sexual activity may have been mostly pleasant or mostly painful, it was often a mixture of pleasure and pain. There was also a mixture of excitement and dread. Such children have some sense of being chosen and rewarded, but also a sense of being used and abused.

The girl who has been sexually violated grows into a woman who tends to sexualize all human relationships. She may use her sexuality to get what she thinks will give her satisfaction, or she may try to avoid all sexual expression. Usually, she vacillates between the two extremes. She views herself as a hole, a nothing, a nonperson. She expects men to violate her. When she has a child she may respond sexually, because that is the only emotion of closeness she knows. To defend herself against sexual arousal, she may ignore or attack her child.

Typically, a sexually abused boy was not engaged in overt sexual acts, but he may have slept with his mother through his adolescent years. He may have been held close and fondled, but was not supposed to have an

8. See Lucile Cantoni, *Parents Anonymous of Michigan Self Assessment Schedule: Report of the First Three Administrations* (Detroit: Parents Anonymous of Michigan, 1979), p. 12; and Suzanne Prescott and Carolyn Letko, "Battered Women: A Social Psychological Perspective," in *Battered Women,* ed. Maria Roy (New York: Van Nostrand Reinhold, 1977), p. 81.

9. Marian G. Morris and Robert W. Gould, "Role Reversal: A Concept in Dealing with the Neglected/ Battered-Child Syndrome," in *The Neglected Battered-Child Syndrome,* (New York: Child Welfare League of America, 1963), pp. 26–46; and Blair Justice and Rita Justice, *The Abusing Family* (New York: Human Sciences Press, 1976), pp. 69–72.

10. Karin C. Meiselman, *Incest* (San Francisco: Jossey-Bass, 1979).

erection. The mother may have bathed her son and given him enemas into adulthood. One young man said, "She gave me everything I ever wanted except my penis." Such a boy becomes a man who expects women to emasculate him. He may be able to perform sexually only as an attack—through rape. Or, he may be able to perform only after he has physically abused his wife. He expects her to emasculate him, and so he may interpret almost anything she does or says as an attack; he defends himself against her "attacks" by blindly hitting out. His wife is usually his target, but not always; one of his children or any other person may also become the victim of his abuse.

Intense Ambivalence and Inconsistency

In this situation, the yearning for or attachment to other persons, especially family members, is excessive. The need for care and love is great because such individuals have never been properly cared for and loved and they yearn for someone who will make up these losses. But, at the same time, experience has taught that no one can or will give love properly. Even as these individuals yearn for love, they are intensely angry with loved ones for the failure they expect. The pregnant mother, yearning for her child to love her, may beat on her abdomen and rail at the unborn child who kicks her. The formerly sweet and dutiful husband may beat his pregnant wife who is withdrawing her constant attention from him as she invests in the new life.[11] These inconsistencies are the product of ambivalence. When these individuals believe they can get longed-for caring and love, they are giving or compliant. When they believe they are being denied or put off, they respond with rage.

Lack of Trust, with Resulting Isolation

Ideally, infants learn trust from the consistent caring of their parents. Typically, violent people have been handled inconsistently from infancy. Thus, they do not learn trust, which is essential in effective human relationships. They may appear socially as isolates.[12] They may be in marriages or a series of marriages that are observable as formalities only, lacking meaningful exchange between themselves and other family members.

A person who has not learned trust may be intensely involved in defective interactions with family, extended family, and others. These relationships are likely to be characterized by fights, fallings-out, taking sides, and various ways of taking advantage of each other. Sexual activity in these relationships are almost exclusively for exploitation. People who are intensely involved in such defective relationships may not view themselves as isolated, yet the quality of their interaction is so defective that they are actually isolated from meaningful human interaction.

Another type of isolated person is socially very correct. Such people may be economically successful and much involved with structured activities—job-related, civic, or religious activities. They appear to interact with others, but carefully protect themselves from letting others really get to know them. In various ways, they believe that if anyone "really knew" them, they would hate, abandon, and destroy them. Their defense is to go through the motions of social interaction while remaining emotionally isolated.

There is yet another emotionally isolated type of person, the "con" artist. Such individuals go through the motions of social interaction, but their goal is to take advantage of others, to trick others into giving them something they feel they have been cheated of. Basically, the thing they have been cheated out of is the consistent, caring love of a parent. Because nothing can ever make up for this lack, their lives are filled with constant frustration and isolation. They need to be able to "get" people. If they can manipulate people into giving them some satisfaction, they may be able to function reasonably well.

Fear of Dependence or of Independence

Individuals who have been less damaged than the isolates may fear only one or the

---

11. Richard J. Gelles, *The Violent Home* (Beverly Hills, Calif.: Sage Publications, 1972), pp. 145–47.

12. Ibid., pp. 132–35.

other side of interdependence. They may be capable of much closeness, so long as the feared part of the relationship is subdued.

Infants who were used as parents to the parents, and who were able to care for the parents successfully, often experienced tremendous gratification in the relationship. Such people are likely to consider their parents as their best friends throughout their lives. Because of the many gratifications they experienced, they are not aware of the profound lack in the relationship. The lack is that their own dependency needs have never been met. More than that, when they have attempted to gain the caring concern of their parents, they may have had a devastating experience. One week a client with this kind of background may remember having been viciously attacked by his parent, but the next week have no memory of the incident. Such a person cannot understand why he should suddenly feel attacked by someone on whom he feels dependent.

Various patterns may contribute to the development of a person who fears becoming independent. One pattern is the neglected-abused child who becomes a clinging whiner. The child may literally cling to the parent's leg and whimper like a hurt animal. The parent may kick the child across the room. The clinging whiner often marries someone who is constantly attentive—the attention may be positive or negative; the significant factors are the intensity and constancy. However, whenever he or she is not receiving constant attention, unrestrained anger or violence may occur.

Inability to Play

People learn how to interact creatively with their surroundings and with other human beings through play. However, people who have never been permitted to play do not learn the most basic skills of living. The author's clinical observations indicate that violent family members usually are lacking in their ability to play. Further investigation is needed in this area.

Inadequate Ego Structure

In this situation, the individual has never had enough consistent care by a stable adult

so that a role model is developed. Instead, life is constantly lived through external involvement. Such individuals seem to crave excitement; life is one long soap opera. There seems to be a fear that if something is not going on incessantly, the story may be over, the television go off, and the person cease to exist. Therefore, there is an intense craving for excitement. Violence may or may not be involved in the excitement, but the danger of possible violence is ever present.

The Expectation of Perfection

There is an almost universal expectation among violence-prone individuals that human beings are supposed to be perfect.[13] They may not be sure what constitutes perfection, but they are sure that it does exist. And because they know that they are imperfect, each assumes that he or she is a totally unacceptable human being.

There are several ways such individuals can react to the expectations of perfection. One way is to devote a lifetime to making one's self and one's family members perfect. Any evidence of imperfection may throw this person into a rage. Conversely, the person may simply give up, accept the negative self-image, and make no attempt to behave like a responsible human being. The expectation of perfection is a perfect setup for failure.

Lack of Self-Control

The above characteristics add up to the lack of self-control seen in this population. These individuals were not consistently controlled by a caring adult in their infancy and childhood. Moreover, they were expected to control the adult, or they were blamed for causing major life events:
"Your father left us because of you."
"If you don't behave, I'm going to leave."
"You keep that up and you'll kill me."
"You are driving me crazy."
"If you don't shut up, I'm going to kill you."

These accusations may be made in many households. But when this kind of accusation is made regularly and with intensity, the child believes he or she is responsible for his family.

---

13. Justice and Justice, *Abusing Family,* p. 60.

The child cannot provide the control that is needed, therefore the child learns to believe that he or she is the cause of major family disasters. Thus, the child develops a distorted concept of control—self-control and the control of others.

Individuals who have grown up in this kind of situation may seem to make no effort to control themselves. They seem totally impulse-oriented. Yet, at times, they may admit to fear of their own unbridled impulses. They yearn for control, even more than for love. In fact, they may equate the two, and rightly so. For the love they lacked was the love of a consistent, caring, controlling parent. As adults, they may seek relationships with cruel persons, who are somehow conceived as capable of control.

Excessive Control

The opposite reaction to impulsivity is the excessively controlled individual. The major life energy of such individuals is devoted to controlling themselves and others. Successful military or police personnel may be individuals who have achieved a satisfactory resolution to the need for self-control. Some successful business people also invest their lives in efforts to gain control. A career breakdown for such individuals might destroy them. Yet, it may be more possible to gain control over a career than over a family. Growing children cannot be so carefully controlled. A sassy look by a spouse or child might be experienced by such persons as posing a major threat to their ability to control themselves; so slight a provocation may throw them into a rage, during which they may attack the offending family member.

It must be realized that persons who have serious problems with self-control are afraid of themselves. They may try to act cool, tough, macho, but in a quiet moment, with a concerned counselor, they will admit their great fear of themselves.

Psychosis and Organic Factors

Most of the people whose characteristics have been described in this article do not demonstrate classic psychotic symptoms.[14] Yet they often feel like they are "going crazy" as they lose control of themselves. They have had such extreme losses throughout life that their underlying personality structure is one of intense depression. With the depressive underlay, there is a sense of nothingness, of nonexistence.

Such people may defend against depression by aggressive efforts to be involved with others. They try to "get" people or things. Their efforts may be regarded as noble, deplorable, sweet, annoying, and so on. Their life energies are devoted to figuring people out, and then behaving in such a way as to get what they think they want from others. As long as these techniques work and they are able to get from others, they can function. When their techniques fail, they fall into a characteristic depressive psychosis.[15]

Other violence-prone individuals recognize when they are losing control and know that they need to be cared for until they can regain it. They present themselves at psychiatric hospitals, pleading for needed care. Often, they are turned away because they do not demonstrate classic symptoms of psychosis. This is a serious problem; there needs to be some place in the community where potentially violent people can receive care.

Various organic conditions may be directly or indirectly related to a person's violent behavior. Explosive rage may be associated with epilepsy, hypoglycemia, or other organic conditions.[16] Violent behavior in chronic schizophrenic patients can usually be controlled by medication, unless the patient is caught in a family pattern conducive to violence.[17]

14. Brandt F. Steele and Carl B. Pollock, "A Psychiatric Study of Parents Who Abuse Infants and Small Children," in *The Battered Child*, ed. Ray E. Helfer and C. Henry Kempe (Chicago: University of Chicago Press, 1968), pp. 108–11; and M. Faulk, "Men Who Assault Their Wives," in *Battered Women*, ed. Roy, pp. 119–26.

15. Garfield Tourney, Peter G.S. Beckett and Jacques S. Gottlieb, "The Atypical Depressive Illnesses," *Journal of Iowa Medical Society* (May 1965): 253–59.

16. Frank A. Elliott, "The Neurology of Explosive Rage: The Dyscontrol Syndrome," in *Battered Women*, ed. Roy, pp. 98–109.

17. Melvin Cohen, "Family Interaction Patterns, Drug Treatment, and Change in Social Aggression," in *Violence in the Family*, ed. Suzanne K. Steinmetz and Murray A. Straus (New York: Harper and Row, 1974), pp. 120–26.

Drugs of all sorts should be considered as causative or complicating factors in domestic violence. These include prescription medication, across-the-counter drugs, illegal drugs, and alcohol.[18] The relationship of the drug to the violence is not always as clear as the example of the man getting drunk and beating up his wife. The author worked with one violence-prone family in which the man regularly had a violent episode on Tuesdays. Every Saturday night he went to parties at which he took "speed." When he stopped taking the Saturday drugs, the Tuesday violence also stopped. Apparently, he suffered withdrawal symptoms on the third day.

Stress

A violent person is not always violent. Often it is possible to recognize a stressful event that triggers violence. Virtually anyone might react to some situations with violence, given enough stress. In battle, the soldier who kills the enemy may be regarded as a hero. The victim of a concentration camp may be regarded as a tragically destroyed human being. This kind of stress is readily understood, but the kind of stress that is likely to trigger domestic violence tends to be more subtle.

Often a family fight erupts and family members demean each other. The fighting escalates, and the contestants feel increasingly pushed, until one or more of them reacts with blind rage. At other times, however, the violent outburst seems to come from nowhere. Sometimes it is possible to recognize the build-up of many frustrations, so that the final stress is the proverbial straw that broke the camel's back. Sometimes stress on the job may be taken out on a spouse. Sometimes it is possible to recognize an anniversary reaction to past loss. Often an apparently innocuous event triggers memories of old pain, and today's victim is merely a stand-in for yesterday's attacker.

The Violent Episode

The violent episode may be experienced in a variety of ways. However, a common pattern appears among the kinds of violent

18. Maria Roy, "A Current Survey of 150 Cases," in *Battered Women,* ed. Roy, p. 39.

people described in this article. During the violent episode, the violent person is beyond concern for right or wrong. They experience a sense of release; there may be a sense of exhilaration, but most often the experience is neither satisfying nor unsatisfying, it is just an uncontrollable release. As soon as the rage is spent, the individual may go into deep depression. Despair, helplessness, and intense pain accompany the depression.

During the violent episode, the attacking person identifies with those who previously attacked him or her and, at the same time, revenges himself or herself against them. In the post-attack depression, the attacker identifies with the victim; the attacker may experience every wound that has been inflicted, and this pain is compounded by the memory of the many experiences of being victimized. Recognizing the intensity of the attacker's identification with the victim in the post-attack depression helps the therapist to realize how intensely binding the violent relationship becomes.

Treatment and the Therapeutic Relationship

There are three basic beliefs that underlie therapeutic efforts on behalf of violent families. First, domestic violence is unacceptable. This message must ring loud and clear throughout the community. Parents do not have the right to harm their children. Wife beating is intolerable and in no sense a display of macho superiority. Second, violent family members are not to blame for having this problem, they learn to be violent. There is a hurt child within the attacking adult and the victim does not cause the attack. Both the attacker and the victim—and the entire family—need help. Third, each member of a violent family must assume responsibility for change. No one outside the family can bestow peace. The community is responsible to provide help to the violent family and to each of its members. With community support and assistance for violent family members, change becomes possible.

It is often difficult to establish a sound working relationship with clients whose principal problem is domestic violence. As mentioned previously, these people have experienced such defective relationships with their parents that they have become isolates; they have never learned to trust others. They are usually convinced that anyone who ever saw their real self would hate and possibly destroy them. Thus, despite their yearning for change, they are terribly threatened by any therapeutic relationship, as the following case examples illustrate.

Mrs. A called her local family service agency six times over a two-year period; however, she would fail or cancel her appointments. Finally, a worker confronted her with her ambivalence about getting help, insisting that she discuss her fears. In the telephone confrontation, the worker's tone was light but firm. He insisted that her repeated calls indicated she did need help. She said nobody could help her. He responded, "Is that what you fear, that you will tell me your problems and then I won't be able to help you? That your problems are hopeless?" Mrs. A then began a lengthy discussion of her family situation. The worker gently but firmly cut her off, saying, "We need to sit down together for an hour to discuss your family situation and your fears. Do you think, now, that you can come in for an interview?" After two or three more minutes of discussing the practical and emotional complications of getting into the office, an appointment was made.

Mrs. A arrived for her interview twenty minutes late. The focus of the interview was on the client's fear of treatment. She revealed that her husband was physically abusive to her and her children, that she abused her children. Her husband had threatened to kill them all, and she sometimes has the urge to kill her husband. In a calm, empathic way the worker said he realized why it was so hard for her to start treatment. Mrs. A then revealed that many times during the past two years she drove back and forth in front of the agency, trying to get up enough nerve to come in, trying to believe that someone could help her. The worker said that others who had problems similar to hers had been helped, and he would like to help her obtain a more satisfactory family life.

Mrs. B came to her intake and all subsequent appointments on time. She filled up her interviews with an abundance of information and feelings. However, she completely con-

trolled the focus of treatment. She insisted that her son's enuresis was the family problem. Mrs. B discussed her interfering mother and her own career plans. She shrugged and passed over any questions regarding her husband with comments indicating he was a "lost cause" and she would divorce him as soon as she could afford to do so. Her comments about his rage and jealousy were hidden in verbiage.

Only on reflection did the worker realize that over several interviews Mrs. B had mentioned that her husband had threatened to kill the whole family if he caught Mrs. B with another man, and that Mrs. B was having an affair in a manner in which she was likely to get caught. Initially, Mrs. B tried to avoid the worker's efforts to confront her on this issue. Finally, the worker said, "I cannot sit here and listen to you talking about Bobby wetting his pants when the lives of your entire family are in danger." Only then did Mrs. B stop her incessant talk and admit multigenerational problems of sexual and physical violence.

Establishing New Relationship Patterns

Issues of isolation, trust, dependence, control, seduction, and ambivalence must be dealt with early in the therapeutic relationship. Sometimes a badly damaged client is unable to form an appropriate relationship with an individual worker because he or she finds the intensity of the relationship too threatening. Such a client may be able to get help in a group setting where the relationship with the worker is diluted. The author's agency has had good success with groups of abusive parents both in the district offices and through Parents Anonymous.[19] The agency has also worked successfully with groups of married couples whose major problem was spouse abuse.

A parent-surrogate relationship is the principal treatment tool for helping violence-prone families. Caseworkers often speak of "reparenting the parents." This should not be taken literally. Adults should not be encouraged to regress. The worker does not live

19. Sally A. Holmes, "Parents Anonymous: A Treatment Method for Child Abuse," *Social Work* 23 (May 1978): 245–47.

with the client; the worker is available to him or her only on a well-defined basis. The worker cannot control the client directly and must carefully avoid suggesting that he or she won't "let" the client do something. The client will repeatedly try to use the relationship in a characteristic, defective way. Each time it happens the worker points out the defect and redefines the relationship. The client learns new relationship patterns by interacting with the caseworker. These new patterns can become the basis for positive family change.

Understanding the Dynamics

A client new to treatment often considers his actual or potential violence either as (1) normal—the community or other family member who objects is "off base" or "out to get me," (2) caused by "my intrinsic badness" or the "badness" of a family member, or (3) "going crazy." None of these assumptions provides a basis for treatment. The social worker's assumptions are that (1) all the family members learned how to relate to others, and (2) the violent behavior is one aspect of a total interactional pattern. Then the worker joins the client in an adventure of exploration.

The C family came in because John, age nine, and Bill, age eleven, had stolen money from a neighbor. The father "beat them good" and brought them to the agency as further punishment. Their sad, quiet little mother came along, with four-year-old Martha in her arms. When asked what they liked best about their family, the boys said "gifts." What was worst was having to do all the work and "getting beat up on." The mother liked the house itself (a surprise to the father), but was angry because nobody ever took care of her; she was sick a lot. Mr. C was proud of his family, but they didn't "do what they were supposed to."

Mrs. C was an illegitimate child who had been shifted from one home to another all her life. Her thirteen years living with Mr. C was the longest she had ever been in one household. She was a school drop-out, grateful to Mr. C for rescuing her. He beat her up sometimes, but she considered wife-beating normal. She was physically ill much of the time, remaining in bed hours and days at a

time. She expected the boys to do the housework and cook the meals. She wanted her daughter near her, in and out of her bed. Mr. C's parents lived a few blocks from them. They demanded regular attention and expected about one day of work each week, in addition to many gifts, from their son. They considered Mr. C the family "dummy" and demeaned his work, despite the fact that his job was more highly skilled than his father's. Mr. C was constantly worried about his job and thought he could never please his boss.

Everyone in the system made excessive demands on Mr. C. He would bear up for a while and then explode, beating up his wife or his sons, or all of them. Mrs. C expected the boys to take care of the house and her. When they did not do so, she beat them. Lately they were becoming too big for this, so she would tell Mr. C to beat them. The boys were jealous of all the attention and physical closeness Mrs. C gave to Martha. When Martha was away from her mother's protection, the boys attacked her. John had difficulty learning, but when his teacher sent a note to the parents suggesting that they help John with his schoolwork, the parents beat the child viciously. Both Mr. and Mrs. C regarded themselves as "dummies"; they were determined to beat the "dumbness" out of John.

Mr. C remembered that when he was a boy he used to run away after his dad beat him up, and that sometimes he would steal. In treatment he realized that the stealing had to do with the violence. The violence was part of a total family pattern. As the family became aware of their dynamics, they were able to change together.

Mrs. J came for help after severely beating her daughter, Dolores. She requested placement for Dolores until she could get herself together. Dolores remained in placement one week before the foster parents sent her back home. Mrs. J had two other children whom she occasionally abused. However, Dolores was the child in whom she had the greatest investment, and Dolores was the most frequent target of her abuse. Mrs. J's mother was also named Dolores. The day of the most recent beating Mrs. J had visited her mother and the mother had demanded that Mrs. J provide inappropriately intimate ablutions for her. Mrs.

J went home and found Dolores dirty, needing to be cleaned up. All the rage that she felt toward her mother was taken out on her child.

In treatment, Mrs. J soon realized that she could not control her rage against Dolores unless she asserted herself appropriately against her mother. Mrs. J had always taken care of her mother and did not recognize how much she resented her. She also did not realize that daily visits with her mother were excessive. During treatment, Mrs. J also remembered that her mother had physically abused and abandoned her several times when she was a child. She considered herself a "whore," but with help realized that from the time she was a baby her mother had often called her a whore. She also remembered being sexually molested by her uncle and telling her mother, who slapped her and called her a whore.

As Mrs. J recognized her anger toward her mother, she wanted to do something against her mother. She fantasied how she would tell her off and do things that would hurt her. The worker encouraged Mrs. J to ventilate in the counselor's office and to assert herself with the mother by refusing inappropriate services and by visiting less frequently. The worker helped Mrs. J realize that she had never separated from her mother enough to become an individual in her own right. Once this was accomplished, the worker was able to help Mrs. J lessen the intensity of her relationships, both with mother-Dolores and daughter-Dolores. Only as Mrs. J recognized the intergenerational family dynamics was she able to change the patterns, become a person in her own right, and develop a non-abusive relationship with her daughter.

Education and Advice

There are such serious deficits in the backgrounds of most violent adults that they need some explicit education and advice. Role reversal is an intergenerational pattern. As noted earlier, babies are perceived as a source of emotional nurture for the parents. But, if a baby's own dependency needs are not met, the baby grows up to have a baby to care for him or her. The parent was never permitted to be a child, and thus he or she does not know what behavior is appropriate for his or her offspring at various ages. Parents may need to be taught that babies cry from internal needs, not as a condemnation of parents. Parents may need to learn that toddlers reach for everything in sight because they need to explore the world, not because they want to break valuable items.

Knowledge about marital interaction may be equally sparse. The author once conducted a group of five deprived marital couples. The couples were first asked to introduce each other, giving the best-liked characteristic of the spouse, but the response was weak. Next each was asked to report the best thing about the marriage, then the best thing in their parents' marriage. No one was able to contribute much. The final question, "How has anyone shown love to you?" was met with silence. Then, gradually, group members offered pitiful contributions that demonstrated dramatically their lacks and their losses. Much time was spent in that group teaching spouses how to talk with each other, how to arrive at joint decisions, and so on.

The timing on educational inputs and advice is critical. The parent usually needs much nurturing, much supportive concern for his or her own needs before he or she can use cognitive inputs. As clients become emotionally stronger, they become more receptive to education and advice.

Ego-syntonic sex education should be included in treatment as soon as a relationship of trust is developed. The clients should be advised that bathroom and bedroom doors should be closed while bathing and dressing. Sleeping quarters need to be divided by sexes; "bed hopping" during the night is unacceptable. Simple discussions of day-to-day living habits can help establish intergenerational boundaries even before the family discusses possible infractions of the boundaries. Most violence-prone families also need to learn how to be creative, how to play, as the following example indicates.

Mrs. E, who had recently divorced her abusive husband, was making valentine cards with her five-year-old daughter. The child was making a mess of the project, and Mrs. E became so upset she beat her with her fists. At the next interview she sobbed with remorse, "I was trying to do something nice with my daughter, but I was concentrating on a

81

product, not on sharing a creative experience." Mrs. Evans had some artistic ability, but needed to learn creative play. She was a long way from being able to mess with finger paints. She decided to try stringing beads. The next week she reported how she and her daughter had shared a delightful evening stringing beads. She had even complimented her daughter on her ability. She showed the worker her own fine craftsmanship, which the worker praised.

The author has had some experiences with groups and with family camps where the therapist, or someone brought in by the therapist, provided direct play experiences for clients. However, the usual process is to talk about creative play in individual and group sessions, offering suggestions and referring to support groups. This is in contrast to traditional therapy, which tends to be problem focused. Paying attention to creative, healthy activity represents a fresh emphasis in mental health.

Crisis Calls

Violence-prone family members are crisis-prone. Some arrangement must be made for them to reach a helping source in times of emergency. If the agency does not have twenty-four-hour availability, there is usually a crisis line in the community. Some workers give their home numbers selectively. Parents Anonymous has a system whereby members help each other through the crisis.

Termination

Many violence-prone family members have suffered severe losses throughout their lives. Separations have been death, desertion, or failure. They need to learn that separations are not always tragedies, parting can be leaving a successful experience to go on to other new experiences. Violence-prone family members who have had close relationships with their own parents have generally been unable to individuate. They need to learn emancipation.

Terminating the relationship provides an opportunity for reviewing the original problem and the course of progress. Clients can recognize their own growth, their own strengths. They can consider how best to respond to stress in the future, including the possibility of a return to the agency.

Termination is separation, somewhat like death. Clients grieve again over past losses, realizing that they have survived such losses. They grieve the loss of the casework relationship, realizing that they have grown through it and can survive alone. Successful termination gives the client an experience in emancipation.

Summary

Domestic violence occurs when a person loses control of him or herself and injures a family member or intimate associate. The counselor addresses the issues of domestic violence whenever family members demonstrate a loss of control, a fear of losing control, or are perceived by others as being out of control.

The violence-prone individual discussed in this article does not usually demonstrate psychotic behavior. However, psychoses and organic factors as well as drugs can be causative or complicating factors. The stress that triggers a violent outburst may or may not be directly related to the victim. The violent episode may be experienced by the attacker in a variety of ways. Characteristically, the individual explodes in an uncontrollable release of rage, followed by a depression in which he or she identifies with the victim.

Treatment of the violence-prone family is accomplished through the therapeutic relationship. Clients are given support and nurture by a caring worker with whom they experience a new way of interacting. Clients gain some understanding of the dynamic interactions between themselves and family members so that they recognize those aspects of their family system needing change. Violence-prone clients have such serious deficiencies in their life experiences that they need cognitive education and advice regarding effective marital interaction and child management. Cognitive inputs must be carefully timed and adapted to the ability of clients to use such inputs. Violence-prone clients must have service available when they have a crisis. Termination of casework treatment gives clients an experience in emancipation. The agency remains available to these clients should they again need service.

PART 3
Homemakers and Mutual Aid

BY MIRIAM SHAMES

Use of Homemaker Service in Families That Neglect Their Children

"THE PROBLEM OF dependent poverty in California is extensive, and increasingly stubborn. It is increasingly specialized and concentrated and self-perpetuating." [1] Judging from newspaper reports it is "increasingly stubborn . . . and self-perpetuating" all over the country, and new ways of meeting the problem will have to be devised if there is to be any hope of reversing the present trend.

The project described in this paper, in which homemakers were placed with seriously neglecting families receiving Aid to Needy Children (as AFDC is referred to in California), had for its purpose a demonstration of what homemakers could do as teachers in homes in which standards of household management were so poor as to seriously jeopardize the health and welfare of the children in the family. What came out of the project was far more than this, and it is with the purpose of describing the project and pointing out some of its implications for work with the multiproblem family and with long-standing dependency that this paper was written.

MIRIAM SHAMES, MA, *was Acting Project Director with Homemaker Service of the Los Angeles Region, Los Angeles, California, and supervisor of the project described. This project, financed by the U.S. Children's Bureau, was conducted co-operatively by Homemaker Service and a Neglect Unit of the Los Angeles County Bureau of Public Assistance Aid to Needy Children Program.*

SELECTING FAMILIES AND HOMEMAKERS

The "Neglect Unit" in the Los Angeles County ANC program is a unit to which cases in which there is serious and long-standing neglect of children are referred. Case loads in this unit are comparatively small and casework is more intensive than in the regular ANC case load. The unit chosen for this project is located in a part of the city that is predominantly Negro in population, and consists of one supervisor and five caseworkers, with a total case load of 240.

Each worker selected five cases he felt would benefit from a homemaker. A total of twelve cases were included in the project, comprising fourteen adults and sixty-seven children. The first six were selected randomly from the initial twenty-five designated by the workers and the second six were chosen from the remaining nineteen by the ANC supervisor, the ANC worker, and the homemaker supervisor on the basis of the families' apparent ability to make use of the service. Factors considered in selection of the latter group were largely the bases from which the neglect seemed to stem, such as lack of acculturation, absence of standards of care in the mother's own family, or early marriage with no op-

[1] Earl Raab and Hugh Folk, *The Pattern of Dependent Poverty in California* (Berkeley, Calif.: Welfare Study Commission, 1963), p. 382.

Reprinted from SOCIAL WORK, 9 (January 1964), pp. 12–18.
Copyright © 1964 by the National Association of Social Workers, Inc.

portunity for learning family and child-rearing skills. Also looked for were some evidence of positive feelings and ego strengths on the part of the mother.

Five homemakers were selected from the staff of Homemaker Service of the Los Angeles Region. With one exception they had been with the agency for a period of three or more years. It was felt that in addition to qualifications required of all homemakers in the agency those confronted with the difficult and complicated situations presented by project families needed to have a fairly high native intelligence not necessarily correlated with the amount of their formal education. They must, to an even greater degree than is called for in all homemakers, have the ability to behave in an accepting and nonjudgmental way, an intuitive understanding of human behavior, and some diagnostic ability. They must be outgoing and able to verbalize fairly freely. In addition to being able to accept the limitations of her own agency, the homemaker on a project of this type has to be able to work co-operatively with and be accepting of the limitations of the Bureau of Public Assistance. Since these cases are uniformly difficult, it was desirable that the homemaker have a fairly wide range of life experience herself and a real understanding of the significance of extremely severe economic and emotional deprivation and the limitations this places on the abilities of both mother and children to function well. In actual practice, the selection of homemakers was made on the basis of past performance in the agency, especially with complicated family situations, and on the homemaker supervisor's knowledge of their work and personality.

One of the significant facets of this project was the growth and development of the homemakers. Originally it had been anticipated that the possible impact of the problem situations encountered might necessitate alternating the more simple type of cases usually carried by this agency with project cases. As it turned out, the en-

thusiasm of the homemakers grew as they developed an increasing understanding—especially of the emotional factors underlying the neglect they encountered—and as they were able to see the many tangible improvements that took place during their duty on a case.

Placed in homes to act as teachers to the mothers, they found conditions that they had never before encountered, and a degree of maternal rejection in some of the cases that could not fail to shock these warm, giving women. The economic problems posed by the ANC budget was the least of their concerns—they were well versed in the art of doing a lot with limited funds and well grounded in nutrition and the physical needs of children.

As had been anticipated, it was found that supervision and education of the homemakers would have to be intensive and continuous. This was accomplished by means of staff meetings and personal conferences with the homemaker supervisor and the ANC worker. Conferences were begun before the actual initiation of the project work, when participation in the project was offered each homemaker and some of the situations she might encounter were discussed.

Staff meetings were held weekly. Of the four meetings held each month, one was a joint staff meeting including the ANC Neglect Unit workers and their supervisor, and another involved participation of the psychiatric consultant, provided for this project by the California State Department of Mental Hygiene. The remaining two meetings were attended only by the homemakers and their supervisor. The purposes of these staff meetings was support and education, the support aspect being essential because of the emotional impact of this type of case on the homemaker. Interpretation of the causes of observed behavior was extremely important, especially with regard to the homemaker's need to understand and therefore accept the reasons for the maternal rejection encountered so frequently. Support was also provided during the course of these meetings by the homemaker's presentation and discussion of her cases and participation of the other homemakers in the discussion. The presence of the consulting psychiatrist was invaluable not only for his suggestions and evaluation of techniques utilized by the homemakers, but also because of his interpretation to them of the background and causative factors of the behavior encountered.

SERVICES OFFERED

On her initial contact with the family (homemakers were usually introduced by the caseworker), the homemaker did little more than become acquainted with the mother and perhaps meet some of the children. The average period of time spent in the home on the first day was from one to two hours. In the first (random) group of cases there was always some resistance on the part of the mother to the homemaker. This resistance was usually implied and indicated in disguised ways, with the mother verbally expressing delight at the homemaker's coming to help her.

In all cases the following general conditions were found: The children were dirty and unkempt and homemakers had the impression that their hair had not been washed or combed for weeks. Many of these children had been sent home from school by the school nurse because they were too dirty to stay. Dirty clothes were scattered throughout the house—in two cases a whole room was given over to dirty laundry. There was garbage and filth all over the house and the care of food was so poor as to constitute a real health hazard. Budgeting was always a problem, with the family running out of money long before the monthly check was due. In some cases there was neither gas nor electricity turned on. School attendance was sporadic or nonexistent in all but two cases, and complaints from school authorities, neighbors, and sometimes relatives ranged from accusa-

tions of neglect to reports about the children foraging in the neighborhood garbage cans for food. Of course each family also had its own special problems in addition to these.

One of the first services the homemaker always gave was to do some of the housework, especially the laundry, for the simple reason that none of the family members had anything clean to wear. Soon after her advent the homemaker was able to engage the mother in working along with her, and through this method techniques of housecleaning, food preparation, child care, and personal hygiene were taught. Through these means the homemaker related herself to the mother, completed some of the preliminary work that absolutely had to be done, and demonstrated what a clean house and clean children looked like.

Direct services also included child care in order to free the mother for tasks that necessitated her absence from the home, such as househunting, clinic attendance, or enrolling a child in school. Isolated as these families were found to be—even in the midst of a highly populated neighborhood—they had not found it possible, or had not had enough motivation, to find such child care for themselves.

Another activity universally engaged in by the homemakers was to beautify the house once a certain amount of cleanliness and order had been achieved. By the time this process was begun there was enough relationship between the homemaker and the mother to engage the latter's interest sufficiently for active co-operation in these efforts. This included hanging curtains, painting furniture and walls, and obtaining some type of floor covering and bedding. At this point the homemaker could introduce the mother to new sources of inexpensive household supplies in the community. Most of them did not, for instance, know what could be obtained in "thrift shops" and, prior to the advent of the homemaker, had felt that everything had to be purchased new and on credit.

Here the basic home management knowledge of the homemaker was brought into play and the mother taught not only about local sources of supply, but also how to do such elementary tasks as hanging curtains, ironing, and mending. Woven into all this and ever present were the homemaker's services to the children in the family—first in the way of direct physical care (to which, incidentally, the children responded with delight). In some cases the homemaker had to introduce the concept that eating was a social and family activity and should have a special place in the home, such as a table with chairs around it. In several families there was no such thing as "meals." The children fended for themselves, with the younger ones often going unfed. Dishes and silverware also had to be introduced in some cases.

Other services to clients included an introduction to community resources for recreation and cultural purposes—community centers, churches, and the like. Often there was some direct interpretation by the homemaker to relatives, and an effort made to re-enlist the interest of these relatives in the family—in two cases with notable success.

FAMILY CHARACTERISTICS

Families in the project have been receiving assistance in this county continuously from four to twenty years. The average time on assistance is just under nine years, but this tells only a small part of the story, since at this time many of the families have numerous small children and the outlook for independence in the near future is dim. A striking fact is that the cases almost always began with the application of a young unmarried girl (age range at time of application from 16 to 20 years) either pregnant or with one baby. This, of course, would have been the ideal time for active rehabilitation of the mother. The problem becomes much more difficult with each ensuing year and child.

Although each family had its unique features and problems, in the words of one homemaker, "Two things you find in all cases—dirty laundry and depression." Loneliness of the mother was another characteristic. One said that when she first came to Los Angeles she felt that no one would ever talk to her again. When mothers were asked on follow-up visits by the homemaker supervisor how the homemaker had been most helpful, it was her friendship, conversation, and company that were mentioned—not the work she did. "By being here," said one mother. Other answers given were: "She was my first friend." "She was the first person who showed me respect." "She listened to me." "She made me feel like a real human being for the first time." The woman who felt that no one would ever talk to her again said that when she awakened in the morning and looked forward to a day with only the children for company she felt so discouraged that she just went back to sleep again. In this case none of the children—five of them school age—attended school, partly because no one got them ready or sent them off in the morning. After the assignment of the homemaker, who came daily for half a day, she would look forward to the coming day, and she eventually became "self-starting" in the morning.

The multiplicity of children was also common. One of these families had only two children, but the others had five or more, the total for the twelve families being sixty-seven. Efforts have been made in various communities to bring a knowledge of contraception to ANC mothers. The availability of such information, however, cannot alone solve the problem of illegitimacy. There are too many and too complex reasons behind the birth of these children. Expert birth control information is readily available in Los Angeles, but is rarely used by the type of mother found in this kind of a case load. Many of the encounters that result in pregnancy are unplanned and are but one result of the bitter loneliness of the mother. One of the mothers, for example, who has had a child a year for the last six years, is fearful of the prospect of all of them reaching school age. She is afraid that she will "die of lonesomeness." Another has illegitimate children to punish her own extremely religious and moral—but severely rejecting—mother. Each time she becomes pregnant she fantasies that her mother will have to take the new baby and "bring it up." At the age of 25 she is now in her eighth pregnancy—the possibilities are rather frightening. Her children range in age from 1 to 9, and it is the 9-year-old boy who assumes the entire responsibility for child care in the family.

In all but three of the cases in this group (in which there are fathers or stepfathers present) the liaisons made by the mothers that resulted in their pregnancies were fleeting, apparently with no thought of a permanent relationship, and were with men who were unreliable and exploitive—the majority of them had been in more or less serious trouble with the law on numerous occasions. This pattern reflects in part the disparaging self-image these mothers have.

In some cases the caseworker was able to revise his estimate of a family situation after the homemaker had been in the home for a while. This was especially true in one case, in which the homemaker had been assigned with the purpose of teaching the grandmother in the family because the mother was considered too retarded to function. After being in the home a while, the homemaker found that, while certainly retarded, the mother was also very much afraid of her mother-in-law, who with her son (the husband) seemed to be terrorizing the family. With casework help and the adroit encouragement of the homemaker, this mother was found to be able to function to a much greater extent than had been thought possible. In another case, in which there was also a father (stepfather to some of the children) present, the homemaker was requested because it was felt that the extreme disorganization in this

family might break up the (common-law) marriage. The father, while himself quite immature in many respects, was the stronger parent and was employed (ANC supplementing for the stepchildren), but was threatening to leave because of the dirt and neglect of the children.

An interesting observation was that the mothers made of their relationship with the homemakers what they needed. In many cases what they needed was a mother themselves and this was how they viewed the homemaker, without regard either to her age or race. This is a situation similar to the use made of relationship in therapy. The cases that follow illustrate typical family situations and the homemaker's function.

MORALLY SUPPORTIVE ROLE OF HOMEMAKER

The K family consists of a 26-year-old mother and her six illegitimate children, the oldest of whom is 6. The family first came to the attention of the Bureau of Public Assistance in April 1956 when Miss K, then 19 and pregnant with her first child, applied for assistance. The family was referred to the Neglect Unit in December 1960, but the case record shows neglect long before this. At one time the worker described one of the babies as being so poorly cared for that it hardly resembled a human being. Miss K was highly defensive about her standards of care and seemed unable to improve, although repeatedly adjured to do so by a succession of workers. One child was severely handicapped with cerebral palsy but Miss K had never kept clinic appointments made for him. She herself had a speech defect and severe hearing loss. In appearance she looked like a frightened and defensive teen-ager.

When the homemaker arrived she was met with Miss K's statement that she did not need anyone to tell her how to take care of her children. The homemaker said of course not, but that with so many young children she could surely use a bit of help with the housework. Within a few days Miss K was able to feel that she could trust the homemaker with her children.

The family occupied a tiny, filthy, and inappropriate apartment with no safe play space for the children. Miss K left the house as soon as the homemaker arrived each day and went househunting, until she found an attractive and larger apartment in a quiet, pleasant neighborhood, one that had a large screened-in porch that provided an ideal play area for the children. As soon as the family moved to their new home Miss K resumed weekly clinic attendance for the cerebral palsied child, and no appointment was ever broken.

In her new home she and the homemaker worked together to improve the appearance of the house. It was discovered that she had remarkable energy. She was able to install a pulley clothesline by herself, and the lines were filled early every morning with newly washed clothes. With the helpful suggestions of the homemaker the apartment soon took on an appearance that was comfortable and attractive by anyone's standards.

It was also discovered that Miss K had a talent for sewing, and she made clothing for her children. The homemaker supervisor felt that this talent could well be made the basis for vocational rehabilitation and, in spite of the large number of young children and the severely handicapped child, efforts should be made fairly soon in this direction.

Supportive casework will be needed for quite a while if the long-term plan of rehabilitation is to be successful, but there is a good possibility that this family can become at least partially self-supporting. This should lead to a different feeling about herself on the part of the mother, and might prevent the advent of more illegitimate children.

It is interesting that in this case the role of the homemaker was primarily one of moral support for a long time prior to the case's termination. Once given a good

start, the mother was able to continue on her own impetus remarkably well. The last follow-up visit was made six months after termination of homemaker service, and it was found that the house was still clean and attractive, clinic appointments were kept regularly for the cerebral palsied child, and the two school-age children attended school regularly. At the present time Miss K is not pregnant, even though her youngest baby is now over a year old.

HOMEMAKER AS MOTHER SUBSTITUTE

The L family consists of a mother and six illegitimate children, most, if not all, by different fathers. Miss L has been receiving assistance continuously since 1943. She herself had been reared in numerous foster homes and was often separated from her own siblings. At the time of the initiation of service she was completely cut off from her numerous relatives living in the area, because of their disapproval of her. An attractive woman, she considered herself ugly—a reflection of her low self-esteem. The children were exceptionally attractive but extremely unkempt, and one little girl who was approaching kindergarten age was so extremely shy that she was unable to speak in the presence of anyone outside the family.

This client made of the homemaker a substitute for the mother she never had (in actual fact the homemaker was younger than the client), and wanted very much to please her. She soon took over most of the actual work of running the household, learned much about cooking, and showed great ingenuity in purchasing and mending secondhand clothing for her children. When the house had been cleaned and decorated, she was emboldened to invite several of her relatives to a birthday party for the 5-year-old, using this means to renew her relationship with them.

Several follow-up visits have been made to this home, and six months after the termination of homemaker service Miss L was still maintaining the improved appearance of the house, her children were attending school regularly, and she herself seemed like a different person, efficient and proud of her family. The social worker believes Miss L will probably soon want to seek part-time employment.

Although this case has been discussed here only briefly, Miss L's background includes a great many complex problems that had an effect on her relationship with her own children. This summary is designed only to give some indication of the movement made by the family during the short time it was included in the project.

CONCLUSIONS

Homemakers were assigned to twelve families, all of whom had been receiving assistance for many years and none of whom had shown any response to efforts on the part of social workers to improve their standards of household management or child care. In addition each family had its own special problems.

All the families showed movement in most problem areas, and gains made during the time the homemaker was assigned are holding remarkably well. Much has been learned about which families are likely to benefit most from the assignment of a homemaker. A surprise to everyone involved in the project has been the amount of improvement made in a relatively short period of time in situations so long standing and in which the mother herself was so severely deprived during her own childhood that it would seem only intensive, long-term therapy could reorient her.

Indications are that the progress made was not so much on the basis of the home-maker's skill and proficiency in homemaking and child care as because of her intuitive ability—strengthened and directed by frequent and careful supervision and professional support—to give the mothers in these families the kind of acceptance, respect, and understanding that in many cases they had not encountered before. The significant result was a real strengthening of the mother or, in some cases, a strengthening of the older children to a point at which there was a realignment of relationships within the family. Of course, the hoped-for result is that the young children in the family will now receive the kind of support their own mothers lacked, and perhaps themselves grow up to become independently functioning members of the community. An indication of this possibility is that in eight of the families in which school attendance was sporadic or nonexistent it has been reinstituted and, at the time of the latest follow-up visits, maintained.

Introducing a professionally supervised homemaker to multiproblem families seems to be one way to start them in the direction of rehabilitation, and suggests that there may be many other possible ways of attacking this difficult problem. The importance of instituting active rehabilitation of the young applicant for assistance as soon as possible after intake also seems inescapable. New ways of instituting change leading to the strengthening of individuals caught up in the kinds of situations in which the families in this study are involved must be found. Otherwise the burgeoning load of dependency, which conceivably could result from the sixty-seven children involved in this study alone, could be staggering.

Parents Anonymous: A Treatment Method For Child Abuse

SALLY HOLMES

In recent years self-help groups have been organized to deal with almost every conceivable problem. Parents Anonymous (PA) was founded in Redondo Beach, California, in 1969 to combat the problem of child abuse. A state organization was formed in Detroit, Michigan, in 1972. National PA sends literature for distribution in the community, as well as for use by members. It also provides some leadership. But, as this article shows, the experience of Michigan has been unique to the state in many ways.

PA of Michigan sets up groups in which helping professionals and abusive families cooperate. It is different from the usual group model in that members undergo treatment in chapters defined as groups, consisting of two to ten parents, led by a parent "chairperson" but therapeutically directed by a professional "sponsor." Two major elements of therapy groups are the members and the leader. In most therapy groups the professional thinks in terms of "my" group and assumes responsibility for leadership. In some self-help groups, there is no professional, and members choose their leader from among the group's membership. PA, however, not only chooses the chairperson from its membership, but also recognizes the importance of the professional sponsor's role. In Michigan, community agencies that offer family, mental health, and protective services usually provide sponsors.

Unlike many self-help groups, PA provides no rigid structure of rules to follow, such as the 12 steps in Alcoholics Anonymous or the guidelines for dieting in Weight Watchers. Rather, it depends on the interrelation-

Sally Holmes, MSW, is Senior Caseworker, Family Services of Detroit and Wayne County, Detroit, Michigan. She is a sponsor of a Parents Anonymous group and serves as chairperson for the State Board of Directors for Parents Anonymous of Michigan.

ships among the professional sponsor, chairperson, and members to create the program most beneficial for each member in the group. The national and state organizations are structured mainly to facilitate the development of groups and to publicize their availability to people who need them.

ROLES

PA requires a parent-as-leader group model in which the group is seen as a primary support system for its members. Sponsors need a sound knowledge of small-group dynamics and an ability to form warm, accepting relationships with group members, especially with the chairperson, who is a parent. The role of the sponsor is to support the chairperson. The sponsor is the professional resource for the group and must constantly meet the challenge of knowing when to offer clarification, interpretation, or didactic information to the group and when to remain silent and let the group members make discoveries for themselves.

The sponsor also is able to observe the group process in relation to the growth of each member. Thus he or she can use interventions to help the chairperson set limits, when necessary, and to facilitate the group process, individual growth, and learning. The chairperson may often need help in clarifying issues and sorting out feelings. The sponsor must learn to offer this help so that it complements the chairperson's leadership.

The chairperson assumes leadership of the group, keeps track of the members' progress and setbacks, and recognizes the occurrence of members' behavioral danger signals during the week, between weekly meetings. Making crisis telephone calls is an important part of PA. Members call each other when they feel they may abuse their children; the chairperson often receives the majority of these calls and is responsible for calling each member at least once a week.

The role of group members includes a combination of teaching and learning. Members are expected to become actively involved with each other, to use other members in the process of learning about themselves, and to understand and discuss their feelings openly. To do this, they must learn to trust each other, to increase their tolerance for closeness, and to accept themselves and each other as valuable and important. Group members learn that this involves acceptance of negative, as well as positive, feelings. They learn the dangers of putting people on pedestals, as well as the disastrous effects of trying to disown anger, fear, hate, and love.

A basic explanation of why members have an abuse problem before they join PA is that they have been unable to develop an adequate support system for themselves within their own families and communities. PA members accept the responsibility to provide this support for each other. As in any close interpersonal relationship, feelings of jealousy, rivalry, hurt, and anger become mixed with those of warmth and caring. Although new members may be welcomed as new friends, behavioral patterns may be reactivated in the same way as they appeared in childhood, such as the sibling rivalry the following example shows:

> Sarah had been in the group for only three weeks. She called two of the members separately to tell them that the sponsor did not like her and had said something to make her feel rejected. Sarah was helped to understand that just as she had always played her two sisters against her mother and ended up being rejected, she was reenacting this pattern in the group.

As patterns of problem behavior appear in the group, members learn to recognize them and to feel their impact on the group. More positive ways of relating are learned and practiced in the group; the members gradually learn to use these new behaviors in their families and other relationships.

The telephone is a life preserver for PA members. Making phone calls also enables the chairperson and old members to reach out to new members.

Reprinted from SOCIAL WORK, 23 (May 1978), pp. 245–247.

Often many calls, offering support and reassurance, are necessary to encourage frightened parents to attend their first meeting. At the first meeting, new members are given the telephone numbers of all the other group members, including the sponsor. Members are expected to call at least one other group member at some time during the week, especially if they feel abusive toward their child. Appropriate use of the telephone is a skill reviewed repeatedly in group meetings.

"Reach for the phone instead of the child" is the directive emphasized with new members. But for the new members especially, following this directive is not easy. "I was too depressed to call anyone," a member may say. Or "I didn't know I was that angry." Or "I knew I should call, but I just couldn't pick up the phone."

SETTING GOALS

The first goal in every PA group is to stop abusive behavior, and this goal is carefully emphasized with each new member. The member is assured of the group's support. The chairperson explains that because the new member is one of the group, old members care about him or her. Members' telephone numbers are available night or day. When abuse occurs, this damages the parent as well as the child, and the group members will try in every way possible to prevent this from happening. Because all group members have gone through what the new member is experiencing, the new member is no longer alone with the problem. Emphasis is given to the courage required to come to the group and the strength needed to recognize such a painful problem. The new member is given the responsibility to call another member instead of abusing the child, but is also reminded that it is unrealistic to expect this to work for everyone from the beginning. The group offers reassurance that failure does not mean rejection. Even in the first meeting, the new member hears other members' stories of failure and watches the support system at work as the members struggle for understanding and self-control. An example follows:

Pat had broken the arm of her 4-year-old daughter. After dealing with their shock, anger, fear, and horror, group members were able to recognize the importance of supporting Pat through her ordeal and to explore carefully with her the causes of the abusive situation. The child was placed in temporary foster care while Pat was helped to deal with her rage and fear toward her father, which had been reactivated by the helplessness she had seen in her child.

Learning to handle and express feelings is another goal members set for themselves. Through the group, members learn they have a right to their feelings, can express them openly, and can establish clear communication patterns with each other. When members learn that all feelings are acceptable if expressed in constructive ways, they are better able to deal with their children's feelings, to conceptualize discipline as a learning experience rather than as punishment, and to recognize age-appropriate behavior in their children.

Self-hatred seems to be a common problem to all newcomers to the group. A major goal is to change this self-image. Group members learn to see themselves as valuable and worthwhile individuals and to accept this new image of themselves. They must overcome a fear of success as well as of failure. Individual strengths are recognized and reinforced. Members learn that they do not have to be perfect, that mistakes are allowed. As this idea becomes acceptable, they learn to accept their children's imperfections.

Creating a comfortable relationship between the parent and child within which both can thrive and grow is another important goal. Members learn to deal with their children in positive ways. Because many group members were not allowed to play as children, they must learn to play with their children. They must be taught to appreciate the value of play.

In the initial phase, a new member must find his or her position in the group and get to know other members who are already good friends. The new member must learn what the group

expects of its members and what can be expected of the group. Anxiety is high, not only because of the new situation, but also because the new member has probably only recently faced the abuse problem. A recent injury to a child may have made the parent focus on the problem, or a parent may have become terrified when realizing how close he or she had come to losing self-control. Sometimes members express the anxiety by demanding magic cures, as this example shows:

Nancy came to her first group meeting in such a state of anxiety she could hardly stay in her seat. "I don't know what to do," she wailed. "Just tell me what to do."

The chairperson tried to reassure her, but Nancy could not hear her. She talked nonstop, as though a floodgate had opened and could not be controlled. Nancy remained with the group, even when members confronted her forcefully about her lack of control. Gradually, she learned to accept group control, to talk about her feelings, and to put controls on herself. By the end of four months, she was successful in establishing some self-control in dealing with her daughter.

Nancy handled her anxiety through loss of control. She could not stop talking, she could not sit still, and she often got drunk. Anxiety, however, may be handled through overcontrol. A new member may sit still and remain quiet throughout an entire meeting, able to stammer only a few words when directly questioned. Such behavior is shown here:

Shirley was late for her first group meeting and slipped in so quietly she was hardly noticed. When she was introduced, she almost whispered her response, twisting her hand nervously in her lap.

Shirley did not easily learn to express her feelings in the group. She remained fearful. Group members discovered that she was helpful to them, an excellent listener with good insight into their problems. They began to call and tell her how much they appreciated her ability to listen to them and to understand how they felt. She began to feel valued for the first time in her life and was able to stop abusing her child. Gradually, she began to share the immense burden of guilt and rage that she had carried. She began to relax, to feel less fearful of the rage inside.

SUMMARY

Parents Anonymous is a treatment method uniquely suited to solving the problem of child abuse. People with this problem are typically isolated, dependent individuals who for some reason have been unable to develop relationships that will offer the love and nurture everyone requires. By banding together, members learn to give and receive this nurturing within the group. A single worker cannot be available all the time. It takes a group to provide the support system required.

The anonymous aspect of PA is important to the process of building a trusting relationship within the group. However, it limits the use of the method to those who can recognize their problem and are strong enough to seek help. Courts and protective services workers are encouraged and often do make strong pleas to their clients to use the service offered by PA. Many clients do follow through, but for many others the rebellion against authority is stronger than is the need for service, and they refuse to come. Because attendance is anonymous, of course, it cannot be forced on anyone.

Some people cannot be helped through PA. People who are unable to respond to others within a group will sometimes attend a PA meeting and may be destructive to the group. Such individuals may leave the group voluntarily, or sponsors may need to intervene to "counsel out" the individuals to another form of treatment, if possible, to protect the group.

Although PA cannot help everyone, it is extremely valuable to those able to involve themselves. Through the group, members learn to understand the abused, terrified child within each of them, to understand and control their anger, to express it in more positive ways, and to build a healthy, comfortable relationship with their children. For them, at least the cycle of abuse can be broken successfully. ◀

94

Volunteers as Mentors
for Abusing Parents:
A Natural Helping Relationship

VIRGINIA WITHEY
ROSALIE ANDERSON
MICHAEL LAUDERDALE

The mentoring relationship established by the use of volunteers in programs to help abusive parents is one that can meet the developmental needs of the volunteers as well as promote change in the parents.

Child abuse programs throughout the country are successfully using volunteers in one-to-one relationships with clients to improve parental functioning and to prevent the removal of children from their own homes. Most of these programs appear to be making use of a natural helping relationship only recently receiving overt attention in professional literature. We believe that this resurgence of attention has

Virginia Withey, B.S., M.A., M.S.W., is Training Specialist III, Resource Centers on Child Abuse and Neglect and Adoption, University of Texas at Austin. Rosalie Anderson, M.Ed., is Project Director and Michael Lauderdale, Ph.D., is Associate Professor of Social Work. This paper was made possible by Grant 90-C-1591 from the National Center on Child Abuse and Neglect, Children's Bureau, Administration for Children, Youth and Families, Office of Human Development Services, U.S. Department of Health, Education, and Welfare. Its contents should not be construed as official policy of the National Center of Child Abuse and Neglect or any federal agency.

important psychological dimensions [1]. This "natural" relationship is that of a mentor to an "apprentice." A better understanding of the nature of this relationship, how it evolves, and why it works is needed, especially by the many agencies that are rapidly moving toward the use of volunteers as treatment providers for abusive parents.

There is a great deal of diversity in how child abuse programs describe their use of volunteers with abusive parents. Though most, in fact, use a mentoring model for developing helping relationships, these programs use other descriptive phrases that have resulted in some confusion of the volunteer's role. This confusion has added to the predictable resistance to the use of volunteers in human services programs that use primarily professional staff to deliver services.

Some of the largest child abuse volunteer programs insist that the goal of volunteer activity is to "reparent the parent" [3]. Perhaps the largest and most successful of these programs is the Suspected Child Abuse and Neglect Program (SCAN) in Arkansas. A SCAN publication states:

> What happens between two people when a SCAN lay therapist works with an abusive parent? A therapeutic relationship grows...one which resembles the nurturant parent-child relationship. It is the creation, perhaps for the first time in the life of an abusive parent, of an atmosphere of trust, unconditional acceptance of the person, and security. It is stimulation, having fun together, doing things, learning to solve problems, learning how to play and laugh. It is learning that it's all right to make mistakes, that the world doesn't fall apart, and that it's possible to pick yourself up and start over or do something different. It is all the things that didn't get done the first time around, when the parent was a child. [10]

Parenting Model

The concept of reparenting as the thrust for the volunteer's interventions puts heavy emphasis on the dependency needs of abusive parents. Interventions are made at a basic parent-child level and are designed to supplement the client's parenting experience and to provide the kind of "good" parenting model the client missed during childhood. Other programs, with similar satisfactory records of helping to change abusive behavior, insist with equal conviction that a reparenting concept is not the most appropriate one for work with abusive parents. In the first place, they contend it is an illusion that adults can, in fact, reparent adults. Although abusive parents may be immature in some ways, they are nevertheless adults who must learn to accept responsibility as adults. Secondly, critics of the reparenting model insist that the concept of reparenting is belittling and demeaning to the parents, already likely to have poor self-concepts.

These other programs use terms such as "befriending the parent" or "supporting the parent" as their intervention thrust. In an unpublished description of the work of the Parents Assistance Center in Oklahoma City, the following paragraph partly describes the relationship that program seeks to establish between volunteers and clients:

> The relationship can develop so they can go out for lunch, coffee, visit with each other, etc. The trust the parent finds in this relationship can be transferred to other people. Our parents may never have had a relationship with a friend in which they have felt special and that somebody really cared for them [8].

One goal of the Marin County, CA, Parent Aide Program is "to be supportive to parents in the Child Protective Services program." A volunteer "functions as a mature, reliable friend" in providing that support [7].

There are other noticeable differences in what appear to be equally successful child abuse programs using volunteers. Some have stringent screening systems for volunteers and enroll only those candidates who have professional qualifications. Other programs use extremely informal screening procedures and assign clients to almost all who volunteer. In some programs, many hours of training are required before a volunteer sees a client; in others, clients are assigned after only an initial training session. The quantity and quality of supervision also vary greatly among programs, some using a close, traditional one-to-one style, complete with narrative recording, others using mostly informal peer supervision.

Behavioral Changes

Despite these fundamental program differences, clients in the different programs are being helped to change their abusive behavior. The behavior changes are facilitated by a relationship of mentoring that the various programs have perhaps fostered without awareness. Mentoring relationships are created out of the developmental needs of both the mentor and the client. If human life can be conceptualized as a process of continual growth, with predictable stages or life phases, it is consistent to assume that in human society various growth phases can be and are complementary to other phases. Mentoring relationships are natural complementary growth phases or natural helping relationships that form because of needs that must be satisfied for growth to continue. Child abuse programs have provided a means whereby this well known, but scantily written about relationship of mentoring can be fostered and encouraged.

Needs of the Volunteer

Many volunteer programs in the last few years have moved to a consideration of the self-actualizing needs of the volunteers, using Maslow's hierarchy of needs as a model for volunteer participation [6]. In a 1972 journal article, Knowles noted that if volunteerism were structured around a self-actualizing model, agencies would allow both the volunteers and clients to become enlisted in mutual self-development, and the agency's efforts could appropriately move toward being a part of the continuing education movement rather than the traditional welfare system [4]. We suggest that the concept of mentoring is a refinement of this self-actualization process.

Levinson et al. offer the fullest available written description of the mentoring relationship [5]. The mentor is usually a person 8 to 15 years older than the client. No one word conveys the full nature of the relationship, although "counselor," "guru," "teacher," "adviser" and "sponsor" have been used. The mentor is usually of the same sex as the younger person, and may act as a teacher to guide or enhance the younger person's skills. As a sponsor, he or she may use influence to facilitate the younger person's entry into an adult or a professional role and advancement in that role. As a guide, the mentor introduces the younger person into an occupational and social world and acquaints him or her with its values, customs, resources, and cast of characters. "Through his own virtues, achievements, and way of living, the mentor may be an example that the protege can admire and seek to emulate. He may provide counsel and give moral support in time of stress" [5].

The mentoring relationship is one type of love relationship. But describing any love relationship is difficult, partly because in any relationship between lovers, or parents and their children, or friends or relatives, there is a complicated mixture of needs, affection, attraction and mutual involvement that is brought to the relationship by each person. Perhaps the old adage describing love as "a matter of need and proximity" is as applicable to mentoring relationships as it is to the young lovers with which it was first concerned.

The mentor is not a parent, though he or she may at times symbolize one, nor strictly a peer, though the relationship's goal is toward establishing peers.

The Age Factor

A prime developmental task of a young adult is to incorporate significant older persons into a sense of self. The mentor is one of those persons. The mentor's primary function is to be a transitional figure. Most mentoring relationships last from 6 months to 3 or 4 years, and can be of varying intensities, depending on the needs of both parties in the relationship. Mentors are rarely younger than 30, while apprentices, according to Levinson, are nonexistent after age 40. The relationship evolves out of maturational needs: the passage of the younger person into full adulthood and the passage of the older one into old age.

Though many persons do not use the term "mentor" or "mentoring," the relationship itself is well known and commonly experienced. When the extended family was more common and viable than it is now, aunts and uncles or older cousins frequently served in mentor roles to older adolescents or young adults. In academia, professors are mentors to young graduate students, while in social work, the supervisor or an older caseworker plays the mentor role to young workers. In theological circles, the St. Paul/Titus model for ministry has frequently been used and is enjoying a popular revival in many charismatic groups. In this model, a young adult is paired with an older, more experienced minister in order that the youngster can learn and the older can have the benefit of the assistance and vigor of the younger person.

The child abuse programs using volunteers have developed out of two sets of recognized needs. The first includes the needs of the abusive parents, who are usually isolated, immature, unskilled in parenting, and without internal or external controls to prevent them from venting their rage on their children. The second group of needs are those of the agencies that have difficulty designing treatment programs for abusive parents because of staff limitations and burgeoning caseloads resulting from increased reporting. Staff limitations include not only insufficient workers and lack of time to spend with clients, but the fact that many agency staff persons are not old enough to have reached a stage of growth when mentoring is natural.

To meet these two sets of needs, volunteers have been enlisted in programs. Levinson's description of mentoring fits exactly with what volunteers in successful programs do in relationships with abusive parents. They *teach* child rearing, household management, how to have access to resources, and what it means to a responsible adult. They *sponsor* their clients by helping to obtain food stamps or medical care. They *guide* and *counsel,* give moral support in times of stress, and constantly *model* how to solve problems and how to enhance the quality of life for themselves and their families.

A director of a volunteer program states that her agency exists both for the volunteers and the clients. Many volunteer programs, however, have not considered the volunteer in such a focal position. Few programs give sufficient attention to the basic reasons why volunteers do what they do, how their needs can be met, and how their experiences can be enhanced through their participation. Crucial to program planners designing volunteer programs is an understanding of the importance of satisfying the growth needs of the volunteer.

Developmental Tasks

Becoming a mentor is one method that middle-aged adults use to complete their developmental tasks. When Erikson published *Childhood and Society* in 1950, he laid the groundwork for the growing attention being directed to adult developmental processes [2]. He listed eight major developmental phases in an individual's life span. Erikson titles the phases according to the major conflicts that must be resolved to at least some degree during each phase. The first five phases pertain to childhood and adolescent growth: 1) acquiring a sense of basic trust while overcoming a sense of basic mistrust; 2) acquiring a sense of autonomy while combating a sense of doubt and shame; 3) acquiring a sense of initiative and overcoming a sense of guilt; 4) acquiring a sense of industry and fending off a sense of inferiority; and 5) acquiring a sense of identity while overcoming a sense of identity diffusion. The last three phases pertain to adulthood: 6) acquiring a sense of intimacy and solidarity and avoiding a sense of isolation; 7) acquiring a sense of generativity and avoiding a sense of self-absorption; and 8) acquiring a sense of integrity and avoiding a sense of despair.

Of particular concern to the authors is phase 7, a phase usually reached between ages 30 and 45. Erikson said that unless a sense of generativity is established during these years, the individual will become self-absorbed and will experience a kind of personal stagnation that will prevent him or her from becoming a fully integrated person. Generativity is the developmental stage in which the key quality is the person's need to be needed and the need to care. Growing individuals need to experience a continuity in their lives by investing energy and ideas into something new, both in their children and in their communities. "Generativity is the natural developmental stage which serves to guard and guide the next generation [10]." Without a sense of generativity, individuals are unable to experience competency in using that which they have so far learned.

Some of one's need to care for and guide the next generation is worked out within the nuclear family, but because of the complexity of needs represented in the family and the emotion-laden nature of those relationships, the sense of competency so needed by the growing adult is often undermined. Then, too, at the very time when many parents have a need to reach out, protect and guide the next generation, their own children are teen-agers, and have an even stronger need to "move out" of their family of origin, perhaps physically, but always emotionally. The parents' needs, in conflict with the needs of their offspring, often create a sense of failure in the parents and feelings of incompetence and ineffectiveness. Thus, a mentoring relationship outside the nuclear family is often more satisfying for one in the generative phase than such relationships within the family.

Mentoring relationships that are formed, for instance, in the business and academic worlds usually occur spontaneously out of a natural attraction between two persons. However, deliberate or designed mentoring relationships can be formed that have the same qualities and mutual benefits as those occurring spontaneously. Once the relationship is formed, no matter how it happens, the processes and benefits are identical.

Basic Factors

Program planners should be aware that for a mentoring relationship to evolve, the following factors are basic.

1) Mentors must have reached the generativity stage of adult development.

2) Mentors should be at least several years older than their clients and should have successfully mastered earlier developmental tasks.

3) Mentors should have the skills, or should be helped to develop the skills, to encourage their clients to like and trust them. Then, as the relationships develop, mentors will have maximum opportunities to receive satisfactory degrees of admiration and status, and a validation of their competency from the relationships.

Program managers using volunteers to work with abusive parents can maximize the potential help for clients, as well as the potential for the volunteers' satisfaction from their experiences with clients, by carefully matching volunteers and clients to allow for the development of this natural helping relationship. ♦

References

1. Collins, A.H., and Pancoast, D.L. Natural Helping Network. Washington, DC: National Association of Social Workers (undated).

2. Erikson, E. Childhood and Society. New York: W.W. Norton, 1950.

3. Kempe, H., and Helfer, R.E. Helping the Battered Child and His Family. Philadelphia: J.B. Lippincott, 1972.

4. Knowles, M.S. "Motivation in Volunteerism: Synopsis of a Theory," Journal of Voluntary Action Research I, 2 (1972).

5. Levinson, D.J. et al. The Seasons of a Man's Life. New York: Ballantine, 1978.

6. Maslow, A.H. Motivation and Personality. New York: Harper and Brothers, 1954.

7. Parent Aide Program of the Division of Public Social Services, Marin County. San Rafael, CA.

8. Parents Assistance Center, Program Design Brochure. Oklahoma City.

9. Simon, A.W. The New Years: A New Middle Age. New York: Knopf, 1968.

10. Tweraser, G., et al. "Every Parent's Birthright: Bonding as the Key to Effective Lay Therapy," unpublished, SCAN Services of Arkansas.

PART 4
Emerging Problems

Meeting the needs of mistreated youths

James Garbarino

The abuse of adolescents is a problem endemic to the institutional and cultural structure of American life and is not an ephemeral phenomenon. The author presents information and theories concerning such abuse as a basis for offering the best strategies to meet the needs of these youths.

James Garbarino, Ph.D., is Fellow at the Center for the Study of Youth Development, Boys Town, Nebraska.

THE CURRENT MEDICAL, psychological, and social welfare establishments have delineated the mistreatment of children and adolescents as a discrete social problem. As well-defined public issues, the abuse and neglect of children are young, dating from the early 1960s. Moreover, only since the 1970s have social service professionals and the public "discovered" the abuse and neglect of adolescents, although teenagers as well as children have always been subject to mistreatment by their parents, guardians, and custodians.[1] Because of the growing concern for mistreated adolescents, social service professionals now seek to broaden the definition of mistreatment. They have raised the following question: Under what circumstances and at what stage of the life cycle is one protected from mistreatment by law, custom, and practice?

This article attempts to bring together the factual information and theories concerning the mistreatment of adolescents as a basis for offering the best strategies to meet the needs of these youths, aged 12–18. Although this article is not a review of the literature on the mistreatment and neglect of children (under age 12), it refers to this literature as a basis for contrasting child abuse and neglect with the etiology and dynamics of adolescent abuse. It not only deals with the various patterns of behavior by adults that harm teenagers but also discusses the mistreated adolescent's need for social services. In this article the definition of mistreatment includes physical assault, coercive sexual relations, and rejection. Although the evidence on sexual abuse is full of contradictory and inconsistent messages, it is clear that when sex is coerced, it qualifies as abuse. Similarly, when emotional privation (rejection) is imposed, it has deleterious developmental consequences.[2] When sexual and emotional "misuse" do not fall into this definition of abuse, they are not discussed in this article.

Factual information about the mistreatment of youths is underdeveloped. Because of this, social service professionals tend to adopt their own hypotheses when responding to the increasing public pressure to do something for and about these teenagers and their families. The relatively new awareness of adolescent abuse affords these professionals the chance to avoid some of the false starts, blind alleys, and misconceived programs that have plagued efforts to understand and deal with child abuse and neglect.

PATTERNS OF ABUSE

The mistreatment of adolescents is a problem endemic to the institutional and cultural structure of American life, not an ephemeral phenomenon. Patterns of abuse can be divided into the following categories: [3]

■ Mistreatment that begins with the onset of puberty.

■ Mistreatment that represents a change in the quality or form of punishment (for example, from slapping to punching), a change in parental affect (from tolerance to rejection), or a change in sexual conduct (from normal kissing to genital fondling).

■ Mistreatment that is present only when the child is in the "terrible twos," and recurs when the youngster becomes an "ornery adolescent."

■ Mistreatment that merely continues a pattern of abuse begun in childhood.

Each pattern may represent special needs of clients and thus challenges to social service professionals. The first three imply the existence of a conflict between parent and adolescent over the youth's behavior. The fourth pattern seems to be a residual category that will gradually disappear now that early identification and treatment of child abusers are widespread, although this assumption may be unfounded because the rate of "cure" reported by those who use conventional and innovative treatment approaches ranges between 30 and 70 percent.[4] It appears that because many cases of child abuse are chronic, a pattern of abuse continues during the youngster's adolescence. Furthermore, as social service agencies improve their case-finding system for mistreated adolescents, it is likely that more youths will be placed in institu-

Reprinted from SOCIAL WORK, 25 (March 1980), pp. 122–126.

tional facilities in which they are at risk for further mistreatment. To prevent this risk, social service professionals must devise and implement ways to serve these youth without institutionalizing them.

According to Garbarino and his colleagues, the American Humane Association has reported that adolescents are the victims in approximately one-third of the abuse cases reported to state central registries.[5] Moreover, the data gathered by these researchers support the view held by others that the mistreatment of adolescents is not so strongly related to socioeconomic deprivation as is the mistreatment of children. This view suggests that the mistreatment of adolescents is about as prevalent in affluent areas as it is in impoverished areas. In the latter, infants and young children are more likely than are adolescents to be mistreated because of the frustration and family isolation related to social and economic stress. However, the abuse of adolescents, compared with child abuse, seems to be less a correlate of social class.

In another study, Lourie has found that 50 percent of the mistreated cases in an affluent county involve adolescents.[6] However, percentages reported for a more representative metropolitan midwestern county almost replicate the national data presented by the American Humane Association.[7] All such percentages are suspect, of course, because in the early stages of developing a case-finding system, it is easy to influence the number and pattern of reports by conducting specialized and intensive programs aimed at making professionals and the public aware of adolescent abuse, as has been the case in the area of sexual abuse.

Most epidemiological issues concerning the mistreatment of adolescents are moot. Finding answers will require the same investment in research that has been devoted to documenting incidence patterns for the mistreatment of children. All these issues must be addressed in the context of what is known about the epidemiology of domestic violence and the adequacy of health care. Straus has found that some 15 percent of families in a

nationally representative sample engage in some "serious violence" (punching, kicking, or assaulting with an object or a weapon).[8] In addition, lower socioeconomic groups have a substantially higher rate of domestic violence than do upper socioeconomic groups. In relation to the health care of adolescents, experts who convened at a recent conference drew parallel conclusions regarding such care:

a substantial proportion of teenagers need medical attention because of socially linked health problems such as venereal disease, and these problems are associated with social and economic impoverishment.[9]

CHILD AND ADOLESCENT ABUSE

American ambivalence about violence is well known. On the one hand, people respond negatively to "crime in the streets," which is usually front-page news when it involves violent assault. Yet films, magazines, television, and sports are saturated with violence. On the other hand, more than 90 percent of American families use physical force to punish children.[10] Yet Americans express outrage about child abuse. Furthermore, although most people abhor violence directed at innocent and helpless infants, many are willing to accept violence directed at wives by their husbands. Efforts to deal with the scientific, legal, and service issues surrounding the mistreatment of adolescents are often confounded by the fact that this form of domestic violence falls somewhere between child abuse and wife battering on the continuum of public and institutional acceptability.

Infants are viewed as innocent and defenseless, and teenagers as provocative and capable of taking care of themselves. Adolescents, like wives, sometimes engage in retaliatory assault. For example, one child protective services agency reports that some 20 percent of its cases involving adolescents are brought to its attention by an adolescent's assault on a parent.[11] Studies of adolescents who murder their parents often reveal a history of serious abuse in the youths' back-

ground.[12] Like abused wives, mistreated adolescents usually face a difficult time receiving justice in the courts and services if their cases reach law enforcement and judicial agencies. Their status as minors does not permit them to choose such options as running away to escape mistreatment. If they leave home, mistreated adolescents are likely to be labeled by those in the court system as "status offenders" or as delinquents. They are most likely to come to the public's attention because of their own antisocial behavior, for example, running away or truancy. In addition, because many social service professionals believe that the judicial system is partial to parents, they prefer to seek a "person-in-need-of-supervision" petition rather than a maltreatment petition.[13] The former petition seeks to "prosecute" the victim and in many jurisdictions leads to incarceration; the latter seeks to prosecute the perpetrator. Given the current state of services to youngsters in foster care and to status offenders receiving institutional care, neither form of care seems appealing as a developmentally enhancing experience. Mistreated youngsters need assistance if they are to overcome the effects of their experience. However, as "criminals" they are less likely to receive that assistance than they would as victims.

Another way in which the mistreatment of adolescents differs from child abuse and more closely resembles wife battering lies in the goals and dynamics of case management and treatment. In the overwhelming majority of child abuse cases, the overt treatment goal is to return the child to a healthy familial environment; in many cases involving adolescents, a more modest goal is to "stabilize" and "maintain" the teenager outside the home. Many social service professionals believe that mistreated adolescents may be better off in the short run, and even in the long run, if these youths have a safe and developmentally enhancing alternative to strife-torn homes. The author contends, however, that adolescent victims should be involved in case-management and placement decisions because they need to have a sense of control over their destiny and because they can actively resist decisions and placements that are imposed on them.

Why do so many cases involving mistreated adolescents reveal behavioral problems on the part of the youngster? By and large, youths in trouble are youths who have been hurt. At least three factors conspire to produce the relationship between mistreatment and problem behavior.

First, in abusive families there is a dearth of positive social interaction and a lack of relationships with others outside the home. Children in these families learn to be socially and interpersonally deficient through the experience of being mistreated. Moreover, some studies document the existence of a strong relationship between the mistreatment of children and delinquent behavior; for example, Alfaro has reported that nearly 70 percent of delinquents have a history of reported mistreatment.[14]

Second, child abuse often leads to institutional care, which in itself tends to cause problem behavior. Although there are many capable and dedicated foster parents, the foster care system is a major social problem in its own right. With the number of foster placements experienced by children in care averaging about five and the number of years in care averaging about seven, it is little wonder that many children fed into the system emerge from it as psychosocially impoverished teenagers. Moreover, because of the lack of interest among foster parents in dealing with adolescents, teenagers are more likely than are young children to be placed in institutions.

Third, many adolescents who run away to escape mistreatment in the home engage in prostitution, use illicit drugs, and become vagrants. As a result of such illegal acts, they tend to come into contact with law enforcement authorities. A recent study conducted in Arizona has compared the "crimes" committed by adolescents with a known history of mistreatment with crimes committed by those without such a history.[15] "Escape" offenses (running away, truancy, and the like) accounted for 35 percent of the crimes by youngsters coming from homes in which abuse was present, "aggression" (assault) for 5 percent, and offenses such as theft for 60 percent. For the comparison group, escape offenses accounted for only 18 percent of the offenses, aggression for 5 percent, and other offenses for 77 percent. These data are consistent with the experiences of youth service agencies around the country. In addition, the Arizona study has found a link between mistreatment and suicide among adolescents.

Another study conducted by Grisso has revealed that adolescents who expressed a low desire to be released from a state correctional youth camp and who returned home were likely to have a history of mistreatment in the home.[16] These youths dealt with difficulties encountered in the school and home by withdrawing from them.

This is not the whole story, however. According to researchers who developed a questionnaire to identify adolescents who would be high-risk parents, mistreated youths lack life-management skills and reveal attitudes and beliefs about child rearing that make them likely to become involved in mistreating their own future children.[17] Because of this, the long-term goal of youth service agencies in serving mistreated youths is to help these adolescents develop the life-management skills and concepts of family life that will prevent them from becoming the next generation of troubled parents involved in the mistreatment of children.

CAN NEEDS BE MET?

Can child protective services meet the needs of mistreated youths? A recent nationwide review of services for abused adolescents has concluded that "to a large extent, child protective agencies are not providing adequate protective services for adolescent youths."[18] Workers in these agencies are usually not trained to deal with adolescents and often do not view serving them as part of the primary mission in child protective services. And because most of the workers are overburdened with cases involving infants and young children, they elect to serve the young children rather than adolescents. In many agencies there is little or no provision for involving teenagers in the decision process of case management and placement. Moreover, the "alternative" agencies (for example, runaway houses) that deal with troubled adolescents often do not have effective working relationships with child protective agencies. A coordinator who specializes in dealing with cases involving mistreated adolescents may be essential. Agencies can provide specialized training in the area of adolescent abuse by reorganizing the tasks of existing staff members or by obtaining an increase in regular funding to train personnel.

Are special-purpose programs for mistreated adolescents needed? The reaction against single-purpose agencies and categorical grants is well founded in the area of abuse and neglect of adolescents. Networks of services, such as youth hotlines, and comprehensive youth-serving agencies appear to be the answer. These networks and agencies provide services to the mistreated adolescent who may need to receive help initially as a runaway, as a school failure, as a gynecological patient, or in some other role that can be a manifestation of mistreatment. To permit effective identification and referral of abuse-related problems, youth hotlines should remain generic in scope while providing specialized training in adolescent abuse. In addition, the training of front-line workers who offer services to adolescents is probably wiser than the creation of new agencies to deal with these youths. Furthermore, because study findings reveal that the judicial system is a major stumbling block to meeting the needs of mistreated youths, programs should educate lawyers, prosecutors, judges, and other court personnel about their responsibilities in this matter and stimulate more effective "watchdog" activities by the mass media and advocacy groups.[19]

Can the schools help? Any solution to the problems of mistreated youths must involve the schools. Schools are the primary source for reporting the mistreatment of children between the ages of 6 and 18, and their effectiveness as a reporting source has improved. However, despite the work of such groups as the Education Commission of the States, many schools offer few services to these youths. Indeed, as the Children's Defense Fund reports, most children who are not in schools are out because the schools cannot or will not deal with them.[20] These adolescents are often victims of neglect and may have been abused. Schools can play a part in identifying, preventing, and treating abuse and neglect. For example, they can provide parent and "life-management" education, improve adolescents' awareness of abuse and neglect, and help youngsters in foster or institutional care become integrated into the social and academic life of the classroom. Few schools cope adequately with these challenges. For many, abuse and neglect are either taboo topics or are tacitly accepted as part of the normal routine of family life.

Given the manifest concern of many individual teachers and administrators, school personnel should be included in a community's network of services for helping mistreated youths. The current pessimism in many circles about the potency and good intentions of schools, although well founded in many cases, should not lead to the exclusion of school personnel from the helping process. The assistance of teachers and administrators is essential if mistreated teenagers are to acquire social behavior of which society approves.

Where do runaway houses fit into the picture? One-third to one-half of the clientele in most runaway houses are adolescents who have been sexually and physically assaulted.[21] When teenagers run away to escape domestic violence, sexual exploitation, or rejection, they run a high risk of being victimized or becoming involved in delinquent acts unless they try to obtain shelter in secure runaway houses. Because these youngsters often require special management, runaway houses and group homes need well-trained staff. Programs that have adopted the "Teaching-Family Model" provide an approach that gives the adults in charge of group homes the strategies and tactics needed to stabilize behavior and teach social skills.[22]

Can teenagers play an active role? By and large, self-help groups for victims, cadres of trained volunteers to act as peer counselors in adult-run service programs, and programs aimed at making teenagers aware of abuse are all effective in dealing with the problem of child abuse and neglect, especially the mistreatment of adolescents.[23] Moreover, the strengthening of links between peer groups and concerned adults can lead to a better flow of information relevant to prevention, case identification, and even "treatment." These peer networks can become an important adjunct to youth-serving institutions, be they conventional health programs or "alternative" services such as Face-to-Face in St. Paul, Minnesota, and The Door in New York City. They encourage a greater reliance on volunteers to handle the more manageable cases involving mistreated youths while saving professional expertise for the most intractable cases. Innovative use of volunteers in all facets of such cases is an idea whose time has come. For example, one promising innovation introduced in California is the use of trained volunteers as lay advocates for mistreated youths.

CONCLUSION

The history of services for youths has been dominated by a debate over the relative importance of control versus support in those programs. This is a false and misleading dichotomy. Successful programs have recognized that young people need a healthy mixture of order and nurturance. The two go hand in hand in a well-run program, a healthy family, and a society that knows how to care for its youths. Current efforts to deal with the mistreatment of youths will succeed to the degree that social service professionals recognize the need to link youths and their families to support systems that provide both nurturance and feedback.

Youths in trouble are often youths who have been hurt. The hurt may be unintentional, or it may be calculated by individuals and institutions that inflict their problems on the youngsters they serve. Rearing a child, especially in early adolescence, is a challenge. However, the difficulty of that challenge cannot excuse individual and institutional abuse and neglect.

As researchers shed light on the mistreatment of youths and on society's efforts to cope with this problem, professionals must play a continuing role in defining the issues related to such abuse and in organizing community support for these youths. The many dedicated friends of mistreated youngsters are well represented in the words of Father Flanagan, a midwestern priest who spent his life ministering to the needs of yesterday's "throwaway youth":

> There were no bad boys. There were only bad parents, bad environments, and bad examples. It's wrong even to call it juvenile delinquency. Why not call it what it generally is—the delinquency of a callous and indifferent society?[24]

Why not? Why not stimulate and nurture the motivation and ability of communities to meet the needs of mistreated youths?

Notes and References

1. For discussions of how the abuse and neglect of adolescents were "discovered," see Eli Newberger and Richard Bourne, "The Medicalization and Legalization of Child Abuse," American Journal of Orthopsychiatry, 48 (October 1978), pp. 593–607; and Stephen Pfohl, "The Discovery of Child Abuse," Social Problems, 24 (February 1977), pp. 310–323.

2. See Ronald P. Rohner, They Love Me, They Love Me Not: A Worldwide Study of the Effects of Parental Acceptance and Rejection (New Haven, Conn.: Human Relations File Press, 1975).

3. Ira Lourie, "Family Dynamics and the Abuse of Adolescents," paper presented at the Second International Congress on Child Abuse and Neglect, London, England, September 13, 1978; and

Monica Mahan, "Differential Diagnosis and Treatment Planning in Working with Adolescent Abuse and Neglect," pp. 1–25, unpublished manuscript, Youth in Crisis, Inc., Chicago, 1978.

4. *See Evaluation of Child Abuse and Neglect Projects, 1974–1977* (Berkeley, Calif.: Berkeley Planning Associates, 1978); and Richard Herrenkohl et al., "The Repetition of Child Abuse: How Frequently Does It Occur?" paper presented at the Second International Congress on Child Abuse and Neglect, London, England, September 12, 1978.

5. James Garbarino, Alan Potter, and Barbara Carson, "Comparing Adolescent Versus Child Abuse Cases," pp. 1–17. Unpublished manuscript, Center for the Study of Youth Development, Boys Town, Nebr., 1979.

6. Lourie, op. cit.

7. James Garbarino and Barbara Carson, "Comparing Child and Adolescent Abuse Cases." Unpublished manuscript, Center for the Study of Youth Development, Boys Town, Nebr., 1979.

8. Murry Straus, "Family Patterns and Child Abuse in a Representative American Sample." Paper presented at the Second International Congress on Child Abuse and Neglect, London, England, September 12, 1978.

9. Institute of Medicine, *Issues in Adolescent Health,* preliminary conference report (Washington, D.C.: National Academy of Sciences, 1978); and Hillary Millar, *Approaches to Adolescent Health Care in the 1970s* (Washington, D.C.: U.S. Department of Health, Education & Welfare, 1975).

10. Straus, op. cit.

11. Bruce Fisher, personal communication. Conference on Adolescent Abuse and Neglect, Monterey, Calif., October 1978.

12. *See* James Duncan and Glen Duncan, "Murder in the Family: A Study of Some Homicidal Adolescents," *American Journal of Psychiatry,* 127 (May 1971), pp. 1498–1502; Charles H. King, "The Ego and Integration of Violence in Homicidal Youth," *American Journal of Orthopsychiatry,* 45 (January 1975), pp. 134–145; and Emanual Tanay, "Adolescents Who Kill Parents—Reactive Parricide," *Australian and New Zealand Journal of Psychiatry,* 7 (December 1973), pp. 263–277.

13. *See* Lis Harris, "Persons in Need of Supervision," *New Yorker,* August 14, 1978, p. 55ff.

14. *See* James Garbarino, "Child Abuse and Juvenile Delinquency: The Developmental Impact of Social Isolation," in Yvonne Walker, ed., *Exploring the Relationship between Child Abuse and Juvenile Delinquency* (Seattle, Wash.: Northwest Institute for Human Services, 1978); and Jose Alfaro, *Summary Report on the Relationship between Child Abuse and Neglect and Later Socially Deviant Behavior* (New York: Select Committee on Child Abuse, 1978).

15. F. G. Bolton, J. W. Reich, and S. E. Gutierres, "Delinquency Patterns in Maltreated Children and Siblings." Unpublished manuscript, Arizona Community Development for Abuse and Neglect, Phoenix, Ariz., 1977.

16. J. Thomas Grisso, "Conflict about Release: Environmental and Personal Correlates among Institutionalized Delinquents," *Journal of Community Psychology,* 3 (October 1975), pp. 396–399.

17. Steven Bavolek et al., "The Development of the Adolescent Parenting Inventory (API): Identification of High Risk Adolescents Prior to Parenthood." Unpublished manuscript, Department of Special Education, Utah State University, Logan, Utah, 1977.

18. Bruce Fisher and Jane Berdie, "Adolescent Abuse and Neglect: Issues of Incidence, Intervention and Service Delivery," *Child Abuse and Neglect,* 2 (Summer 1978), p. 173.

19. *See* James Garbarino, "Investigating Child Abuse and Neglect." Paper presented at the National Conference of the Investigative Reporters and Editors Association, Boston, June 1979.

20. Children's Defense Fund, *Children Out of School in America* (Washington, D.C.: Washington Research Project, 1974).

21. Fisher and Berdie, op. cit.; and U.S. Department of Health, Education, and Welfare, *Runaway Youth: A Status Report and Summary of Project,* report of the Intradepartmental Committee on Runaway Youth (Washington, D.C.: National Technical Information Service, NTIS-PB 255836, 1976).

22. Dennis M. Maloney, Gary D. Timbers, and Karen B. Maloney, "BIABH Project: Regional Adaptation of the Teaching-Family Model Group Home for Adolescents," *Child Welfare,* 56 (January 1977), pp. 787–796; and Montrose M. Wolf et al., "Achievement Place: The Teaching-Family Model," *Child Care,* 5 (Spring 1976), pp. 92–103.

23. *Evaluation of Child Abuse and Neglect Projects, 1974–1977.*

24. Fulton Oursler and Will Oursler, *Father Flanagan of Boys Town* (New York: Doubleday & Co., 1959), pp. 191–192. ◀

A perspective on childhood sexual abuse

Jerilyn A. Shamroy

In 1977, the Cincinnati Children's Hospital treated seventy-eight pre-adolescent children for symptoms, signs, or complaints of sexual abuse. The alleged abuser was known to the children in 72 percent of the cases. This article describes the hospital's procedure for identifying these children and the follow-up services necessary for their protection and emotional adjustment.

Jerilyn A. Shamroy, MSW, is Hospital Social Worker, Social Service Department, Children's Hospital Medical Center, Cincinnati, Ohio.

SEXUAL ABUSE OF preadolescent children is being reported with alarming frequency. This increase is a result of professionals' growing awareness of the incidence of sexual abuse, more open communication regarding sexuality, the availability of community services for abused children, and reporting techniques that are more protective of sexually abused children.

Previous studies indicate children are often the victims of sexual assault by persons known to them.[1] The dynamics of affected families have been explored, and DeFrancis suggests that a large percentage of such families were multiproblem with the father suffering from hostile, aggressive behavior.[2] He concluded that approximately two-thirds of the victims developed emotional disturbances as a result of the sexual abuse. Brant and Tisza suggest factors in the family's constellation that may increase a child's risk of sexual abuse, including a parent who was sexually "misused" as a child or a parent who is single.[3] It is clear that physicians and social workers in the field of health must respond to sexually abused children and provide the necessary services for their protection.

In 1977, 292 children ranging in age from 3 weeks to almost 15 years were treated at Children's Hospital Medical Center in Cincinnati, Ohio, for suspected child abuse. Seventy-eight of these children were treated for complaints or symptoms of sexual abuse, over five times as many as the number treated for sexual abuse in 1976. These seventy-eight cases were studied to explore how the medical center treats sexual abuse in preadolescent children. The center's method of identification, the availability of follow-up services, and the judicial process involving the victimized child were specifically evaluated. Family dynamics and the circumstances of the molestation were reviewed in an effort to identify situations that put children at risk in order to develop more effective interventions and follow-up.

CHILD ABUSE TEAM

The Child Abuse Team of the Children's Hospital Medical Center is composed of social workers, physicians, and a child psychiatrist. In addition, the team uses consultants from the Youth Aid Section of the Cincinnati Police Department and the Hamilton County Welfare Department. This multidisciplinary team meets on a weekly basis to focus on the following five tasks: (1) review all cases of child abuse at Children's Hospital Medical Center, (2) coordinate follow-up services, (3) provide peer support and suggestions, (4) clarify problem areas in the community service programs, and (5) coordinate educational services to the community.

At the medical center, either in the emergency room or outpatient clinic, the social worker is usually the first person to see a child who has symptoms or complaints of sexual abuse. As soon as the child's complaint is known, the registration desk contacts the social worker. (From 8:30 A.M. to 10:30 P.M., Monday through Friday, a team social worker is in the hospital. After these hours and on weekends, a team social worker is on call.) An interview with the child and family focuses on the circumstances of the abuse, the family's social history, the relationship of the parents and child, family stability, ability of the family to cope, previous history of abuse, and an assessment of the family's needs and strengths. Mandatory reporting of suspected child abuse to the appropriate child welfare agency designated for the protection of children or law enforcement agency is also explained to the parents.[4] A sexual assault protocol has been developed at Children's Hospital to aid emergency room staff in their treatment of the sexually abused child.

The team physician, normally with the social worker present, explains the nature of the medical examination to the child and parents. After the examination, the physician and social worker confer regarding the most appropriate plan for the child considering the child's injuries, age, suspected abuser, and whether the child will receive adequate protection by the primary caretaker. The child may be admitted to the hospital, return home with the parents, or be placed in a

Reprinted from SOCIAL WORK, 25 (March 1980), pp. 128–131.

relative's home or foster care institution.

The social worker and physician discuss their recommendations for the child with the family. If a law enforcement officer or representative from a children's protective agency is present, they share in the decision-making process. A twenty-four-hour emergency unit of the county welfare department, known as 241-KIDS, has been a valuable resource to the Children's Hospital staff. It is within the jurisdiction of 241-KIDS to make foster care placements to avoid the need for hospitalization or, conversely, to obtain an emergency court order to admit a child to the hospital.

If a child is admitted to the hospital, the social worker coordinates the discharge and psychosocial follow-up when the child is medically ready to leave. Follow-up counseling by the team social worker is also available for children not admitted to the hospital. If long-term therapy is indicated, community counseling agencies are used. The team social worker also supports the family through any judical procedures.

CASES

From January 1977 through December 1977, seventy-eight children were treated at Children's Hospital for sexual abuse based on medical evidence, venereal disease, or the child's account of molestation. Their ages ranged from 1 year, 11 months to 12 years, 7 months. Sixty-four were females, and fourteen were males. Children from 1 to 5 years of age constituted 47 percent of the total. Twenty-four of the seventy-eight children were admitted to Children's Hospital for injuries, venereal disease, or because of the family's inability to protect the child adequately.

Sexual abuse must always be considered when a child is seen with venereal disease, vaginal discharge, or genital irritation. Gonorrhea is being documented more frequently in preadolescent children.[5] Fifteen children in this sample were treated for gonorrhea; six in the 1- to 5-year-old group and nine in the 6- to 12-year-old group. Twelve were females; three were

males. Twelve of the children were admitted to the hospital for medical treatment, including an intensive social service evaluation. Follow-up for cooperating family members included gonorrhea cultures done by the Cincinnati Health Department. Two 12-year-old brothers and an 11-year-old female were treated as outpatients. A 5-year-old female had secondary syphilis in addition to gonorrhea. A 9-year-old female was treated for gonorrhea for the second time, having been treated once before in 1976. Eight of the children named specific individuals as their abuser, in each case someone known to the child. The remaining seven children were either too young to give accurate information or stated that their abuser was unknown.

As previous studies indicate, the offender is often well known and trusted by the child.[6] Table 1 shows the alleged abuser in this sample was known to the child in 72 percent of the cases. In the case of one 4-year-old female victim, information revealed that the child had been abused by a known juvenile male and a known adult male; thus both persons were counted. Persons known to the victims included family friends, relatives, and neighbors.

Children abused by persons known to them, including a natural father or stepfather, experienced a high degree of anxiety and ambivalence. If the abuser subsequently was excluded from the family, the child's guilt and ambivalence increased, particularly if court action was involved and testimony from the child was needed. Many of these children had experienced affection from the abuser and

TABLE 1. RELATIONSHIP OF ALLEGED
ABUSER TO CHILD

Alleged Abuser	Number of Cases
Natural father or stepfather	16
Known adult male (not father or stepfather)	17
Known juvenile male (less than 18 years old)	22
Known juvenile female (less than 18 years old)	1
Unknown adult male	7
Unknown juvenile male	4
No information	12

wanted the family to reunite. When the abuser was an extended family member or neighbor, the child was often criticized or ostracized because family loyalties were divided. The most common reaction of the victim's mother was avoidance. She wished to forget that the incident had occurred and believed that follow-up counseling would make it more difficult for herself and her child. All the victimized children and their families were offered counseling to help them express and work through their feelings. The majority of families did not follow through, however. The families most willing to accept follow-up therapy were the ones faced with impending court action.

The following cases illustrate the family relationships and the conflicts present in a child who has been a victim of sexual abuse.

Case 1 Tina was a 7-year-old white female brought to the emergency room by her 27-year-old mother, Mrs. C. A medical examination found that Tina had vaginal irritation and a ruptured hymen. The physician believed the examination pointed to a history of sexual abuse. Tina had told her mother that her stepfather had been having intercourse with her and she had witnessed his masturbation with ejaculation. The stepfather had been unemployed for approximately five months and took care of the children after school while the mother worked. Mrs. C was regularly employed and a good housekeeper, and the children seemed well cared for physically. Mr. and Mrs. C had been married for over two years, and Tina called her stepfather "daddy." Mr. and Mrs. C experienced some marital and financial difficulties, although Mrs. C believed the marriage was basically sound. She based their difficulties on Mr. C's unemployment.

Additional social history revealed that Mrs. C had a poor relationship with her parents and had married at a young age to get away from home. Her father died when she was 14 years old, and she had the responsibility of caring for her invalid mother. She married Tina's father, who drank heavily and physically abused her. She then married Mr. C. Although information on Mr. C was limited, he was clearly a weak man and regularly unemployed. After the sexual abuse of Tina became known, Mr. C was banished from the home. Tina felt affection for her stepfather, however, and felt she was to blame for his banishment. Mrs. C's reluctance to talk with Tina regarding the abuse, and her statements in Tina's presence that she loved her husband, compounded Tina's guilt. Preliminary court proceedings were difficult for Tina. She cried and would not testify against her stepfather, stating that she loved him and wanted him home. Mrs. C later entered a therapy group for parents, which helped her gain insight into her past and present behavior and offered support through her divorce.

Case 2 Mary was a 6-year-old black female who was experiencing vaginal discharge that proved (by culture) to be gonorrhea. She related a history of sexual abuse by her step-uncle for approximately six months. The uncle lived with her mother, Mary's grandmother, who cared for Mary while Mary's mother worked. After the abuse became known and court action was initiated, the grandmother would no longer talk with Mary or her mother except in attempts to persuade them to drop the charges. Mary, a bright, verbal child, became withdrawn and felt increasingly guilty because of her grandmother's rejection. She complained of vague abdominal and vaginal pains with no apparent medical basis. Following a court verdict of guilty, the hostilities within the family became unbearable, and Mary went to live out of town with her natural father, who had been supportive during the ordeal. Therapy was recommended, although it is not known if the family followed through on it.

Family Situation A review of the family situation indicates that all seventy-eight children resided with their natural mothers except in one family where the mother was deceased. The natural father resided in the home in twenty-nine cases, a stepfather in nine cases, and a male friend of the

mother in three cases. In thirty-seven families, the mother was the only known parent present, and the majority of these women were under the age of 30. Whether one or both parents are in the home does not seem to contribute to a risk of sexual abuse as suggested by a previous study.[7] Instead, factors such as consistency and stability in the family structure and transiency of persons in the home may be a better gauge of risk and require further investigation.

Sixty-three of the children treated for suspected sexual abuse resided within the Cincinnati city limits, and the Youth Aid Section of the Cincinnati Police Department investigated the complaints. Appropriate county or city police departments investigated the complaints involving the other fifteen children. In the majority of cases, arrests could not be made because of lack of evidence or uncooperative families. Fifteen arrests were known to have been made. Nine offenders were adults, and six were juveniles (under 16 years of age). The adult offenders pleaded guilty or were adjudged guilty by a criminal trial process. The juvenile offenders usually received an informal hearing in the judge's chambers.

DISCUSSION

Children's Hospital Medical Center is the primary pediatric facility in the Cincinnati area. Hospital personnel work in a coordinated effort to identify and explore thoroughly all complaints of alleged child sexual abuse. A child's verbal history of abuse, even when physical evidence is not present, receives further investigation. If a child has venereal disease, the source is assumed to be sexual contact and is investigated accordingly.

The child victimized by sexual abuse must be approached in a nonjudgmental manner to learn the facts and circumstances of the abuse. Often, the child is asked to draw a picture of the incident and write in the names of the persons involved, which is less traumatic and frightening than a verbal account may be. A younger child can use dolls to point out male and female

anatomy and to show how the abuse occurred. Shame and guilt are common feelings experienced by the child, and it is often difficult for the child to describe the abuse while several persons are present. It is often easier for the child to sit and talk directly to one person while others sit out of sight and listen.

The Child Abuse Team works with community agencies to provide comprehensive investigation and follow-up services. Close contact with the Youth Aid Section of the police department and children's protective agencies insures that a family referred by the hospital will not be lost in follow-up. An agreement with the Cincinnati Health Department defines the role of their health workers and of hospital personnel and insures that follow-up will be made with members of a family with a child with gonorrhea. A person is not legally required to have a culture for gonorrhea, however, even if strongly suspected or accused of sexual abuse by the abused child. An additional problem is that culture results are private, and it is questionable whether this information can be used in a criminal proceeding without the individual's consent.

All the above measures are needed to protect a child from further abuse, although, in the final analysis, the primary caretaker is the only person who could prevent a repeat of the abuse. All but six of the seventy-eight children returned to their mother's home. Programs must be developed to help the mother in protective planning. In addition, she needs to verbalize her own anxieties and feelings of guilt to be in a better position to help with her child's anxieties and questions.

The author believes that a family approach is the best method of treatment. Even if the abuser is a stranger, the entire family will be affected by the incident, and family life will be altered. Often the reaction of adults disturb the child more than the sexual activity. Some children seem to react with apparent indifference or to relish the attention of the abuser until they observe the shock and anger of the adults around them. Community agencies such as rape crisis centers, mental health clinics, and family service associations are valuable resources, although many have long waiting lists.

The Family Development Center, a project of the Social Service Department at Children's Hospital Medical Center, was conceived in response to the need for ongoing treatment of families in which one or more children have been either physically or sexually abused and the child remains in the home. The program operates twelve months a year and includes a four-day-a-week preschool class for abused children, mandatory biweekly meetings for parents, and an opportunity for the parents to participate in the classroom. Preschoolers are at high risk of sexual abuse because they are in the home more often, are dependent on their primary caretaker for protection, are more trusting of adults, are subjected to various babysitters, and do not have enough experience to avoid a potentially abusive situation. The hospital's program serves a limited number of families, and children must be between the ages of 2½ and 5 years. It is hoped that other community agencies will use the Family Development Center as a model to develop additional programs of this type.

Finally, the judicial process involving the victimized child should be reformed. Regardless of age, the child must testify at a preliminary hearing, grand jury hearing, and trial in an open courtroom. The courtroom is crowded with persons the child does not know, which is always disturbing for the child. In addition, the all-day process is tiring for a youngster. It is important that a close friend or member of the family, who is not to be a witness, accompany the family to court. Often witnesses are excluded from the courtroom, leaving the child alone. The child will not feel isolated and fearful if a familiar person is present in the room.

The agency social worker who is assisting the family should also be present to explain the court procedure and to give emotional support. Prior to the official proceedings, the social worker should take the child to the courtroom to become visually accustomed to the setting, to learn where certain persons will sit, and to engage the child in role-playing so anxieties and fears can be expressed. The psychosocial trauma that the child experiences in testifying in front of numerous strangers and the offender might be alleviated by closing the courtroom or through the use of videotape.

The child's family is often unprepared for the court process, and, although initially cooperative, they may withdraw their support when they learn that a series of hearings will be held or when they witness their child's emotional upset in court. Families should be informed of the steps in prosecution and should be involved in decisions regarding their child. Many families stated that if they had known what the legal proceedings entailed, they would not have pressed charges.

In summary, early identification and comprehensive medical, social, and psychological services are needed for the sexually abused child. It is imperative that the laws and procedures that affect the child victimized by sexual assault be examined and reforms be initiated as necessary. Additional community programs are also needed to deal with the psychological trauma and family disorganization that occurs when a child is sexually abused.

NOTES AND REFERENCES

1. *See* Charles R. Hayman and Charlene Lanza, "Sexual Assault on Women and Girls," *American Journal of Obstetrics and Gynecology*, 109 (February 1971), pp. 480–486; and Barbara Herjanic and Ronald Wilbois, "Sexual Abuse of Children," *Journal of the American Medical Association*, 239 (January 1978), pp. 331–333.

2. Vincent DeFrancis, *Protecting the Child Victim of Sex Crimes Committed by Adults* (Denver, Colo.: American Humane Association, 1969).

3. Benee Brant and Veronica Tisza, "The Sexually Misused Child," *American Journal of Orthopsychiatry*, 47 (January 1977), pp. 80–90.

4. Ohio, *Child Abuse Reporting Laws* (1975), sec. 2151.031(A), 2151.421.

5. Hayman and Lanza, op. cit.

6. DeFrancis, op. cit.

7. Brant and Tisza, op. cit.

Child Protection Records: Issues of Confidentiality

RICHARD STEVEN LEVINE

The entire procedure of child protection has been drastically altered in recent years. Since the development of legal services programs for the poor and the trend toward adversary proceedings in child protection hearings, social workers and lawyers clash regularly in the nation's family and juvenile courts.[1] Parents supected of abusing or neglecting their children are now entitled to appointed counsel and a due process hearing, and children now have the right to representation independent of the social service agency.[2] If these adversary concepts are alien to the traditional view of child protection, certainly nothing could be more drastic or revolutionary than the idea of allowing attorneys to examine the heretofore inviolate client records kept by social service agen-

cies. If the right of attorneys to do this were established, administrative chaos might well result and a reassessment of both case-record and casework methodology would be necessary.

Attorneys are now successfully arguing that due process is equivalent to the social scientist's empirical search for the truth and that records maintained on clients by a social service agency are essential for the advocate in the pursuit of the client's cause and in the interest of justice.[3] This partic-

Richard Steven Levine, JD, LL.M., is Instructor of Child Advocacy, University of Pittsburgh School of Social Work, Pittsburgh, Pennsylvania.

---

[1] Patrick R. Tamilia, "Neglect Proceedings and the Conflict between Law and Social Work," *Duquesne Law Review,* 9 (1970–71), p. 579.

[2] Robert S. Catz and John T. Kuelbs, "The Requirement of Counsel for Indigent Parents in Neglect or Termination Proceedings: A Developing Area," *Journal of Family Law,* 13 (1973–74), p. 233; and "Domestic Relations: Appointment of Counsel for the Abused Child," *Cornell Law Review,* 58 (November 1972), p. 177.

[3] Richard Steven Levine, "Caveat Parens: A Demystification of the Child Protection System," *University of Pittsburgh Law Review,* 35 (Fall 1973), p. 1.

Reprinted from SOCIAL WORK, 21 (July 1976), pp. 323–324.

ular argument has been especially persuasive to the courts because, in addition to containing the usual medical, psychological, and social histories, social services files have been known to be notorious repositories of opinion, hearsay, and gossip.[4] Although the experienced caseworker would give little weight to such suspect data, decisions that are influenced by unsound information occur all too often, and the child's attorney and the parent should be given ample opportunity to expose them in open court. Even attorneys who represent agencies agree that many cases are lost because the caseworker did not understand elementary evidentiary considerations.[5] Also, notations by caseworkers often reveal conscious or unconscious biases. Thus, access to the material gives the advocate an opportunity to probe and test the underlying basis for the caseworker's decision-making processes and judgments.

In spite of the recent judicial trend to allow access to formerly confidential information, agencies have continued to resist such intrusions on the premise that confidentiality is essential to both efficient administration and successful therapy in the areas of child protection and public welfare. The key question is whether there are any legitimate legal or therapeutic grounds for this presumptive privilege.

An exhaustive search of the law reveals that the genesis of confidentiality provisions in federal statutes and regulations was the Social Security Act. Special portions of the act were created to protect welfare recipients from abuse and exploitation because of their vulnerability and dependence on the public.[6] For this reason, lists of welfare recipients are generally unavailable for public scrutiny, and particular prohibitions are delineated by statute and regulation. What is more, elementary legal doctrine holds that

if "privileged" communication is said to exist between caseworker and client, the privilege of disclosure belongs exclusively to the client imparting the information, not to the agency personnel recording the communication.[7] Thus, it appears that current record-keeping practices violate even the most elementary legal principles.

Federal and state bureaucracies, however, have apparently gone beyond this original mandate and have construed the Social Security Act and its attendant regulations to limit the access of recipients to their own records. This permutation of the law has been a purely self-serving bureaucratic contrivance that has no legal foundation. Succinctly stated, state laws and regulations that prevent or have been interpreted to prohibit the recipients of social services from having any access to their own records are probably invalid.

However, it appears that the client's access to sensitive materials in his own records can be granted as a matter of constitutional right only during litigation and that the courts have refused to recognize any property interest in the records. Thus, any merely curious recipients of social services could be lawfully precluded from casually inspecting their own records as long as the prohibition did not interfere with any constitutionally protected interests.

Social workers who vehemently oppose the notion of attorneys "fishing" through their case records point out that some materials may be damaging to the client-caseworker relationship and that disclosure might discourage informants from reporting abuse and neglect for fear of exposure and retribution. The counterargument is that guidelines would be adopted to prevent the indiscriminate use of the records. Access to agency records would be under court supervision, and the attorney could be prevented from disseminating the contents under penalty of contempt. It has been frequently noted, however, that if the social service agency must resort to court proceed-

ings to insure the welfare of a child, there is substantial reason to believe that the client-caseworker relationship was never developed in a positive manner and thus never jeopardized.[8]

Finally, public policy clearly favors the disclosure of records simply because public agencies should not be permitted to use the claim of confidentiality to mask potential or actual wrongdoings. In fact, access to the records might be one way that the child protection system could be made more responsible to its consumers.

The professional relationship between lawyers and social workers has been one of cynicism and distrust. Indeed, social worker elitism and the mercenary image of many attorneys has not encouraged positive communications. The issue of accessibility to social service records is likely to be argued for some time. It is to be hoped that this conflict will eventually lead to a more productive interdisciplinary dialogue. ◀

4 Lee Teitelbaum, "The Use of Social Reports in Juvenile Court Adjudications," *Journal of Family Law*, 7 (1967–68), p. 425.

5 Cynthia Bell and Wallace J. Mulniec, "Preparing for a Neglect Proceeding: A Guide for the Social Worker," *Juvenile Justice*, 26 (November 1975), p. 29.

6 "Confidentiality of Welfare Records," 54 *Annotated Law Reports*, 3d 769 (1973).

7 John H. Wigmore, *The Law of Evidence*, Vol. 8 (Rev. ed., Boston, Mass.: Little, Brown & Co., 1961), p. 531.

8 "Dependent-Neglect Proceedings: A Case for Procedural Due Process," *Duquesne Law Review*, 9 (1970–71), p. 651.

PART 5
Protecting the Child Protective Worker

'Burnout': smoldering problem in protective services

Michael R. Daley

Inability to handle continued stress on the job that results in demoralization, frustration, and reduced efficiency has come to be termed "burnout." This article explores why caseworkers in protective services are especially susceptible to becoming emotionally burned-out and describes various strategies for the management of stress and prevention of burnout among workers.

Michael R. Daley, MSW, is a doctoral student, School of Social Work, University of Wisconsin–Madison. This article is a revised version of a paper presented at the Southwest Regional Conference of the American Public Welfare Association, Dallas, Texas, April 1978 and develops further and in detail the beginning conceptualization of "burnout" as it was presented in an earlier piece for the Practice Forum section of Child Welfare, 58 (July/August 1979), p. 443.

WORKERS IN THE AREA of child protective services usually do not start on the job as autonomously functioning professionals. This is particularly true in the public sector. Traditionally, new workers possess only formal education and credentials and are thus partially prepared to perform their role in protective services. Therefore, agencies must bear the additional expense of training these workers and providing them with supervision for long periods to develop their potential fully. Often, agencies invest considerable time and money in the training of workers only to see them become emotionally drained, or "burned-out," within a year or two.

It has long been recognized that caseworkers in child protective services function in a stressful environment. The effects of the pressure they experience can be seen in high rates of turnover and decreased effectiveness among workers, which are commonly regarded as the manifestations of what has been termed "burnout." The recruitment and training of new workers and the revitalization of workers who have become emotionally burned-out are at best an expensive proposition. Given the limited resources available to child protective services programs, burnout among workers constitutes a major drain on an agency's capacity to help its clients.

Although the phenomenon of burnout presents a serious problem to protective services agencies, the precise meaning of the term itself is somewhat confused. A gap exists between the practice definition of burnout, which tends to focus on job turnover among workers, and definitions presented in the literature. Therefore, the author will undertake a formal definition of burnout before discussing how this phenomenon occurs and exploring potential solutions.

DEFINITION

Burnout has been defined as a wearing out, exhaustion, or failure resulting from excessive demands made on energy, strength, or resources.[1] However, a definition that is more specific to a particular job situation, takes into account the nature of the stressors involved, and identifies the major characteristics of burnout may be more useful. According to such a definition, burnout might be defined as a reaction to job-related stress that varies in nature with the intensity and duration of the stress itself. It may be manifested in workers' becoming emotionally detached from their jobs and may ultimately lead them to leave their jobs altogether.

Using this definition, it is possible to conceptualize burnout as a dynamic process and to identify various stages in its development. Maslach views burnout as a reaction to job-related stress that results in the worker's becoming emotionally detached from clients, treating clients in a dehumanizing way, and becoming less effective on the job.[2] The problem of burnout is manifested in a variety of forms, and this is indicative of the many ways in which different individuals can respond to the same type of stress. The following are some examples of behavior that have been characterized as typical of burnout:

- The worker makes a sharp distinction between his or her personal and professional selves by, for example, not discussing work at home.
- The worker minimizes his or her involvement with clients by keeping physically distant from them or by sharply curtailing the interviews.
- The worker becomes a petty bureaucrat, going strictly by the book and viewing clients as cases rather than as people.[3]

Freudenberger has suggested that burnout develops within the worker via a process so gradual he or she is unaware it is happening and may even refuse to believe anything is wrong.[4] One of the primary warning signals of burnout can be seen in workers who are exerting increasing amounts of effort but seem to be accomplishing less.[5] If such workers were to continue in this manner, they would soon become exhausted, isolated, and dysfunctional within their organization. Viewed collectively, these symptoms of burnout might be noted as low worker morale, high rates of absenteeism, and high rates of turnover.

Reprinted from SOCIAL WORK, 24 (September 1979), pp. 375–379.

STAGES OF BURNOUT

Costello and Zalkind have described a model representing human behavior under stress that is an appropriate paradigm of burnout.[6] They state that environmental stressors interact with aspects of the individual's personality to produce tensions, which may vary in intensity and duration.

As stress increases in both intensity and duration, stronger mechanisms of resistance develop within the individual. In the initial stage of this reaction, termed the "alarm state," an emergency mobilization of the body's defense mechanisms takes place. This may result in either increased striving to maintain levels of aspiration and effective performance, or in internal conflict produced by the continual inability to obtain objectives, which in turn leads to frustration. According to Costello and Zalkind's model, this stage may then progress into what is termed the "resistance state," in which the individual's energies are constantly exerted to manage stress. This state may correspond to the stage of detached concern that has been identified by Maslach.[7]

Finally, the resistance state gives way to exhaustion, which represents a breakdown in the individual's adaptive capability. At this stage, the worker is no longer able to manage job-related stress, and frustration and severe anxiety consequently develop. The worker is now faced with two choices: either get out of the job or break down. Many workers get out at this point by leaving their agency or seeking less stressful jobs within it.

The process just described is probably familiar to the supervisor in protective services. The initial stage of the outlined reaction to stress is exemplified by the behavior of new workers who expend excessive amounts of energy to do a good job. These workers inevitably spend evenings and weekends trying to complete what is basically an open-ended job. They put in large amounts of overtime and soon approach exhaustion, only to become frustrated by the additional tasks that demand their attention.

Many workers, especially those who have not made a career commitment to the profession of social work, choose to leave their job at this point rather than compromise their values concerning quality of service. Those who remain often move into a resistance state and become petty bureaucrats, isolated and inflexible. Characteristically, these workers become cynical and tend to view clients as cases rather than people.

Finally, the stress experienced by workers reaches a point where they must leave their situation. Some choose to remain with their agency and effect an intraagency transfer; many others simply quit. Surprisingly, many workers return to school to pursue careers in social work at either a different organizational level or in a different field of practice.

Despite its negative aspects, job-related stress is functional in its earlier

---

"Often, agencies invest considerable time and money in training workers only to see them become emotionally drained, or 'burnedout,' within a year or two."

---

stages because it represents a challenge to workers, increases their motivation, and results in increased productivity. Unfortunately, when tension increases beyond a certain level or persists over a long period of time, its negative effects on workers' behavior can be seen. Thus, a process that is beneficial to employees' performance in its initial stages becomes the vehicle for burnout if left unchecked.

However, it should not be assumed that burnout is a linear phenomenon or the resultant buildup of job-related stress that continues unchecked. Periodic rewards or rest periods replenish workers' energies and allow them to reduce the degree of burnout that they experience. Nevertheless, these rewards tend to become less effective as the worker's length of time on the job increases. It is therefore necessary either to increase the number of rewards and rests given to workers or periodically remove them from sources

of stress. The remedial strategies that this suggests are the elimination of the sources of job-related stress or the provision of mechanisms that periodically interrupt the process of burnout and thus allow workers to recoup their energies. These strategies presuppose that it is possible to identify relevant stressors and diffuse their effect on workers.

SOURCES OF STRESS

Job-related stress is not caused by a simple stimulus or category of stimuli. Rather, objects, emotions, or personal interactions that produce tensions in the individual all fall under the general heading of the causes of job-related stress. However, the problem inherent in defining stressors on an individual basis is that a person's perceptions of stress are related to his or her personality. In other words, what may provoke a stress reaction in one individual may not do so in another. This implies that the remediation of stress must be conducted on the basis of individual diagnoses and that plans to prevent burnout must be individually tailored to each worker.

Nevertheless, certain common elements relating to stress do exist among caseworkers. Because of this, some stressors produce tension in the majority of workers, and this enables the administrators of agencies to develop agencywide or programmatic strategies for reducing burnout. The following are factors in the worker's environment that might prove stressful for caseworkers:

■ Barriers to the attainment of goals, which generate frustration.

■ Uncomfortable working conditions.

■ The necessity of reconciling incompatible demands.

■ Ambiguous role prescriptions.[8]

To understand fully why workers become emotionally burned-out and how frustration concerning the attainment of goals contributes to this, one must first understand why individuals become caseworkers. Although people seek out work to obtain certain types of rewards, whether financial or emotional in nature or related to status, all job seekers are not interested in the same rewards. They therefore look for employment in a particular profession or job on the basis of their perception of the likelihood that their own needs will be met.[9] Rosenberg, for example, has pointed out the contrast in the values held by those entering business because they prefer economic rewards and those seeking social work careers, who generally place worth on working with people.[10]

However, there is more to a job in protective services than just dealing with people. In fact, workers probably spend only about 25 percent of their time in direct contact with clients. The rest of their time is spent transporting clients, filling out forms, keeping case records, attending staff meetings, and participating in other related activities. This severely limits the time available to them for working directly with clients and therefore generates a considerable amount of frustration. Workers frequently refer with disdain to the inordinate amount of paperwork they have to complete and to the fact that they have to "chauffeur" clients around, and they often complain about the number of irrelevant meetings they have to attend. To them, direct service is the only important feature of their job and the one they enjoy most.

Another problem confronting the worker is frustration about completing the job. Many workers like to take pride in a job well done. Unfortunately, because of pressures stemming from large caseloads and arbitrary deadlines, they are frequently unable to see a case through to completion.

A related source of frustration for workers has to do with the fact that clients' cases are usually closed when their problems are sufficiently resolved to rule out the possibility of overt danger to any children in the situation. However, people may still require services, particularly supportive services, beyond this point, and services are often not provided once a client's case has been closed. Nothing is more discouraging to a worker than to see clients return to an agency for help after their case has been closed because they did not receive supportive services that they needed. Moreover, in those instances in which such services are provided, the original worker is still denied seeing his or her case through to completion because clients often receive the services through referral to another agency.

Nevertheless, probably the most frustrating problem faced by caseworkers is the lack of a tangible index of success for use with clients. Clearly, workers make decisions about what constitutes success or failure, but these evaluations are based on subjective criteria. The worker is therefore often uneasy about their validity. To compound this problem, almost everyone in the community feels qualified to offer critical comments about the appropriateness of workers' decisions and does not hesitate to do so. This criticism is a devastating blow to workers, particularly new workers, who are basically insecure about the soundness of their decisions anyway.

Although barriers to the attainment of goals represent one category of stressors for caseworkers, working conditions induce stress as well. Often workers must come to grips with some of the stressful realities that clients confront daily. Middle-class workers are frequently surrounded on the job by decaying slums infested with lice and rats. They may often enter neighborhoods in which they are the only member of their race within miles and in which their status as intruder is painfully apparent. They must also conduct interviews in buildings that are extremely hot or cold and smell of garbage, and they regularly have to talk in competition with radios and television sets. In addition, they frequently work with clients who have severely injured their own children. It is thus understandable why workers become emotionally burned-out.

Furthermore, in the normal course of duty, the protective services caseworker has to reconcile incompatible demands and cope with institutionalized role conflict. Workers may face contrary demands from the courts, their agency, clients, relatives of clients, members of the community, other social service agencies, and a variety of other individuals and groups, each of which may have some kind of investment in a given situation and seek to have input into the disposition of a case. Moreover, the individual worker is asked to perform the roles of resource broker, arbitrator, case manager, therapist, and investigator, but the last two roles are basically contradictory. With role ambiguity stimulating doubt about how to behave at any particular moment and irreconcilable demands being pressed by various groups, the worker undoubtedly experiences considerable stress.

Admittedly, this is a bleak picture. If the job of protective services worker is so stressful, how does anyone manage to survive emotionally, and how could anyone hope to prevent burnout in this type of environment? Fortunately, job-related stress is not always as intense or persistent as has been suggested. If it were, little hope of reducing burnout would remain.

A number of strategies for reducing job-related stress have been developed, and many of these seem relevant to the area of protective services. These strategies attack the problem of stress at the personal and the organizational level. Those focused on the personal level seem more appropriate for use by supervisory staff and the administrators of programs, whereas those put into effect on the organizational level seem more germane to the executives of agencies.

STRATEGIES

Preventive approaches to burnout that are most relevant to the supervisor in protective services involve the use of sanctioned time-outs, or time away from the job; supervisory support; and peer group support systems and the judicious rotation of job assignments.[11] Research indicates that workers who spend a large proportion of their time in direct contact with clients are more likely to become emotionally burned-out.[12] Therefore, occasional periods in which workers can escape from job pressures are essential to the effective management of stress.

Protective services workers expend tremendous amounts of emotional

> *"What may provoke a stress reaction in one individual may not do so in another. This implies that the remediation of stress must be conducted on the basis of individual diagnoses and that plans to prevent burn-out must be specifically tailored to each worker."*

energy in attempting to meet the needs of their clients. Unfortunately, contacts with collateral sources such as relatives and other community agencies are as emotionally demanding as contacts with clients are, leading the worker to feel continually under fire. To escape this pressure and recoup their emotional strength, workers need to have time away from the job and to be able to retreat from unnerving phone calls and bad news. Examples of the use of time-outs would include the following: having workers retreat into their office while someone else answers phone calls for them, allowing workers to engage in social conversation with colleagues, and permitting workers to leave the office early on especially difficult days.

However, simply making time-outs available to workers may not be sufficient insurance against burnout. Workers in the throes of becoming emotionally burned-out may not be aware of what is happening, and they may not avail themselves of time-outs. It is incumbent on their supervisors to recognize what is taking place and to approach the problem with them in a nonthreatening manner to avoid alienating them or producing feelings of guilt. If the situation warrants, and particularly when a worker is approaching exhaustion, the supervisor should seriously consider suggesting that the worker take a vacation.

It should be noted that time-outs can represent a dilemma for the administrator in public welfare who is concerned with being accountable to the public. On one hand, the suggestion that workers take extra time off at public expense may be interpreted as a waste of the public's money. On the other hand, the chief criterion for evaluating this practice should be whether it achieves the goal of increasing workers' overall productivity. Far more money is wasted in the constant turnover of trained staff than in allowing dedicated workers some time off.

Nevertheless, supervisors may want to consider the use of supportive techniques as an adjunct to time-outs. The most basic of these techniques involves a simple discussion of problems with the individual worker, thereby allowing him or her to ventilate pent-up feelings. In the course of such discussions, supervisors should attempt to demonstrate empathy for their workers by offering understanding for the workers' problems, helping the workers gain insight into the nature and source of the problems, and discussing the quality of the workers' performance. This should help reduce the workers' tendency to become alienated and their uncertainty over their performance on the job. Supervisors may need to initiate contact with workers in order to offer their support. Regularly scheduled supervisory conferences may be a convenient and nonthreatening way to accomplish this.

In addition, supervisors can help reduce job-related stress for workers through their control over work assignments. Careful consideration should be given to the assignment of new cases. Workers who have recently been under a great deal of stress should be assigned cases requiring relatively smaller investments of time and energy, which should allow them some relief from pressure. Furthermore, supervisors should try to avoid assigning difficult cases to new workers because such assignments inevitably result in frustration. Unfortunately, the realities of the flow of cases in protective services agencies do not often permit supervisors the freedom in assigning cases that is needed to implement the foregoing suggestions.

One should not underestimate the effect of periodic merit raises and promotions on employees' motivation. The use of these measures is a formal but effective way of demonstrating confidence in an employee. Clearly, limitations exist regarding their use. Agencies' funds are limited, and increases in pay must, of necessity, be infrequent. Nevertheless, it is probable that if promotions are not forthcoming, a worker will leave his or her job in less than two years.[13]

Finally, supervisors should encourage workers to meet as a group. Peer support is a powerful means of counteracting stress and is readily available. Formalized encounters such as unit meetings and informal discussions help reduce workers' feelings of isolation, make them aware that others are having problems similar to theirs, and enable them to obtain information on case-related problems.

Though supervisors can play a key role in reducing the stress experienced by workers, the part to be played by the agency's administration should not be underestimated. If administrators take the initiative in rotating jobs, developing career ladders in direct service, opening two-way channels of communication with staff, and implementing sound training programs for workers, they will decrease the likelihood of burnout among workers in their agency.

Protective services agencies tacitly encourage turnover among workers by failing to devise career ladders in the area of direct services. Frequently, jobs in protective services are entry-level openings requiring little previous experience. As workers develop expertise, they may advance one or two levels in the organization's salary structure but still remain caseworkers. Once they reach such a level, they have little hope of advancement other than by pursuing supervisory or administrative jobs. Unfortunately, many of these positions are closed to workers because they serve as entry-level jobs for those with more advanced educational credentials. Workers are therefore faced with the choice of following a career path in which their lack of formal qualifications may slow their advancement or returning to school to gain their professional credentials. Many return to school.

One remedy to this problem lies in the development of career ladders that offer expanded opportunities to those with competence in direct service.[14] Career ladders such as these would provide individuals having high levels of direct service or treatment skills with opportunities for advancement and would at the same time represent traditional career paths in the area of supervision and administration. This would allow for the longer retention of workers who wished to remain in direct service as well as for the retention of workers who did not choose to seek administrative jobs. Such a scenario would essentially involve the creation of direct service jobs that financially reward those with high levels of skills in the area of direct service. Perhaps the development of positions like "advanced therapist" and "direct service consultant" would provide the additional positions necessary to reduce turnover among workers.

The rotation of workers into less stressful jobs would also help prevent burnout by allowing individuals time to relax and recover their emotional strength. Once rested, these workers could return to jobs that were more emotionally demanding. However, this type of approach may not prove useful if it takes workers longer to recover than to become burned-out or if they strongly resist giving up jobs that are less pressured.

In addition, keeping lines of communication with direct service staff open is crucial to preventing burnout. Supervisory staff can help facilitate this process, but it is essential that communication be reciprocal. Freudenberger has noted that workers who are emotionally burned-out become isolated and feel that no one cares about their particular problems.[15] Effective communication can alleviate this situation as well as obtain support for the agency's policies and goals.[16]

Finally, the importance of training programs should not be overlooked. Being in training allows the worker time away from the office and is thus one means of offering time-outs. Well-designed training programs help workers sharpen their skills, which should in turn reduce their frustration over any inability to deal with case-related problems. An interesting and relevant topic to be explored in such programs would be personal stress management techniques, including instruction in deep breathing, transcendental meditation, yoga, or physical exercise. If workers learn how to manage stress, the probability of burnout will be reduced.

CONCLUSION

Although burnout is generally perceived as having negative implications for agencies, this is not always the case. A number of the workers who have sought employment in social services have made an incorrect career choice. They learn through experience on the job that they either intensely dislike working in protective services or that they may be incapable of performing satisfactorily in this field. The loss of these employees does not present a major problem for an agency. However, if they become burned-out and remain on the job, difficulties inevitably ensue. Therefore, burnout among such workers represents an opportunity for them to be counseled to leave the profession.

Clearly, the response of burnout to job-related stress is a highly individual phenomenon. Factors that may cause one worker to become burned-out may represent a challenge to another. It is thus unlikely that a single preventive strategy will be effective in significantly reducing burnout among workers. A broad-based approach tailored to specific elements in the organizational environment and to the particular needs of workers would be most effective.

Waiting for signs of burnout to appear before instituting preventive measures will probably result in failure. If workers become emotionally detached from their job, the commitment needed to remediate job-related stress may no longer be forthcoming from them. It is important for both workers and supervisors to identify sources of stress that may lead to burnout and together commit their energies to the efficient management of such factors.

NOTES AND REFERENCES

1. Herbert J. Freudenberger, "Burnout: Occupational Hazard of the Child Care Worker," *Child Care Quarterly*, 6 (Summer 1977), p. 90.

2. Christina Maslach, "Burned Out," *Human Behavior*, 5 (September 1976), pp. 16–18.

3. Ibid.; and Gary R. Collins, "Burnout: The Hazard of Professional Helpers," *Christianity Today*, 21 (April 1977), pp. 12–14.

4. Herbert J. Freudenberger, "Burnout: The Organizational Menace," *Training and Development Journal*, 31 (July 1977), pp. 26–27.

5. *See* Timothy W. Costello and Sheldon S. Zalkind, "Introduction to Part 3," in Costello and Zalkind, eds., *Psychology in Administration: A Research Orientation* (Englewood Cliffs, N.J.: Prentice-Hall, 1963), pp. 125–129.

6. Ibid., p. 126.

7. *See* Maslach, op. cit.

8. Costello and Zalkind, op. cit., p. 128.

9. Edward E. Lawler, *Motivation in Work Organizations* (Monterey, Calif.: Brooks/Cole Publishing Co., 1973), pp. 89–96.

10. Morris Rosenberg, *Occupations and Values* (Glencoe, Ill.: Free Press, 1957), pp. 18–22.

11. Maslach, op. cit., pp. 18–19; and Freudenberger, "Burnout: Occupational Hazard of the Child Care Worker," p. 94.

12. *See Project Management and Worker Burnout Report* (Berkeley, Calif.: Berkeley Planning Associates, 1977), p. 34; and Ayala Pines and Ditsa Kafry, "Occupational Tedium in the Social Services," *Social Work*, 23 (November 1978), p. 506.

13. Freudenberger, "Burnout: Occupational Hazard of the Child Care Worker," p. 95.

14. Carl L. Bellas, "The Dual Track Career System within the Internal Revenue Service," in Robert T. Golembiewski and Michael Cohen, eds., *People in Public Service* (Itasca, Ill.: F. E. Peacock Publishers, 1976), pp. 116–121.

15. Freudenberger, "Burnout: The Organizational Menace."

16. Lester Coch and John P. French, "Overcoming Resistance to Change," in Costello and Zalkind, op. cit., pp. 228–241. ◀

Leaderless Support Groups in Child Protective Services

LARRY R. BANDOLI

Working with abusive and neglectful parents is an extremely demanding task. As Davoren has expressed it: "It requires workers who are themselves exceptionally sensitive to other human beings, who can accept hostility and rejection without feeling the need to retaliate." [1] Social workers practicing in the protection area need to feel a high degree of self-worth because "services to children who are abused or neglected are probably the most difficult and complicated in the whole area of social services." [2]

Workers who sustain emotionally draining experiences from day to day need a good support system, both on and off the job. Because of the lack of adequate support systems or inadequacies of those in existence, the leaderless support group has emerged. Such groups have been described as "staff get-togethers where newer techniques of role-playing, validation exercises and facilitating are used to raise consciousness and to allow group support for each worker who needs it." [3] The use of the leaderless support group technique is an excellent and needed addition to more traditional supervisory support methods in child protective services. The high turnover in protective service personnel is, in the author's opinion, mainly a result of emotional exhaustion. If this depleted condition is not corrected it can lead to lowered feelings of self-worth, projected blame, and eventually to unit morale problems.

BACKGROUND

In 1964, in his book *The New Group Therapy*, Mowrer gave some clear and concrete reasons why leaderless support groups had been established in many parts of the country:

Larry R. Bandoli, MSW, is Social Service Supervisor II, Kern County Welfare Department, Bakersfield, California.

I refer to the spontaneous appearance of a wide variety of special groups and associations, inspired . . . by laymen, whose main objective is to provide restorative experiences which scores of people have sought, but failed to find, at the hands of would-be professionals. . . . They reflect the pervasive failure of existing natural groups to perform the ideological and therapeutic functions which they should have been performing.[4]

In his recent book on group psychotherapy, Yalom explains further why this particular phenomenon came about:

In part the self-directed group has sprung into being as a result of the shortage of professional manpower; in part it is a reflection of a humanistic trend which decries the need for an authority structure that is perceived as restrictive and growth inhibiting.[5]

The group itself is the primary helping force. It must collect and direct its energy without the aid of a formal, designated leader.

The use of leaderless support groups in protective services is a result of the "humanistic trend" mentioned by Yalom and the desire for individuals to be "self-directed," as illustrated by Mowrer. In management terms, social service personnel desire to participate with as little bureaucratic red tape as possible in events that influence their lives. This may be the beginning of a trend against what May and Riesman identify as the prevalent American character—the "outer-directed" person who "seeks not to be under-

standing but to 'fit in'; he lives as though he were directed by what other people expect of him." [6]

This conceptualization may be viewed as narrow and as failing to take into account older therapeutic approaches. While the argument is beyond the scope of this article, the author does not believe this to be true. "Trust is the pacemaker variable in group growth" no matter how the process is conceptualized.[7]

GROUP EXPERIENCE

In response to the new national awareness and concern for the abused and neglected child, the Kern County Welfare Department, Bakersfield, California, separated the intake and investigation responsibility from the ongoing field services in July 1974. The newly formed unit participated in several workshops and seminars designed to raise consciousness and to upgrade the quality of its child protective services. At one of the sessions conducted by a group from the Trauma Center for Abusive Parents of Oakland, California, the idea of a leaderless support group was discussed briefly. They challenged participants to experiment with the idea.

In the weeks that followed, several members of the unit suggested that the newly discovered support method be tried. The idea was first presented at a regular staff meeting. While some doubt and anxiety were evident, the unit decided to proceed, although cautiously. Several major preliminary decisions were made. The group meeting would be voluntary, and it would meet for 90-minute sessions on a regular weekly basis. The supervisor would participate as a regular member in the group, not as the leader. And finally it was agreed to meet again in one month to discuss the progress of the

[1] Elizabeth Davoren, "Working with Abusive Parents: A Social Worker's View," *Children Today*, 4 (May–June 1975), p. 39.

[2] Christina Zawisza, Geraldine McKinney, and Janet Hartnett, *Child Abuse and Neglect: Report of a Survey Conducted in Ten States and Thirty Local Public Departments of Social Services* (Washington, D.C.: Community Services Administration, December 1974), p. 4.

[3] Davoren, op. cit., p. 40.

[4] O. Hobart Mowrer, *The New Group Therapy* (Princeton, N.J.: D. Van Nostrand Co., 1964), pp. iii and v.

[5] Irvin D. Yalom, *The Theory and Practice of Group Psychotherapy* (New York: Basic Books, 1970), p. 325.

[6] Rollo May, *Man's Search for Himself* (New York: W. W. Norton & Co., 1953), pp. 17–18; and David Riesman, *The Lonely Crowd: A Study of the American Character* (New Haven, Conn: Yale University Press, 1950).

[7] Jack R. Gibb and Lorraine M. Gibb, "Humanistic Elements in Group Growth," in Jong S. Jun and William B. Storm, eds., *Tomorrow's Organizations: Challenges and Strategies* (Glenview, Ill.: Scott, Foresman & Co., 1973), p. 132.

Reprinted from SOCIAL WORK, 22 (March 1977), pp. 150–151.
Copyright © 1977 by the National Association of Social Workers, Inc.

group. The leaderless group is now in its 11th month of operation. Participation has been excellent.

In the "orientation stage," the group was still just a "collection of persons." [8] Its purpose did not evolve quickly, and the group frequently strayed from the goal of support. Eventually, trust developed; all members felt they had something in common and could help one another. Mutual support was essential to develop maximum individual potential with the clients. The "exploring and testing stage" was nearly nonexistent or may have been mixed with the orientation stage, probably because the group had already been working and meeting together for a few months as a unit.

The group has spent most of its time on the problem-solving process, dealing primarily with the individual problems of group members, but also with difficulties concerning the functioning of the group as a unit. It has also renegotiated its purpose and renewed its commitment to the project several times. Members are truly dependent on one another for needed support. They receive confirmation from others that they are not alone in experiencing emotionally draining and trying situations with the protective service clientele. The group is both cohesive and a "vehicle for working through of problems." [9]

The leaderless group can be invaluable as an aid to the supervisor with the task of sustaining protective service personnel. The success of such a group may be contingent on the participation of mature, highly motivated individuals who have already developed some trust in one another. A clearly defined goal, which all can easily identify, adds to the group's potential for success. ◀

[8] Helen Northen, *Social Work with Groups* (New York: Columbia University Press, 1969), p. 117.
[9] Ibid.

Protecting the Child Protective Service Worker

Child protective service cases involving severe child abuse are coming increasingly to the attention of the public through an aware and attentive press. Information concerning child abuse is also coming to the attention of professionals in the human services field through professional journals.[1] Added to the awareness and information is an interest in implementing new state protection laws.

Social workers are becoming more aware of these laws. An implication of this is an increased awareness of the legal responsibilities of child protective service workers assigned cases involving possible violations of the new protection laws. Unfortunately, child protective service workers are often inexperienced, with limited knowledge of social work and legal policies. Even so, they must handle difficult cases.[2] It is important, therefore, to examine the needs of child protective service workers in light of the complicated legal implications and the pressures placed on these workers and on welfare departments. Needs include improved review and appeal procedures in disputed cases and adequate legal consultation during case planning.[3]

This article suggests that the concept of case review boards is potentially useful for increasing the availability of administrative due process for child protective service workers and supervisors. This concept complements the developing technique of using interdisciplinary teams to plan case management. The interdisciplinary team could consist of a social worker, a child protective service worker, a representative of a voluntary or private helping agency, and a physician or psychiatrist. Interdisciplinary teams usually function during the early phases of a case. The review board would handle disputed cases during the later stages.

The decision to institute abuse proceedings is a serious one and errors can be made in the process. For example, the decision to institute such proceedings, rather than pursue a case on the basis of neglect, may result in the accused seeking legal counsel and instituting a legal challenge. In that event, public welfare departments, cooperating agencies, and employees may have to defend their actions in court.

SAFEGUARDS AND SUPPORTS

The interdisciplinary team approach can insure that errors do not occur in case planning. Collaborative decisions regarding actions to be initiated (investigation, removal, placement, return, continuing contact, termination) can provide administrative safeguards for workers, supervisors, and agencies when case decisions or case management is challenged. The interdisciplinary team approach can also result in improved case planning and improved service and can reduce the potential for workers not to act for fear of personal liability, particularly if the family threatens to sue.[4]

Another recent development is the leaderless support group used to help child protective service workers face emotionally demanding job situations —an unavoidable condition of this type of work. This concept is being added to the resources of child protective service supervisors and is seen as helpful in preventing the emotional exhaustion of workers and the resulting high turnover rate among protective service personnel.[5]

Interdisciplinary teams and support groups are useful innovations but additional safeguards and supports are needed. The death or serious abuse of a child returned to a family from which he or she had been removed can result in caseworkers and supervisors being demoted or relieved of their positions. Demotion and dismissal are based on such errors as apparently faulty case management, lack of case follow-up, inaccurate interpretation of the law, and failure to recognize legal evidence. This is not dissimilar to the outcome of mishandled police work resulting in the mistreatment, injury, or death of a citizen. But for police work, many cities have an established police review process available to the parties involved. The review process was instituted mainly because of the volatile nature of urban environments.

Child protective service workers, working with cases involving complex human interactions and possible legal implications, encounter demands and problems similar to those faced by police officers. Both police officers and child protective service workers encounter human relations problems in which legal requirements and priorities are often unclear because of the nature of the human interactions and the speed of unfolding events. For years the law enforcement community has been aware of the difficulties and pressures faced by undertrained and underpaid police officers, since inexperience and limited training contribute to negative events and experiences with the public that result in negative public attitudes. Similar dilemmas are encountered in the delivery of child protective services.

Interest in existing and potential relationships between law enforcement workers and social workers is increasing. For example, Roberts's article "Police Social Workers: A History," identifies historical precedents for current interactions of police forces and social work professionals.[6] In the

[1] See, for example, Srinika Jayaratne, "Child Abusers as Parents and Children: A Review," *Social Work*, 22 (January 1977), pp. 5–9.

[2] Cynthia Bell and Wallace J. Mlyniec, "Preparing for a Neglect Proceeding: A Guide for the Social Worker," *Public Welfare*, 32 (Fall 1974), p. 26.

[3] Cynthia Bell, "Legal Consultation for Child Welfare Workers," *Public Welfare*, 33 (Summer 1975), p. 33.

[4] Ibid., p. 36.

[5] Larry R. Bandoli, "Leaderless Support Groups in Child Protective Services," *Social Work*, 22 (March 1977), p. 50.

[6] Albert R. Roberts, "Police Social Workers: A History," *Social Work*, 21 (July 1976), pp. 294–299.

126

Reprinted from SOCIAL WORK, 23 (January 1978), pp. 62–64.
Copyright © 1978 by the National Association of Social Workers, Inc.

article "Helping Families in Crisis: Police and Social Work Intervention," Henderson describes the linking of police and social work knowledge, skills, and resources for intervention with family disturbances and mental health emergencies.[7] Similarly, it is becoming apparent that in child protective service cases, frontline caseworkers (like front-line police officers) face problems of legal accountability. This problem is compounded because the background and education of front-line caseworkers in dealing with intertwined legal and human problems are limited.

Social work professionals training police officers to cope with the complexities of combined legal and human problems recognize such development of personnel as a long, slow process.[8] Public welfare departments face similar situations when they employ persons, often with limited experience and training, for child protective service work. In addition, salaries are not always as high as they should be. It is difficult to attract qualified police officers or caseworkers with low entry salaries. It is also difficult to provide ongoing and intensive on-the-job training while these persons are on the firing line carrying out their assignments.

Although there are similarities between law enforcement work and social work, there is one notable difference: seldom is there an established review process for child protective service cases involving disputes that question the appropriateness or the legality of actions taken by the child protective service worker. In disputed police cases, a police or citizen review board reviews the facts of a case and the opposing views prior to the completion of action concerning officers accused of negligence of duty or similar charges. In the field of social welfare, administrative review procedures and legal implications are not so

---

[7] Howard E. Henderson, "Helping Families in Crises: Police and Social Work Intervention," *Social Work*, 21 (July 1976), pp. 314–315.

[8] John L. Hipple and Lee Hipple, "Training Law Enforcement Officers," *Social Work*, 21 (July 1976), pp. 316–317.

clearly defined, and further development of administrative due process is needed.

DUE PROCESS

Certainly child protective service workers should also have administrative due process available to them, given the difficulty of their work and its sometimes controversial nature. The review board concept should be incorporated into the child protective service field for use in disputed child protective service cases. Safeguards for both clients and workers would result if both "precase" interdisciplinary team planning and "postcase" review boards were used. A postcase review board would provide an additional resource if workers or supervisors, or both, are accused of actions that may be detrimental to the interests of a family or community or that may be illegal. The postcase review process would be particularly useful when workers or supervisors are confronted with administrative disciplinary action.

It should be noted that one controversial aspect of review boards in the law enforcement field is that of the designation and membership composition of review boards. A "police review board" implies a board composed either entirely or primarily of law enforcement officials. A "citizen review board" implies a board composed either entirely or primarily of citizens. Generally, law enforcement officials would rather keep the review of disputed cases within the confines of their departments. In some cases a balance of membership is struck between representatives of the community and law enforcement officials. It is evident that many possibilities exist for the membership structure of protective service case review boards, given social work's outlook on the rights of clients, participation of citizens, professionalization, and ethics.

This concept is new to the child welfare field, and it would be useful to examine how review boards might function. Case review boards would function once a dispute evolved concerning action taken in a case and would be available at the initiation of

either clients or agency employees. This procedure is comparable to that of an administrative hearing. Case review boards could be employed as an accepted form of administrative review prior to final agency administrative action against employees or prior to the initiation of legal action by the client.

Essentially the review board could provide a means for review of disputed cases. It would offer clients access to administrative review and give child protective service workers and supervisors administrative due process when an accusation of case mismanagement is the basis of potential agency disciplinary action. Thus, when workers or supervisors are accused of inappropriate, illegal, or unprofessional action, the case review board could protect the worker's right to due process by providing for a review hearing by uninvolved peers and citizens prior to initiation of administrative disciplinary action or legal proceedings. The case review board employed in disputed cases would be distinct and separate from the interdisciplinary team approach used in case planning. An agency that uses both bodies would offer maximum safeguards to both clients and workers.

SUMMARY

The case review process would include a review of the facts of each case, a presentation of accusations or points of dispute, and an administrative finding or recommendation as to the final disposition of the case in question. The review process and its outcome would precede, but not preclude, possible further administrative action or client-initiated legal proceedings. The case review process should insure due process for both the client and the child protective service worker or supervisor.

Progress is being made in improving the delivery of child protective services. It is important, however, to recognize the pressures encountered by workers, supervisors, and agencies and to look for ways to provide legal counsel, knowledge of policies, and administrative due process. The provision of these safeguards will strengthen the administrative and legal aspects of child protective services and contribute to the development and maintenance of positive organizational frameworks for serving the interests of children.[9] In seeking long-term improvement in the delivery of child protective services, the case review board concept would be a useful addition to existing procedures because it insures a formalized and explicit process to protect clients, child protective service workers, and supervisors.

DAVID P. FAURI

School of Social Work
University of Tennessee, Nashville

---

[9] James J. Delaney, "The Legal Process—A Positive Force in the Interest of Children," Fourth National Symposium on Child Abuse, Charleston, South Carolina, October 23, 1973 (Denver: American Humane Association, Children's Division, 1975); and George Hoshino and George Yoder, "Administrative Discretion in the Implementation of Child-Abuse Legislation," *Child Welfare*, 52 (July 1973), p. 414.

Judith E. Gourse and Martha W. Chescheir

Authority Issues in Treating Resistant Families

Clinicians were queried about using authority to obtain parental
cooperation in treatment with troubled children. Consideration
of the issues of client self-determination and the effect of court
involvement on resistance and on treatment efforts revealed a positive
attitude toward the use of authority in working with these parents.

Judith E. Gourse is a Diagnostic Probation Officer,
Superior Court of the District of Columbia, Social Ser-
vices, Washington, D.C. Martha W. Chescheir is an
associate professor and clinical social worker, National
Catholic School of Social Service, Catholic University of
America, Washington, D.C.

A MENTION OF AUTHORITY in social work
often brings to mind negative images of coercion of clients, interference with client self-
determination, and a generally inferior therapeutic outcome. In the treatment of children
it is increasingly accepted that parents' continued involvement is essential; however,
there is much uncertainty as to how social
workers can approach parents who do not
enthusiastically offer their full cooperation.

The futility of working with a child without
full parental cooperation is a constant source
of concern and frustration for social workers.
They are often hesitant to deal with parents
who see the child as the only one in need of
attention and who are reluctant to seek understanding of themselves or their relationship with the child. In the light of an ambivalence about hard-to-reach clients, social
workers may overlook parents' consternation
over having a child who needs professional
help. Clinicians might also question whether a
role has been clearly defined for the parents in
the effort, and if they have helped the parents
understand how to involve themselves in the
child's treatment. Two general issues of authority are frequently present in instances of

parental resistance to involvement in treatment: (1) the social worker's authority based
on competence and role, and (2) authority
based on the implicit power of referral
sources such as the courts or school.

The interest in exploring the issue of
authority in clinical work with resistant
parents stems from observations of just how
uncomfortable social workers are with the
idea of using authority. Social workers are
generally ambivalent about court involvement in their cases. For this reason, it was
decided to study clinicians' attitudes toward
authority as a component of resistance itself,
as might occur when a family is court-referred for treatment, and to determine if and
when social workers use authority as a practice tool to bring clients into treatment. This
might include such practices as calling on
court personnel for back-up or involving a
school official in a treatment plan. With increasing involvement of courts in mental
health areas, the effect of such authority on
treatment is a subject of more than casual
concern to social workers.

With this in mind, experienced social
workers were asked for their views on what
they have found helpful in working with hard-
to-reach parents. Of particular concern was
the issue of authority—its contribution to
parental resistance and the social worker's attitudes toward its presence and/or use in
treatment.

Authority in Casework

Throughout the literature there are observations that the social work profession has "in general been uncertain about the place of authority in the dynamics of helping" and "that many practitioners experience uneasiness in social work positions which call for the use of authority."[1] Contributing to this uneasiness are such factors as concern for client self-determination, juxtaposed against the demands and limitations of both the agency and society as a whole. Because it is generally agreed that the attitude of the social worker toward the use of authority significantly affects treatment outcome,[2] an uneasiness with the presence or use of authority in treatment raises important issues for clinical practice.

In this study, the concept of authority is applied in two ways: as a possible component of parental resistance to treatment, and as a potential tool in engaging some resistant parents. Central to both is Elliot Studt's analysis of social worker-client authority relationships in which authority appears as a relationship between people only in an organization of persons aiming to accomplish specific tasks. It is always legitimized power, occurring as a special form of influence when one person has certain official responsibilities toward the behavior of another: "Authority is created when, in order to get the job done properly, a person in one position of an organization is authorized to direct the role activities of a person in another position."[3]

The client of a social agency becomes a functioning member of the social organization and participates in its authority relationships. The social worker is invested with whatever authority is inherent in the agency to guide the client's role behavior, so that the goal for which he or she and the organization

came together can be achieved. In the case of a voluntary client of a private agency, the social worker's authority stems from the voluntary contract agreed to by worker and client, incorporating policies and procedures of the agency. When dealing with involuntary clients of such public agencies as protective services and probation, the social worker's authority ultimately rests in the very real power of the legal system to intervene in a person's activities.

Elliot Studt describes a graded series of definitions of the client role that reflect the differing abilities of individuals to manage their behavior. At one end of the continuum is the self-actualizing client who is voluntarily seeking assistance, usually found in private family agencies and in outpatient psychiatric clinics. At the other extreme are involuntary clients who are assigned to work with authority persons on extended areas of personal functioning. Abuse and neglect agencies, institutional care for the mentally ill or severely retarded, and correctional services are most frequently involved in such situations. Additionally, courts now refer clients to psychiatric and family service agencies as a mandatory component of their sentence or disposition, thus creating an intermediate group of involuntary clients who must work on specific areas of behavior with authority persons.

It is this diverse group of involuntary clients for whom the authority issues under discussion are particularly germane. The social worker whose client resists intervention, yet is obliged by some authority to participate in treatment, faces important questions regarding client self-determination. How far can a social worker go to secure client compliance with treatment plans? Studt distinguishes between confronting the client with the reality of the situation, that is, what is expected of the client and what may happen if the client does not cooperate, and authoritarian actions that may in some instances compromise the self-determination of the client. For example, attempting to terminate parental rights legally is certainly more intrusive than urging clients to attend parent education classes and warning them of eventual court involvement if they do not cooperate with the treatment plan. That some

1. Lloyd Ohlin, Herman Piven, and Donnell Pappenfort, "Major Dilemmas of the Social Worker in Probation and Parole," in *Social Perspectives on Behavior,* ed. Herman Stein and Richard Cloward (Glencoe, Ill.: Free Press, 1958), p. 251.

2. Elliot Studt, "Worker-Client Authority Relationships in Social Work," *Social Work* 4 (January 1959): 25.

3. Ibid., p. 18.

worker actions interfere with client self-determination cannot be denied. These strong measures are surely more discomforting than simple reminders of the social worker's real power to involve the agency or legal system in the client's life. But, ultimately, to engage in or avoid socially unacceptable behavior or to engage in or avoid problem-solving efforts is the client's decision. Any authoritarian action taken by a social worker within the limits of the role cannot be simply rejected as a total violation of the client's right of self-determination, for there are many decision points for the client along the way to such worker actions.

In correctional literature, examples of using authority as an aid in engaging resistant clients abound. The use of authority is not usually viewed as compromising client self-determination. In fact, it may be seen as having a far more positive role in fostering client participation. Charles Shireman, in his work in juvenile probation, gives a cogent portrayal of social workers' use of authority in a court setting to urge children and their families into a therapeutic enterprise. He submits that probation officers are responsible for expressions of support for the troubled family, but also must confront the family with reality—with the precise nature of the demands imposed upon them by the court —and the probable consequences of failure to respond to such demands. He adds that many young people logically expect some surveillance and setting of limits when they have transgressed and interpret lack of surveillance as a lack of concern for them, or as a sign that the institution with which they are dealing is powerless and therefore worthy of their disdain.[4] Harres Gottesfeld[5] found that an authoritative approach characterized by a blunt statement of the possible results of violative behavior and the worker's ability to enact punishment, combined with an "almost parent-surrogate approach stressing true con-

cern for them," was preferred by the clients.

Yehuda Nir and Rhoda Cutler describe a collaborative program between an adolescent psychiatric clinic and a juvenile court that has resulted in successful handling of previously "unworkable" court-referred adolescents. They point out that court authority is positive and useful for engaging clients whose limited self-esteem is overwhelmed by asking for help. They describe the therapist as using the authority of the court from afar, saying "the court forces us to meet; we might as well work on some of these problems," and by aligning with the client in this contact enforced by others.[6]

Rhoda Michaels and Harvey Treger also found in their work with social work—police collaborations that the clear threat of further intervention by the court helps engage clients who would certainly not participate in voluntary counseling.[7] In their study, they found that, after a few interviews, client families often became engaged and participated in therapy without it being a mandatory part of probation. An interesting finding in their study of adolescent offenders was that several called for police-aligned social workers to help solve discord with their parents and used the police-based authority of these therapists to pressure parents into family counseling, even without a pending law violation.

Social workers use their authority both as clinicians and as representatives of social institutions by (1) the authority of a role position that can be used to engage resistant clients, and (2) a continuum of authority actions that allow for client decisions at each point, and that lead from simple confrontation with reality to serious legal intervention in clients' lives and activities. A gap remains, however, in the criteria workers use in deciding when to take firmer authoritarian actions with resistant parents. This study attempts to examine workers' attitudes toward the use of authority and how this is applied to work with parents who tend to resist service.

4. Charles Shireman, "Perspective on Juvenile Probation," in *Pursuing Justice for the Child*, ed. Margaret Rosenheim (Chicago: University of Chicago Press, 1976), p. 146.

5. Harres Gottesfeld, "Professionals and Delinquents Evaluate Professional Methods with Delinquents," *Social Problems* 13 (Summer 1965): 45-49.

6. Yehuda Nir and Rhoda Cutler, "The Therapeutic Utilization of the Juvenile Court," *American Journal of Psychiatry* 130 (October 1973): 1116.

7. Rhoda Michaels and Harvey Treger, "Social Work in Police Departments," *Social Work* 18 (September 1973): 74.

The Study

The questions raised here were part of a general study on worker attitudes toward parents.[8] In the original study, questionnaires were submitted to fifty-seven experienced social workers and psychologists in a metropolitan area. Forty-one were completed and returned. The majority of the respondents, 68.3 percent, was composed of clinicians in private practice and private family service agencies. The remaining respondents worked in hospital, court, or public social service departments. The average length of clinical work experience was twelve years. In addition to being given the questionnaire, eleven of the most experienced workers were interviewed. The questionnaire consisted of demographic data and a series of multiple-choice and open-end questions asking for a reaction to three case vignettes depicting three families who differed in their level of resistance to treatment. The family configuration and the child's behavioral difficulties remained constant, while the referral source and parents' attitude toward treatment varied. In all three cases, the family consisted of father, mother, son, and younger daughter. The thirteen-year-old son was stealing from neighbors and doing poorly in school. The first case stated that a neighbor referred the family to the agency. Although hesitant, the parents were willing to cooperate. In the second vignette, the case was referred by a court worker. There were previous complaints of child abuse made to the public protective service agency. The parents expressed great anger about the referral. In the third case vignette, a school counselor referred the parents, who denied any problems existed in their child's behavior. The questionnaire was pretested three times to ensure that it distinguished the three levels of resistance sufficiently.

The questionnaire contained several statements designed to tap social workers' attitudes toward authority as (1) contributing to the formation of resistance and (2) as a tool or technique used in the treatment of resisting

families. They were asked to describe how the presence of authority, such as the school or court, in a case affected treatment and their therapeutic approaches. Because no prior studies had been conducted on the relationship between parental resistance and authority, exploratory questions were asked on the subject and attitudes toward court involvement came from responses to questions about treatment. It was expected, however, that workers would name both pros and cons of court involvement. The purpose was to collect clinicians' views on when and how authority is a help or hindrance in work with parents.

The eleven workers interviewed were asked four open-end questions about their experience with resistant parents. Information was sought on their views about the use of authority in promoting parent engagement. They were also asked to describe their most frustrating client and to describe the qualities a social worker would require to engage such a client effectively.

Responses to Questionnaires

The study was designed to assess if clinicians' attitudes toward the use of authority varied in accordance with differing levels of parental resistance. To elicit information about preferred treatment techniques, the question, "Which techniques would you be inclined to emphasize in helping this family?" was asked after each case vignette. The clinicians were asked to check three techniques from a list of twelve drawn from the pretests. The twelve techniques included: (1) focus on problem solving; (2) draw attention to unconscious patterns and defenses; (3) teach behavioral management; (4) suggest task assignments; (5) offer training in child development; (6) focus on improving communication patterns; (7) use humor and flexibility; (8) make connections between historical past and present difficulties; (9) actively reach out, that is, visit the home; (10) clarify interpersonal patterns; (11) use the authority of the school and the court; and (12) use support, sustainment, and empathy.

The clinicians did alter their selection of treatment techniques according to case. In the case vignette portraying the most extreme parental resistance, the clinicians over-

8. Martha W. Chescheir, Judith E. Gourse, and Victoria Siltman, "Treating Resistant Parents," National Catholic School of Social Service, Catholic University of America, Washington, D.C.

whelmingly preferred two techniques of treatment: active reaching out (home visits, school visits, telephone sessions) and use of the authority of the school and court. Outreach was not selected by any respondent for the other two cases of lesser resistance. The authority referral was selected by a small percentage of the sample for the moderately resistant parents and by no one for the least resistant parents.

The hypotheses regarding worker use of authority as a tool of treatment was explored further in a separate question. It was anticipated that (1) when parental resistance was low, social workers would feel uncomfortable involving an authoritarian agency; (2) when parental resistance was moderate, workers would have higher degrees of comfort in enlisting the help of an authoritarian agency to obtain parental cooperation; and (3) when parental resistance was high, workers would feel most comfortable in enlisting the help of an authoritarian agency to obtain cooperation.

Based on the returned questionnaires, there was an association between the level of parental resistance and the workers' willingness to use the authority of the court or legal system. Specifically, the question asked was, "Would you feel comfortable enlisting the help of an authoritarian agency at some point to obtain parental cooperation in this case?" In the case portraying extremely resistant parents, 87 percent of the respondents stated that they would feel comfortable calling in authority. In the case of moderately resistant parents, 49 percent answered that they would feel comfortable. In the case judged least resistant, none (0 percent) would use an authority referral. These findings support the hypotheses that when lower levels of resistance are present, clinicians feel uncomfortable involving an authoritarian agency, and that, as resistance increases, more of them feel comfortable using authority to involve parents in treatment.

More information was sought through an open-end question: "Under what circumstances would you [the worker] choose the route of enlisting the help of an authoritarian agency?" Responses fell into five categories: (1) when the child continued or increased acting out, (2) when the parents did not attend sessions or cooperate with treatment planning, (3) when the child did not attend, (4) when there was obvious danger to the child from parental abuse or neglect, and (5) when continued collaboration with the referring agency meant court or school contact. Many of the clinicians that indicated that they did not feel comfortable using authority answered this question citing circumstances when they would call in the court or school. The answers differed, depending upon the level of resistance in the family. In the case with the least parental resistance, continued or increased acting out by the child was most frequently cited as a reason for using authority. In the case of moderate resistance, acting out of the child and lack of parental cooperation were about equal in frequency. In the case of highest resistance, lack of parental cooperation was the primary reason for using an authority referral.

The request at the end of the questionnaire, "Please share the ways in which you might engage this family in treatment," was designed to allow for more extensive descriptions of the clinicians' approaches to resistant clients. Twenty-five categories of responses were found. The most useful finding was the preponderance of active, reaching out, and supportive techniques, with a strong emphasis on clarifying the services offered to the client and the reality of the family predicament. The responses could be categorized into three groups: offerings of assistance, evaluative techniques, and confrontational approaches.

In-Person Interviews

It was anticipated that the face-to-face interviews would elicit more personalized responses to questions about clinicians' handling of resistant parents than was possible in the structured questionnaire. Eleven experienced social workers and psychologists were asked how the authority of the court affected treatment when a client was court-referred. Responses ranged from simple acceptance of the idea that court backing may be the only way to get some clients in the door to a very positive view of court authority as a way for the client to seek help while saving face: "The judge was making him (her) come." One respondent believed that this was a "lending of a superego structure to the client" that "frees the ego to engage." Several of those interviewed found that being able to direct hostility at the court for current difficulties rather than at one's self or at the clinician allowed for client engagement. These findings are reminiscent of those of Nir and Cutler and Michaels and Treger.[9] None of those interviewed believed that court involvement interfered with the treatment itself, although several did refer to a greater sense of anger and a heightened distrust of helping professionals when a case came by way of court. More persistence was required on the part of the clinician to deal directly with this anger and initial resistance when the court or other public agency was involved, but it was generally felt that, by dealing immediately with the anger and distrust, treatment could proceed. Most of those questioned said that court involvement was an overall help rather than a hindrance in engaging their more resistant clients. The response was qualified, however, by specifying this to be valid only when the worker was able to accept initial hostility and distrust from the client and to face the resistance calmly and patiently.

The second question asked the clinicians if and how they altered their treatment style when faced with parental resistance. All stated again the need to handle the resistance first by accepting initial hostility and by persistently offering support and empathy in the parents' difficulties with their child's behavior. Aligning with the parents in relation to the child was seen as necessary before attempting to shift focus to the marital couple or family system. Two people stated that they confronted parents with the reality of the consequences of continued acting out on the child's part and urged the parents to assist both the child and the social worker as a kind of team in the change process. These clinicians described such an approach as looking for parental strengths to engage and as creating an expectation of change. Two of the respondents contracted for several meetings with skeptical parents, after which time choice was given to the parents to continue or terminate.

The third question asked clinicians to describe the kind of parents who frustrated them the most. Two main client groups were mentioned: (1) parents with a characterological indifference at best, or truly malevolent feelings toward their child at worst, showing no guilt over their lack of desire to participate in the child's treatment; and (2) sophisticated intellectualizers who "talk a good game," are "super-cooperative yet only give lip service to the ideals of treatment and try to sabotage it subtly." It is essential to note that when asked this question, none of the clinicians mentioned court involvement as a primary frustrating factor.

When asked to describe a therapist who might work well with the most difficult clients, the clinicians described a secure, patient, and active worker who would not take the client's anger personally or intellectually "fence" with the sophisticated client. A supportive, emotionally responsive stance was deemed more appropriate than a neutral position, based on the understanding of the parents' need for support and fears of being judged inadequate. Interpretation was not seen as helpful in the initial states of working with resistant parents. Judged most essential was clarity of planning, with an ability to set realistic goals for both the worker and parents. Overriding all was the importance of a sense of hope and movement and an ability to communicate the idea that change was possible to the parents.

Authority: Help or Hindrance?

Clearly, clinicians do use authoritarian resources to aid them in involving resistant parents in treatment on behalf of their child. As anticipated, the cases portraying higher levels of resistance elicited more active efforts by the therapist to engage the client through outreach and use of an authority to at least get the parents into the office. In fact, some respondents felt more positive about using authority as a tool of treatment than had been anticipated. They felt that being "forced" to deal with a counselor by a judge or a law requiring school attendance saved face for the client, who might have wanted to ask for help but was unable to. Being able to pin any doubts and fear of the therapeutic process on

9. Nir and Cutler, "Utilization of the Juvenile Court," and Michaels and Treger, "Social Work in Police Departments."

a distant judge and system was sometimes seen as helpful to the worker, who could say: "Look, we are being put together for X amount of time because of ABC, so we might as well do something with the time."

There was some ambivalence, however, when it came to the issue of court-referred cases. In a question asking what factors would make a worker more interested in working with a case, some respondents stated that "if it were not referred by an authoritarian agency" they would be more inclined to take on the case. With regard to the case of extreme parental resistance in the questionnaire, almost one-half of the respondents would have preferred that the family was not referred by a court worker. Yet, they perceived the court as helpful with this same set of parents as a tool of treatment. Based on the questionnaire responses, this might be interpreted as an impression among clinicians that families involved with the court or authoritarian school official (such as a truant officer) become more resistant through the experience. Perhaps clinicians prefer to try to engage the parents first without the use of authority, and then are comfortable seeking authority if necessary.

However, the clinicians interviewed did not support this interpretation; they held a positive attitude toward court involvement both as a referring agency and as an aid in treatment. No one gave as their "most frustrating client" those with court involvement prior to treatment. The clinicians believed that court involvement from the start made clients more available for intervention and subsequent engagement in treatment than would be expected. Did the questionnaire responses indicating a preference for no authority involvement reflect a troubling factor other than the referral source, such as the extremity of problems that often correlate with court involvement leading to referral for treatment? Those interviewed expressed their belief that court-referred cases included many people who would not seek treatment under any other circumstances and whose dysfunctional patterns were often extensive and seriously entrenched. It was also believed that although court authority may account for the physical presence of the client in the office, it was possible to then lower resistance and obtain a congenial voluntary engagement.

A feeling of discouragement prevailed in discussing highly resistant clients. Most of the clinicians who could choose their cases were not enthusiastic about the idea of working with resistant parents and would turn down some of these cases in their private practices. Yet, these clinicians clearly had found approaches to generate parental interest and movement. A major emphasis was placed on the clinicians' need for persistence, high energy, and optimism in work with this group. They noted that if the worker were insecure or hopeless about working with a particular parent, this could be subtly communicated to the parent, whose resistance to treatment could then be misread as theirs alone.

One of the original interests that precipitated this inquiry dealt with social workers' ambivalence toward using the authority of their own role and agency and that of society's authorities to obtain client participation at even a minimal level. There was concern as to whether practitioners viewed the use of authority with resistant clients as coercive and a violation of client self-determination. Furthermore, information was sought regarding whether experienced practitioners found that the presence of an authoritarian force inhibited engagement or created a less productive relationship between worker and client than might be obtained from approaches used to engage voluntary clients. For the most part, the clinicians thought that the use of authority to get some cooperation from parents was not in violation of this right to self-determination. By contracting for a few sessions and by being very clear about what services were being offered, clinicians felt that they were respecting the clients' freedom of choice to engage in treatment.

Further exploration of these issues would produce useful guidelines for dealing with resistant parents. Clarification would be helpful of how court referrals affect treatment, and at what point in the treatment it is deemed useful to call upon an authoritarian agency for back-up or intervention. As judges and schools increase their referrals to counseling services, it can be expected that issues of authority will affect treatment.

PART 6
Toward Social Policies for Families

Primary Prevention
of Child Mistreatment:
Meeting a National Need

CAROLYN CLARK MILLER

*Greater emphasis on preventive efforts in the growing
problem of child abuse and neglect has become a
national necessity. This article presents a framework
for action on federal, state and local levels.*

According to a recent national study, 1.8 million children, or 27 out of
every 1000 children under 18 in the United States, were receiving public
social services as of March 1977 [19]. Abuse or neglect were reported to be
the primary reasons that almost a quarter of a million of these children
were receiving services [19]. Neglect led the list of the eight most frequently cited reasons, followed by abuse. According to the National Study on
Child Neglect and Abuse Reporting, the number of reports of child
maltreatment increased by 24% nationwide between 1976 and 1977 [15].
Estimates of the actual incidence of neglect and abuse, however, vary
widely, and there is disagreement over how much of the increase in
reporting reflects an actual rise in the incidence rate and how much is a
result of publicity and changes in reporting laws [1]. Consequently, no
one knows how many abused and neglected children never come to the
attention of authorities, and thus, never receive services.

Public responses to the problems have ranged from outrage and demands for imprisonment of guilty parties to compassion and intensive

*Carolyn Clark Miller, B.A., M.P.A., is Research Associate, Human Resources
Group, JWK International Corporation, Annandale, Va. She thanks Mady Kim-
mich, D.S.W., and Martin Sundel, Ph.D., for guidance on this paper.*

supportive services. Nevertheless, these responses have been largely reactive. Although most sources show the reported incidence of child abuse and neglect increasing, almost all services are delivered after a child has already been abused or neglected.

Public agencies at both state and local levels are acutely aware of the need for more primary prevention. The lack of preventive services was one of 15 high priority issues identified by state and local child welfare professionals attending a series of regional meetings in 1976 sponsored by the Department of Health, Education, and Welfare. The meetings were called to identify and clarify needs in the field. With primary preventive services leading the list of needs, the summary report of these meetings observed:

> Few public social service agencies provide services directed toward prevention, or reaching a family before internal problems explode into a crisis [16].

In 1977, a draft manual entitled *Local Child Welfare Services Self-Assessment Manual* [21] was field tested in 17 local social service agencies across the country. One of the seven instruments used was specifically designed to assess "in-home" services, which were defined as preventive in nature. Data from this field test indicated that local agencies felt they were not providing sufficient "in-home" services. This was frequently the greatest shortfall that local agencies identified during their assessments.

A complementary manual, *State Child Welfare Program Self-Assessment Manual* [22], was pilot tested in seven states, and field tested in eight states in 1978. Again, all but one of the states noted significant deficiencies in preventive services.

Why is so little being done to prevent child abuse and neglect before these problems require costly treatment? This paper explores some of the reasons for the shortfall, and suggests ways of meeting this national need.

Obstacles to Provision of Preventive Services

The most important immediate obstacle to increasing primary preventive activity is the shortage of resources. Budget and allocation decisions at all levels of government continue to be influenced largely by the incremental approach. A decision to redirect any amount of program funds from treatment services to preventive services, if there is not a corresponding reduction of active clients, will necessitate a decrease in the number and/or quality of treatment services. Agencies are not likely to opt for reducing the number or quality of other services in order to provide preventive services. Reduction of current and ongoing programs and services usually occurs only when required by stringent budgetary or legislative directives.

Several additional factors contribute to the lack of resources for preventive child welfare services and programs, including: the historical basis for social service in this country; definitional problems concerning both the concepts of prevention and the question of what constitutes abuse or neglect and related services; eligibility requirements; lack of information about the impact of services; the narrow policy framework within which child welfare services are provided; and a fragmented constituency.

Historical Perspective

The values placed on individualism and self-sufficiency in America have contributed to a traditional separation of government and families. Furthermore, parents' rights have in most cases superseded the rights of children. This tradition of noninterference in the affairs of families explains in part why the provision of support and assistance to families has occurred only in response to readily identifiable problems. Social services have never been institutionalized in society the same as have, for example, educational and recreational services. Social services are usually provided to individuals who come to the attention of an agency because they have one or more problems. Consequently, receiving such services involves a certain degree of stigma [7].

Definitional Issues

The goals of two major public programs providing funds for child welfare services, Title IVB and XX of the Social Security Act, include prevention of child abuse and neglect. However, the terms "prevention" and "appropriate services" have not been adequately defined. In child welfare, "prevention" often means either preventing further abuse or neglect, or placement. This narrow focus reflects the fact that most preventive services are provided at the secondary level; that is, after maltreatment has already occurred. Advocates of primary prevention suggest that early intervention should not be labeled prevention [20].

Efforts to define the scope of services designed to prevent and alleviate abuse and neglect are also complicated by variations in both the definitions and the goals of services. "Protective service" is the term that usually identifies service related to abuse and neglect, considered a specialized form of child welfare service. Protective services, however, may include any or all child welfare services. There is little uniformity across states in their definitions of these services. Foster care is rarely categorized as a protective service, despite the fact that it is frequently provided as a remedy for abuse or neglect. Adding further ambiguity is the fact that day care is provided as a social service in cases of substantiated abuse and neglect and as a preventive service. Such definitional problems make cost and impact analyses exceedingly difficult.

Eligibility Requirements

The establishment of eligibility criteria works contrary to the principle of preventive service. If one must manifest the problem characteristics before being eligible for service, how can services be provided to prevent that very manifestation? Diagnoses or eligibility determinations are required to justify prescribed services. Although this requirement could result in premature diagnosis of a situation as pathological, it may be undesirable to defer services until a situation has been thoroughly investigated. Delay can result in clarification of the situation. This clarification, however, often stems from further deterioration in the environment of the client. The problem of such delay is illustrated by the number of children placed in foster care before any services were offered to prevent the placement.

Although the legislative language of programs purports to support preventive efforts, in practice attention to "at risk" groups is discouraged if prior behavior has not been sufficiently dysfunctional. Reimbursement that is contingent on following strict eligibility guidelines serves as a disincentive to preventive efforts and results in a disturbing paradox: Only if and when a parent abuses or neglects a child is either entitled to the services that might have prevented neglect or abuse had they been available earlier.

Information Gap

Agency administrators have a vital interest in learning how effective preventive child welfare programs could be in reducing the need for costly efforts to treat problems. Yet, the cost-effectiveness of preventive services has hardly been explored at all, much less with the goal of specifically reducing the incidence of new cases of abuse and neglect. Why? There are methodological and psychological reasons. Evaluation of primary preventive programs is beset with difficulties. In addition to the definitional problems, funding mechanisms are exceedingly complex and nearly impossible to link to particular clients or outcomes, and external effects are difficult to control. Inability to estimate true costs and benefits means that prevention has tough going when competing with treatment services for limited funds.

The psychological reasons for the absence of impact studies in this area are as compelling as the methodological reasons. Historically, social services have not done well in impact studies. The classic *Girls at Vocational High* damaged the reputation of casework [12]. Research done by Blenkner and associates [3] on the effectiveness of adult protective services led many advocates to fear that such services could never be shown statistically to be effective. Child abuse and neglect treatment programs have also demonstrated mixed success in attempts to rehabilitate families. An evaluation of 11 demonstration programs showed high reincidence rates, and the researchers concluded that an annual reincidence rate of about 50% appeared to be a norm for the field [2]. A study by the General Accounting Office in 1976 indicated that in severe cases of abuse or neglect, at least 10 months of intensive services were required to ensure that 75% of the children could safely remain in their own homes [13].

Narrow Policy Focus

Another major reason for inaction in the preventive area is the domination of a narrow policy framework. Attention is given to children needing treatment, to malfunctioning individuals. There has been a failure to look at the family as a whole or from a developmental perspective. It is generally believed, however, that families have the most basic and significant impact upon children. Recently, social indicators have emphasized the changing nature and increasing vulnerability of families—the growing numbers of women employed outside their homes, for example, and the rising divorce rates resulting in increased numbers of children living with single parents. Although research indicates that violence in families often occurs during crises, few support services are available to meet the needs of those experiencing such stress

Fragmented Constituency

A final factor explaining the lack of attention to preventive needs is the absence of a unified voice on the matter. There is no active, unified constituency pushing for family concerns and a preventive focus. Broskowski and Baker have identified the lack of demand for primary prevention as "...the most serious and potentially insurmountable barrier to widescale prevention programs" [4].

The voluntary sector is a powerful lobbying force, but within it exist important conflicts of interest. On the one hand, there are voluntary agencies that stand to gain. They may develop and provide preventive services that would be purchased by the public agencies. However, agencies that provide purchased treatment services may perceive themselves to be potential losers because the term "prevention" is often used synonymously with avoiding placement in foster care. This group is likely to fear that funds to purchase their services will be cut. Efforts will therefore be focused not on encouraging preventive efforts, but on maintaining or increasing resources for treatment services.

Although advocacy organizations can wield considerable influence in Congress, they continue to work separately on narrow issues and with meager resources. Consequently, the public has little information on which to form opinions about the relative significance of various issues. Congress quietly ignores the programs supported by less vocal constituencies. Legislative decisions are often based on the number of letters supporting various programs that are received by committees. This kind of decision making frequently channels public dollars to popular but less cost-effective programs.

Recommended Actions

Preventive services are a crucial tool in the fight against family breakdown and what appears to be a growing incidence of child maltreatment. But national attention and resources have largely failed to support these services. What feasible alternatives exist at federal, state and local levels to change the situation? Three separate lines of action can be identified, ideally developing together to provide a solid base for preventive efforts in the area of services for children. These lines of action relate to policy, legislation and capacity building.

Policy

Institutionalize primary prevention in a broad-based national family policy. The first line of action is on the philosophical base to children's services. Clearly, primary prevention must be directed toward the factors that impinge upon the welfare of families, the primary socializing environments of children. A strong argument for the development of comprehensive and coherent family policy is made by Kamerman and Kahn:

> There is no real primary prevention for so vaguely delineated a phenomenon as abuse and neglect except good social policy for children and families in interaction with their communities [8].

The lack of such a family policy in the United States has been noted by the National Research Council of the National Academy of Sciences [14] and by Robert M. Rice of the Family Services Association of America [18]. There is growing feeling that the time has come for government to develop a consistent and comprehensive policy on families. The planned White House Conference on Families and the public forums that it presents offer an important opportunity to begin to establish the kind of national family policy that must be the foundation of primary prevention. In addition, an executive-level Office on Family Policy, to be located in the Administration for Children, Youth and Families, is in the planning stage. Proposed to function as a policy review group, this new office could exert considerable influence on broadening the policy framework within which children's services are delivered.

The concept of a continuum of developmental services to coincide with life stages has been discussed by those concerned with institutionalizing social supports [9]. This approach is based on the conviction that these activities are part of what society should offer its citizens. Research indicates that violence in families often occurs in conjunction with predictable life crises such as divorce, and during particular life stages such as adolescence. Development of family policy may require a service orientation that reflects more clearly the developmental experiences of families and the individuals living in them.

Coordinate preventive efforts across human services programs. A significant element in this new family policy should be coordination of federal, state and local programs in education, health, mental health, juvenile justice and social services. Legitimate interest in primary prevention exists within all of these human service areas. Varying definitions, treatment philosophies, eligibility assumptions and service restrictions, however, exist for programs in different agencies and often for programs in the same agency. This is due in part to the categorical nature of most federal programs serving children, youths and families, but also to the continuum of values implicit in the philosophical base of various social programs, which extends from a punitive to a preventive perspective.

More and more experts are coming to the conclusion that no single discipline can provide a comprehensive service program in the area of child abuse and neglect. Rather, several disciplines must provide essential services. This is likely to be the case also in the area of prevention. Education in particular offers the ideal nonproblem-oriented setting for primary prevention. Because the major objectives of primary prevention are to promote healthy development and reduce vulnerability, the schools are a suitable setting for primary preventive activities. Head Start programs are another appropriate location for the development and delivery of primary preventive services.

Legislation

Modify current programs to earmark more funds for primary prevention. If indeed "...simplicity in policies is much to be desired" [17], the undesirable policy is graphically illustrated by the current array of federal, state and local programs that include prevention of abuse and neglect as among their goals. Although both Titles IVB and XX claim the goal of prevention, the goals are vaguely worded and mix prevention with treatment. It is apparent that the drafters of both titles were interested in increasing preventive efforts. Including preventive services in the same funding stream with treatment services, however, will ensure that prevention remains on the bottom rung of the priority ladder.

The new section E under Title IV, although directed toward increasing early intervention, may help establish the credibility of prevention in child welfare, and pave the way for future program expansion as more support is gathered for preventive services and more funds become available. Lawmakers should also consider lifting the ceiling on federal Title XX funds, or adding incentives to provide primary preventive services, such as the higher federal match that is available for family planning services. Additional funds should be targeted to states that are committed to implementing a clearly stated federal policy to increase primary prevention of child maltreatment.

Establish the importance of the family in legislation. Child abuse and neglect legislation varies from state to state in terms of the philosophical response to the problems. Some statutes emphasize observable injury and punishment of parents who have inflicted it. In other states, protection of children is primary, while in a third group of states, rehabilitation of families is the major legislative objective. It seems apparent that states with this last legislative orientation may have more interest in primary prevention than states with more limited statutes. Therefore, one approach to promoting primary prevention is legislative advocacy. It is often far easier to advocate for programs and funds to support a group for which concern has been legitimated.

Capacity Building

Begin a limited program to investigate the effectiveness of alternative preventive services. A small program of demonstration projects should be developed that could be organized and managed at either state or local levels. Grants should be earmarked for agencies that demonstrate an awareness of the key factors in preventing child abuse and neglect. Proposals should include innovative approaches to improve the accessibility of services to the general population, with special outreach to high-risk client groups, and a willingness to include rigorous evaluation components in order to demonstrate whether such programs are cost-effective in preventing child abuse and neglect.

It is probably unlikely that a limited research program such as this could involve systematic experimentation. Nevertheless, even random innovation is a step toward overcoming two significant obstacles to primary prevention: the lack of demonstrated effectiveness, and the lack of a constituency demanding such services. Such a research program could also provide answers to questions about the political feasibility of implementing prevention programs in states. For example, to what extent can the federal government expect states to concur with preventive objectives under the current fiscal pressures? Will states continue funding projects that prove successful?

Develop a constituency for primary prevention through publicity and citizen involvement. A great deal of time and money has been devoted by states and localities to publicize the problems of child abuse and neglect in order to encourage reporting of cases. An educational component should be included in all such publicity campaigns. The focus should be on discussing why the problems occur, information concerning where and how help can be obtained, and suggestions of how interested citizens can help prevent neglect and abuse.

The Federal Standards for Child Abuse and Neglect Prevention and Treatment Programs and Projects encourages the formation of multidisciplinary community councils [6]. Kenneth Keniston of the Carnegie Council on Children also recommends the establishment of councils to increase public involvement in finding solutions to community problems

[10]. According to Keniston, these councils should have a heavy representation of parents, and would:

> 1) assess the need for services in their areas of responsibility; 2) survey how well programs are reaching people with those needs; and 3) evaluate how well programs are actually alleviating the problems they were set up to solve. [10]

An objective of publicity and citizen involvement is the recruitment of organizations and individuals willing to volunteer their time and money in the efforts to prevent child abuse and neglect. The potential of volunteers, often housewives and retired persons, to supplement public child welfare services in a variety of important roles is being increasingly recognized. Although many of these efforts must take place at the local level, states can strongly encourage the development of citizen participation in addressing needs by providing guidelines and ensuring public agency representation on councils.

Establish community networks and resource centers. Community networks can spring up from the coordinated work of community councils. Self-help resource centers have grown out of the desire of citizens to be involved in local planning, decision making and problem solving [5]. The idea has potential for community groups with interest in preventing family violence. Networks and resource centers can operate in a wide variety of local settings: for example, hospitals, schools, community mental health centers, recreation centers, libraries, community colleges, civic centers, day care centers, Head Start programs, social service agencies and churches. Every community has unique needs and characteristics, and these should guide the planning and implementation of unique programs.

Network members should be drawn from the medical, education, law enforcement and social work disciplines and also include key leaders from the business, political and volunteer segments of the community. Committees of network members should concentrate on such areas as: a speakers bureau; media liaison and publicity; parenting and mental health education programs; legislative and family advocacy; staff for hot lines, crisis nurseries, shelters for victims of family violence, and outreach or resource centers; and development of self-help groups and supportive networks through churches and other community social centers.

A variety of nontraditional funding sources can be uncovered to provide full or partial support for such innovative community-based programs. Local foundations and civic or charitable organizations such as the Junior League and the National Council of Jewish Women should not be overlooked. HHS grants should be sought. In addition, federal funds can sometimes be obtained from agencies such as ACTION, the Community Services Administration, and the Department of Housing and Urban Development. HUD has provided funding for a series of workshops to train neighborhood organizations in resource center development, and Community Development Block Grant funds can also be used for community resource centers [5]. In addition, in some cities general revenue-sharing dollars have provided support for social programs.

Conclusions

Alternatives to meet the national need for more primary prevention in child welfare must be realistically considered within the constraints of dwindling service dollars and the varying policy implementation arenas of federal, state and local agencies.

It is important to recognize that the federal government faces limitations in its capacity to implement social policies. It is frequently difficult to induce changes that states and localities do not consider expedient. There are also constraints on states' abilities to establish policy in the area of human services. Variations in size and population and in political, social and economic conditions are substantial. Equally important, however, is the organization of the administration of services. Although approximately two-thirds of the states have state-administered systems, the remaining county-administered systems include over half the child welfare clients nationally. The authority of state-level offices in these states can be limited. At the local level there is often the greatest degree of freedom to innovate and develop unique programs. But here, also, social, financial and political resources vary greatly.

The most effective way to overcome the constraints on the authority of various governmental levels to act is unity of purpose. Actions to overcome the lack of services directed toward primary prevention of child maltreatment must take place concurrently in federal agencies, in state offices and in localities. Furthermore, it is essential that the public also see the need for such actions. Professionals in the field must continue to encourage public involvement in the efforts to prevent neglect and abuse of our nation's voteless citizens, her children. ♦

149

References

1. 1977 Analysis of Child Abuse and Neglect Research. Washington, DC: Children's Bureau, HEW, 1978, p. 11.

2. Berkeley Planning Associates. Evaluation of Child Abuse and Neglect Demonstration Projects, 1974–1977. Washington, DC: National Center for Health Services Research, HEW, 1978, p. 131.

3. Blenkner, Margaret; Bloom, Martin; and Neilson, Margaret. "A Research and Demonstration Project of Protective Services," Social Casework (October 1971).

4. Broskowski, Anthony, and Baker, Frank. "Professional, Organizational and Social Barriers to Primary Prevention," American Journal of Orthopsychiatry XLIV, 5 (October 1974), p. 716.

5. Davis, Susan A. "Community Resource Centers: Need, Reality, Potential," National Civic Review LXVIII, 4 (April 1979), pp. 194, 197.

6. Federal Standards for Child Abuse and Neglect Prevention and Treatment Programs and Projects. Draft. Washington, DC: National Center on Child Abuse and Neglect, Children's Bureau, HEW, March 1978.

7. Geismar, Ludwig L. Preventive Intervention in Social Work. Metuchen, NJ: Scarecrow Press, 1969, p. 116.

8. Kamerman, Sheila B., and Kahn, Alfred J. Social Services in the United States: Policies and Programs. Philadelphia: Temple University Press, 1976, p. 164.

9. Kahn, Alfred J. "Therapy Prevention and Developmental Provision: A Social Work Strategy," Public Health Concepts in Social Work Education. New York: Council on Social Work Education, 1962; and Hirschorn, Larry. "Social Policy and the Life Cycle: A Developmental Perspective," Social Services Review LI, 3 (September 1977).

10. Keniston, Kenneth. "Increasing Parent Power," Public Welfare XXXVI, 2 (Spring 1978), p. 15.

11. Meyer, Carol H. "Preventive Intervention: A Goal in Search of a Method," in Preventive Intervention in Social Work. Washington, DC: National Association of Social Workers, 1974.

12. Meyer, Henry L.; Borgatta, Edgar F.; and Jones, Wyatt C. Girls at Vocational High. New York: Russell Sage Foundation, 1965; and Gordon E. Brown, editor, The Multi-Problem Dilemma. Metuchen, NJ: Scarecrow Press, 1968.

13. More Can Be Done about the Welfare of Children. Washington, DC: U.S. General Accounting Office, April 1976, p. 20.

14. National Research Council. Toward a National Policy for Children and Families. Washington, DC: National Academy of Sciences, 1976.

15. National Study on Child Abuse and Neglect Reporting. Annual Statistical Analysis of Child Neglect and Abuse Reporting, 1977. Englewood, CO: American Humane Association, 1979, p. 3.

16. National Study on Selected Issues of Social Services to Children and Their Families: Summary of Information Needs. Washington, DC: Children's Bureau, HEW, 1977, p. A1.

17. Pressman, Jeffrey, and Wildavsky, Aaron. Implementation. Berkeley: University of California Press, 1973, p. 147.

18. Rice, Robert M. "Reducing Substitute Child Care Through National Family Policy," in Child Welfare Strategy in the Coming Years. Washington, DC: Children's Bureau, HEW, 1978, p. 434.

19. Shyne, Ann W., and Schroeder, Anita G. National Study of Social Services to Children and Their Families. Washington, DC: Children's Bureau, HEW, 1978, pp. 23, 82.

20. Sundel, Martin, and Homan, Carolyn Clark. "Prevention in Child Welfare: A Framework for Management and Practice," Child Welfare LVIII (September-October 1979), p. 514.

21. Sundel, Martin, et al. Local Child Welfare Services Self-Assessment Manual. Washington, DC: Children's Bureau, HEW, 1978.

22. _____. State Child Welfare Program Self-Assessment Manual. Washington, DC: Children's Bureau, HEW, 1979.

Defining the care in child care

Karen Authier

Over the centuries families have made provisions for child care to allow parents to work in agriculture and industry. Changes in family structures and in the role of women require a refocusing of attention on the child care arrangements of families. This article examines historical foundations, current issues, and future concerns related to child care.

Karen Authier, MSW, is Director of Social Services and Instructor of Psychiatric Social Work, Nebraska Psychiatric Institute, Omaha.

DAY CARE POLICY AND PROGRAMS are ensnared in political and philosophical controversy, with opponents and proponents lining up under banners proclaiming women's rights, parents' rights, children's rights, free enterprise, anticommunism, and sanctity of motherhood. Meanwhile, the need for alternate care arrangements for children of working parents continues to increase despite society's confusion and ambivalence regarding needs and priorities for child care. This article will address the issue of child care, particularly in view of the historical perspective, current day care needs and policies, and concerns for the future.

HISTORICAL PERSPECTIVE

Engaging in a reverie of the traditional family of the past might evoke a vision of the ubiquitous earth mother, a babe nursing contentedly at her breast, toddlers playing at her feet, and soup simmering on the family hearth while father toils in the field or marketplace. However, a more realistic encounter with the family in Western history reveals different scenes: infants sent from family homes to live with wet nurses from birth to about age 2 and then returned to parents who were strangers; infant mortality rates accelerated by carelessness, neglect, and ignorance; children age 6 and over routinely sent to the homes of friends, relatives, or strangers to work as apprentices or servants; and both parents engaged in working long hours in the fields, factories, or shops, leaving their young children alone or in the care of older siblings, wet nurses, or relatives.[1]

The goal of enabling mothers of small children to work by providing child care was not an invention of the Work Incentive Program. In a *Letter to Friends of the Poor in Great Britain,* Baron von Voght described such a goal in an "Account of the Management of the Poor in Hamburgh Between the Years of 1777 and 1794":

And we are now busy in preparing in every parish a warm room and bread, milk, and potatoes in plenty, where such parents as go out to work may deposit their children during the day, and thus prevent any obstacle to their own industry, or to that of their elder children.[2]

A standard practice in almost all countries until the proliferation of the baby bottle in the twentieth century was the hiring of wet nurses by upper- and middle-class families. When it was popular to send their infants to wet nurses in country homes, supposedly to protect them from the unhealthy city environment, parents virtually relinquished their children for approximately two years.[3] When wet nurses were hired on a live-in basis, their own children were at risk of malnutrition or starvation. Marvik recounts the plight of wet nurses who were encouraged or forced to place their own children in orphanages so that they could provide better care for infants of upper- and middle-class families.[4] The Nursery for the Children of Poor Women, an early venture into day care in the United States, was established in 1854 by New York Hospital to minimize the risks for children of wet nurses.[5]

Increasing industrialization and urbanization and growing concern about the problems of care for children of working mothers led to the development of day nurseries, the forerunners of modern day care centers. In England and France, day nurseries or crèches proliferated from the first decades of the nineteenth century. Fascination with the idea of day nurseries crossed the Atlantic, and the Boston Infant School was opened in 1828 to care for children between the ages of 18 months and 4 years. For a fee of six cents per family, children were cared for between 6 A.M. and 7 P.M. in the summer and 8 A.M. and 5 P.M. in the winter.[6]

Nationally, the number of day nurseries increased to at least 450 by 1910.[7] Even during their heyday, they were not without their opponents and detractors, who feared that day nurseries would weaken parental responsibility. The opponents criticized them for offering less than adequate care and for providing mothers with the opportunity to leave their rightful place in the home. However, the realities of the time outweighed the homilies and

Reprinted from SOCIAL WORK, 24 (November 1979), pp. 500–505.

pious preachings, and the establishment of day nurseries became a means of discouraging and preventing the abandonment of children to orphanages or the neglect of children who were left alone in locked tenement rooms or were unsupervised on the streets.[8]

The demise of the day nursery movement began after World War I when the United States closed its doors to large-scale immigration. In addition to a decrease in the number of immigrants, Steinfels lists the following converging factors that contributed to this demise: (1) cooling of the fervor for social reform, (2) retreat of militant feminists after the passage of the Nineteenth Amendment, (3) passage of laws providing pensions for mothers, (4) economic prosperity that enabled fathers to provide more adequately for their families, and (5) loss of interest by upper-class philanthropists.[9]

However, in the 1930s the concept of day nurseries was revived. During the Great Depression of the 1930s, the nursery school movement experienced its first spurt in growth when nursery schools were opened under the Works Progress Administration (WPA), which was funded by the federal government. WPA made the first allocation of federal funds for group programs for young children to be operated by public school systems. The primary purpose for the establishment of these schools, however, was to provide jobs for unemployed teachers. By 1937, about two thousand nurseries served approximately forty thousand children.[10] Officially, nursery schools under WPA closed in 1943.

During World War II, attention shifted away from nursery schools to day care centers. Mothers needed day care to enable them to work in war-related industries. In 1942, through the Lanham Act, the Federal Works Administration (FWA) provided funds to local communities engaged in the war effort to operate day care centers. In addition FWA was charged with mobilizing women to work in defense plants. Social workers questioned the lack of standards set for centers and defended the rights of women to stay home with small children without being labeled unpatriotic. FWA ignored state governments and existing social service and child welfare agencies and followed the WPA precedent of placing child care centers in local educational systems. The still unresolved struggle for control over funding of child care became a central issue. Day care centers operated in forty-seven of the forty-eight states, and by the end of the war in 1945 approximately $50 million had been spent to care for about half a million children in 3,102 centers.[11]

As soon as the war ended, federal grants were withdrawn and most centers were closed. Although many mothers left the labor force (but not as many as were expected), many others began to challenge the societal proscription against working outside the home. Some worked despite dire predictions regarding the consequences to young children separated from their mothers. Disciples of Freud, including social workers, were preoccupied with the role of the mother in the psychosocial development of young children. In addition, those who objected to day care formed generalizations from Bowlby's work, which described the destructive effects of institutional care on children.[12] They concluded that all mother-child separations and all types of group care prevented the healthy development of the child.

LEGISLATION

Recognition of the need for day care services for children of working mothers was acknowledged in the recommendations of the 1960 White House Conference on Children and Youth; however, the bias against working mothers was also evident in the following recommendations:

> That to maintain the relationship of infant and mother, children under three remain in their own homes unless there are pressing social or economic reasons for care away from home.
> That social casework and other counseling services be available both before and during employment of the mother, to help parents decide wisely whether her employment will contribute more to family welfare than her presence in the home.[13]

Title IV-B of the 1962 amendments to the Social Security Act marked the reentry of the federal government into day care. It authorized the appropriation of federal funds to state welfare departments for day care services. Later, Title XX of the 1975 social services amendments to the Social Security Act became an authority under which day care services for welfare and low-income families could be funded. The goals of the social services amendments were directed to keeping people off welfare rolls; day care services for children were just one of a number of defined social services that states could opt to include in their plans.

Title XX currently provides the primary federal funding for day care services. Funds from Title XX may be spent by agencies to achieve one of five goals. The goals are (1) to help clients achieve or maintain economic self-support, (2) to help clients achieve or maintain self-sufficiency, which refers to clients' ability to take care of their personal needs, (3) to prevent neglect, abuse, or exploitation of children or to preserve, rehabilitate, or reunite families, (4) to prevent inappropriate institutional care or (5) to assist clients in locating and obtaining the most appropriate institutional care when other forms of care are inappropriate or to provide services to individuals in institutions. Title XX gives states some leeway in defining eligibility for services. In addition, this program supports the renewed interest in day care by providing funds for day care to meet the needs of the working mother and incorporates the child welfare concept of day care as an alternative to institutionalization for the child whose parents are unable to provide adequate care.

During the past decade, several attempts were made to expand the role of the federal government in child care. These efforts were met with cries of emotional outrage and predictions of calamity by opponents who viewed them as attacks on the existence of the nuclear family. Although Congress passed the Comprehensive Child Development Act in 1971, President Nixon vetoed the proposed legislation and portrayed himself as defending the country against a law that

> would commit the vast moral authority of the National Government to the side of communal approaches to child-rearing over against the family centered approach.[14]

Throughout the last several centuries, children have been cared for in facilities outside their homes. But no commitment has been made to the development or expansion of programs to provide adequate care. Society sanctioned child care during the world wars and the depression but withdrew the sanction when the crises were resolved. For the most part, rhetoric supporting the role of the mother as the home-based care-giver discouraged efforts to resolve the child care problems of millions of families with working mothers.

CURRENT NEEDS

Clichés and rhetoric do nothing to provide for the needs of the approximately 6.5 million children under age 6 whose mothers work. This figure represents an increase of 17 percent since 1970.[15] In addition, the number of working mothers of children under age 3 is increasing. In 1974, 31 percent of married women and 46 percent of unmarried women with children under 3 worked outside the home. Furthermore, 18 million children between the ages of 6 and 14 had working mothers, and more than 2 out of 5 children had mothers in the labor force.[16]

Working parents developed a variety of solutions for their day care needs. According to the 1970 figures cited by Emlen and Perry, fathers, other relatives, and nonrelatives provided approximately 50 percent of the child care in the homes of children under 6.[17] Nonmaternal care in the homes of children between the ages of 6 and 14 increased from 66 percent in 1965 to 78 percent in 1970 (these figures did not include situations in which children cared for themselves). Care in the home of a nonrelative for

children under 6 increased from approximately 13 to 19 percent between 1958 and 1970 while remaining relatively stable at 5 percent for children between 6 and 14. Day care centers accounted for the smallest percentage (2 to 10 percent) of child care arrangements. Emlen and Perry also cited the following variables that affected parents' choice of child care arrangements: income, size of family, nonavailability and accessibility of service, and feasibility of fitting the arrangement into family life.

If every parent who needed child care were to seek out a licensed home or center, there would not be enough spaces or "slots" available. However, Emlen and Perry discussed some studies which indicated that most parents were satisfied with their current child care arrangements, which were usually in unlicensed facilities.[18] In addition, they noted that other studies indicating a preference for group day care might be unreliable because of skewed samples that consisted of families waiting for admission to day care centers. A national survey of licensed child care faciilties published in 1975 reported a total of 34,235 licensed child care centers and 81,652 licensed family day care or group day care homes of unknown capacity. However, Mondale estimated that licensed day care centers have a capacity of serving approximately 700,000 preschool children.[19]

Although the federal government carries the burden of responsibility for funding day care, state governments have accepted responsibility for licensing day care facilities. State standards vary significantly in minimum requirements, types of care covered, and enforcement practices. States generally agree on the need for child care regulations, but the agreement stops there. In view of this, advocates for children and providers of day care criticize existing standards for licensing day care and the manner in which they are enforced.

The Federal Interagency Day Care Requirements (FIDCR) were hastily conceived in 1968. Centers receiving federal funds are required to comply with FIDCR. In 1973 the Department

of Health, Education, and Welfare conducted a survey of 552 day care facilities. Of these facilities, four-fifths did not meet federal requirements.[20] To bring these facilities up to the level of FIDCR would have been an expensive undertaking. With this in mind, Congress suspended the requirements for major funding programs such as Title XX. Revisions of FIDCR were proposed in 1972 but did not survive the labyrinth of the federal bureaucracy.

CURRENT ISSUES

Competing philosophies contribute to the lack of coordination, planning, and clarity of purpose in day care policies and services, which results in a haphazard system of day care. One tenet proclaims that a mother's place is in the home and that society should provide the necessary assistance so that she can devote herself full time to the role of mother. According to proponents of that position, the availability of adequate child care can endanger that principle by attracting mothers to the labor force. A variation on that tenet stresses the importance of full-time motherhood to meet the needs of the child but excludes mothers who are single or have no one to support them and their families. For single mothers, child care can be provided so that they can work and thereby avoid becoming financial burdens on taxpayers. Those espousing another, altogether different tenet preach that the road to self-fulfillment crosses the marketplace and that women must have access to free child care so that they can seek and hold jobs. As history has demonstrated, the practical needs of the child get lost in the demand for day care so that adults can move toward their own lofty goals of winning a war, reducing unemployment, or decreasing the amount of funds allocated for welfare.

The needs of children are taken into consideration to the extent that society remembers that working mothers have to make child care arrangements, but day care policy is usually an afterthought. At the other extreme are children's advocates and policymakers who have grandiose notions about child care programs playing fairy god-mother to children who are neglected or abused in their own homes. Some agree with the day nursery worker of 1892 who said that slum children "would all be better off in nurseries." [21] However, somewhere between the status of day care as an afterthought and reliance on day care as a panacea for all social ills lies realistic and reasonable options for child care.

Day care serves four basic purposes: (1) as substitute care while parents work or participate in training or educational programs, (2) as substitute care for parents who are physically or mentally disabled, (3) as a provider of enriching, stimulating, and developmental activities for children from less than adequate home environments, and (4) as an alternative to institutionalization for children living in dangerous home situations. For any one child, the purposes may be overlapping.

Because the purposes are not mutually exclusive, those who favor one purpose over another can opt for peaceful coexistence. But the anticipated rewards of funding, power, and acknowledged superiority; commitment to a cause or a dream; and differences of opinion keep the protagonists contesting in various arenas. Some areas of difference center on questions of who should pay for child care, how much should be spent, who should control day care policy, and what should be the quality of care. The questions are blurred further by the realization that an answer to any one question affects the options available for the others. For example, if day care is subsidized as a public utility, it will be more costly than child care that is subsidized only for the poor. In addition, the level of funding will have implications for the quality of care.

The issue of quality care elicits the use of such adjectives as custodial, comprehensive, educational, and developmental, which purport to classify and describe types of child care but have been so overused that they confuse rather than clarify. Regardless of terminology, however, there is a distinction between care that protects a

"Social workers questioned the lack of standards set for centers and defended the right of women to stay home with small children without being labeled unpatriotic."

child from bodily harm, insures a clean and safe environment, and perhaps even provides nutritious meals and care that provides these features as well as opportunities for emotional physical, and intellectual growth. Despite research that demonstrates the detrimental effects on children of sensory deprivation and lack of nurturing, disagreement continues about the necessity of insisting that day care programs provide a stimulating environment and nurturance. In fact, many day care facilities do not meet the most minimal standards, even in areas of health and safety.

Concerns regarding the control of child care are many faceted and touch on such issues as the desirability of parents' participation in decision-making, local versus federal control, the need for professionalism, and the problems of professional turf. The issue of local versus federal control is further complicated by fierce disagreement over the definition of "local." State governments, as well as state agencies responsible for administering day care policies and programs, believe that they should make decisions about the use of federal funds and should monitor expenditures at the city, county, and agency levels. In addition, minority groups mistrust state governments and demand control of day care programs in their communities.

The issue of professional control in day care hinges on answers to the two-part question, Who knows best, the parent or the professional—and if the professional, which professional? Parents' decision-making can be minimal or instrumental in organizing the program. Parents who have been involved with parent-planned and controlled programs have discovered the difficul-

ties inherent in applying the democratic process to day care decision-making but seem to prefer those difficulties to the problems of dealing with decisions imposed by administrators.

If professionals are to be in control, then which discipline is best qualified? Professionals in education, social work, child development, and health may all agree that the expertise of each discipline is essential but disagree about which profession should captain the ship, which should navigate, and which should have scullery duty. Educators are making a strong bid to designate the public schools as the single service-delivery system for all early childhood programs, including day care. Their arguments have been criticized for focusing more on the need unemployed teachers have for jobs than on the needs of children.

FUTURE CONCERNS

In which direction is society headed, with the need for day care services increasing and lack of consistent direction or well-laid plans for the development of such services? As Steinfels points out, day care policy decisions can be expected to produce ramifications for the institution of the family.[22] Since the government has not yet committed the nation to a well-defined course of action, there is time to examine the benefits and dangers that may derive from various goals and policies.

A study of history indicates that women have worked outside the home for centuries. Women, especially mothers of small children, are joining the labor force in increasing numbers. Society can choose to ignore this and persist in the myth of the male-supported nuclear family, hoping that if child care is not provided, mothers will be discouraged from working, the women's movement will fade away, and the divorce rate will drop. If, however, the nation works toward the development of day care facilities to meet the need for child care services, several considerations should be taken into account.

The development of quality child care may be a noble endeavor, but it is dangerous to expect too much from such care. Quality child care will not be an all-purpose solution for troubled families, much less for a troubled society. By overpromising and overexpecting, child care advocates risk resentment and bitterness, including their own, when unrealistic promises and expectations do not materialize. A dangerous smugness exists in the assumption that eight hours a day or less for five days a week in a quality child care center can equalize a pathological home situation. Day care has value as part of the armamentarium of a child welfare or protective services worker, but it cannot work miracles.

Providing quality day care for a child as an isolated service when an inadequate or impoverished family needs more comprehensive services is another danger. The goal of enhancing a child's development is thwarted if an ideal environment is provided for the child, but the family is ignored. In cases of child abuse, a worker who neglects the family but provides rewarding experiences for the child may only increase parents' hostility toward the child.

In addition, a special incongruity is tied to the question of who cares for the care-giver's children. Unskilled, low-income women are employed in day care facilities and receive training to work in such facilities. There is a degree of absurdity in social policy that encourages mothers to leave their children in the care of other mothers while they care for the children of other mothers, whose mothers may be caring for—ad infinitum. This issue is not new but relates to the century-old concern, discussed previously, for the children of wet nurses.

Struggles continue between those favoring more stringent regulation of child care and those favoring less stringent regulation. There are clear dangers in approaching the Scylla and Charybdis of underregulation versus overregulation. With the lack of regulations, the rights of the business persons or care-givers and the rights of the parents to place children in situations hazardous to their physical or emotional well-being take precedence over the needs of the children. But

there are also dangers with overregulation that stifles creativity. It is difficult to translate quality care into a checklist. Checklists work well to make sure that the water is sufficiently hot for dishwashing and that the fire extinguishers are in place, but it is difficult to monitor warmth, understanding, patience, and enjoyment of children by means of a checklist that can be administered by a licensing representative.

Perhaps society will have to be content with counting what can be counted and measuring what can be measured and then relying on parental discretion to evaluate the more subjective qualities of facilities and care-givers. In any event, parents seem to provide the key to quality control in child care, because they usually are in touch with the center more frequently than the licensing representative. Recent efforts to educate parents to select quality over nonquality day care show promise. Educating parents about day care must be an ongoing process of community and professional groups. Parents can also benefit from published descriptions, evaluations, or ratings of day care facilities in their communities. Such guides can alert parents to centers that provide transportation or have a staff nurse, parent groups, or a toy lending library. Each parent looks for different qualities in child care. No one model can meet the needs of every family. Parents seek child care that complements their own child-rearing practices. Unless these practices are unhealthy for the child, rather than merely unfashionable, the parents have the right to choose arrangements that professionals may question.

Caldwell has suggested that society must make decisions about the qualities it wants young children to develop so that it can fashion child care environments to inculcate those qualities.[23] Perhaps the best response is to ask for a little of each quality in the interest of preserving individual rights to self-determination and a heterogeneous society. The specter of "Kentucky Fried Children" models of franchised day care with standardized equipment, buildings, and curricula

has frightening implications for attempting to standardize children. There is increasing clamor for federal funding of day care on a more extensive and comprehensive basis. It is important that any such plan encourage diversity of models and creative approaches to child care.

NOTES AND REFERENCES

1. See Lloyd DeMause, ed., *The History of Childhood* (New York: Psychohistory Press, 1974); and Philippe Aries, *Centuries of Childhood: A Social History of Family Life* (New York: Alfred A. Knopf, 1962).

2. Quoted in Karl de Schweinitz, *England's Road to Social Security* (New York: A. S. Barnes & Co., 1943), p. 93.

3. DeMause, op. cit.

4. Elizabeth Wirth Marvik, "Nature Versus Nurture: Patterns and Trends in Seventeenth Century French Child Rearing," in DeMause, op. cit., p. 284.

5. See Margaret O'Brien Steinfels, *Who's Minding the Children? The History and Politics of Day Care in America* (New York: Simon & Schuster, 1973); and Virginia Kerr, "One Step Forward—Two Steps Back: Child Care's Long American History," in Pamela Roby, ed., *Child Care—Who Cares? Foreign and Domestic Infant and Early Childhood Development Policies* (New York: Basic Books, 1975), p. 86.

6. Steinfels, op. cit., pp. 35–36.

7. Ibid., p. 34.

8. Ibid., p. 37.

9. Ibid., pp. 64–65.

10. Kerr, op. cit., p. 90.

11. Ibid., p. 91; and Steinfels, op. cit., p. 67.

12. John Bowlby, *Maternal Care and Mental Health*, Monograph No. 2 (Geneva, Switzerland: World Health Organization, 1951).

13. *Conference Proceedings: Golden Anniversary White House Conference on Children and Youth* (Washington, D.C.: U.S. Government Printing Office, 1960), pp. 358–367.

14. *New York Times*, December 10, 1971, p. A1.

15. *America's Children 1976* (Washington, D.C.: National Council of Organization for Children & Youth, 1976), p. 69.

16. See Ibid; and *U.S. Working Woman, Bulletin 1880* (Washington, D.C.: Bureau of Labor Statistics, 1975).

17. Arthur C. Emlen and Joseph B. Perry, Jr., "Child Care Arrangements," in Lois Wlandis Hoffman and F. Ivan Nye, eds., *Working Mothers* (San Francisco: Jossey-Bass, 1974), pp. 104–105 and 114. *See also* Steinfels, op. cit., p. 72.

18. Emlen and Perry, op. cit., p. 113.

19. *Day Care Licensing Policies and Practices: A State Survey, July, 1975,* ECS Report No. 72 and Early Childhood Report No. 13 (Denver, Colo.: Education Commission of the States, 1975), pp. 52–56; and Walter F. Mondale, Foreword, in Stevanne Auerbach and James A. Rivaldo, eds., *Rationale for Child Care Services: Programs Vs. Politics* (New York: Human Sciences Press, 1975), p. xii.

20. Donald J. Cohen and Edward Zigler, "Federal Day Care Standards: Rationale and Recommendations," *American Journal of Orthopsychiatry,* 47 (July 1977), p. 458.

21. Steinfels, op. cit., p. 45.

22. Ibid., pp. 245–249.

23. Bettye Caldwell, "A Timid Giant Grows Bolder," *Saturday Review* (New York), February 20, 1971, p. 49. ◀

Comparative analysis in family policy: a case study

Sheila B. Kamerman
and Alfred J. Kahn

In the belief that there can be clear advantages to analyzing social policy in terms of its impact on families, the authors present a case study in which they compare family policy in five European countries and the United States in relation to the question of how citizens can raise and care for children at the same time as they are productive members of the work force.

Sheila B. Kamerman, DSW, is Associate Professor, and Alfred J. Kahn, DSW, is Professor, Columbia University School of Social Work, New York, New York, where they are also Co-directors, Cross-National Studies of Social Services and Family Policy.
This study here presented was funded by the German Marshall Fund of the United States.

MORE THAN THREE years ago, in an article published in SOCIAL WORK, the present authors wrote about a concept that they thought had immediate relevance for U.S. social policy discussions—a concept that had been used extensively in Europe but was relatively unknown in the United States.[1] That concept was "family policy." In that article, the authors defined the concept and illustrated how it could be used in social policy analysis. Since then, family policy has become an increasingly popular topic in the United States and has been discussed by many people, including some who are uncomfortable with the term. Political leaders such as President Carter, Vice-President Mondale, and former Secretary of Health, Education, and Welfare Joseph Califano have talked of the need to develop policies designed to strengthen rather than undermine family functioning.

National committees, as well as task forces and seminars, have been organized to bring together experts from various fields with the purpose of determining which public policies are clearly good—or bad—for families. For example, the National Research Council of the National Academy of Sciences established two successive committees on child development research and public policy, and a Family Impact Seminar was organized at George Washington University.[2]

Several universities around the country have established research centers in which some academic experts are studying aspects of family life and the child, while others are trying to develop a technology for assessing the impact of policies on families or are attempting in other ways to improve public policymaking as it affects families and children. This interest continues despite a growing awareness of the problems that are inherent in the endeavor.

There seems little doubt that family policy has potential value as an analytic construct, although it is becoming increasingly clear that it is difficult to use family well-being as a criterion in choosing policy. Regardless of the recent spate of research and writing on the subject, the state of knowledge remains limited. Value conflicts that might have remained masked in earlier discussions now emerge at the outset of family policy debates as the dilemmas of choice become clearer. Emotion clouds reason as special interest groups assume narrow and intransigent positions, and successful resolution of differences becomes more and more difficult.

Yet despite all this, family life remains an appropriate area of concern for government, if only because virtually all governmental actions affect families—indirectly if not directly. Therefore, the critical issue is not whether we should have family policy (or "families-policies" as the authors have suggested elsewhere), but what kind of family policy to have—a point that has been stressed by Senator Daniel P. Moynihan and Harvard University political scientist Hugh Heclo.[8] This is not to encourage the creation of one monolithic, uniform policy for one kind of family, but rather to try to bring about an approach that would allow decision-makers to become more sensitive to family-related issues.

CENTRAL QUESTION

The following summary of a case study in comparative family policy analysis illustrates how such an approach could be implemented. The central question addressed is a critical one for families today and has implications for several domains of social policy. The method highlights both knowledge and value choices. The most salient outcome that the study seeks to measure is the effect that alternative policy choices have on families and children.

The question is this: Since all adults, women as well as men, are likely to be fully participating, productive members of the labor force, what actions (if any) should the makers of social policy take to make it possible for citizens to bear, rear, and care for children? Or, in other words, which policies can help people to combine work and family life?

This is the central family policy issue in much of Europe today. It is discussed most often with regard to

Reprinted from SOCIAL WORK, 24 (November 1979), pp. 506–512.

policy that affects families during the years when their children are young and when child care responsibilities are most intense. It is clear that this issue is also becoming significant in the United States. As of March 1978, 60 percent of the mothers of school-aged children in this country were in the labor force, and most worked full time.[4] This was also true of 50 percent of the mothers of children aged 3 to 6 and almost 40 percent of the mothers of children under the age of 3. Sixty percent of the growth in the size of the labor force during the last two decades is attributable to the entry of women into the job market. The most significant increase in the female labor force involved married women who were under the age of 35 and who had at least one child of preschool age. Within the last few years, the most rapid growth in employment has been among women with children under age 3. Indeed, the rate of participation in the labor force for these women increased 11 percent between 1977 and 1978 alone, far more than for any other group.

In Europe, care of children aged 3 and over is assumed to be a public responsibility.[5] That is, in most countries, most children aged 3 to 6 are enrolled in a free, preschool program on a voluntary basis. Such programs may operate either independently or as part of the public school system. Parents in the United States clearly want such programs, since more than half the American children in this age group take part in preschool programs that are largely private and unsubsidized and that often cover only part of the day.[6] Unfortunately, U.S. policy in this field still is not comparable to that of such countries as France, Belgium, West Germany, or Israel, where from 75 percent (West Germany) to over 95 percent (France and Belgium) of children aged 3 to 6 attend publicly subsidized programs that cover at least the normal school day.

Even though in these and many other countries there is a national policy for children who are 3 to 6 years old, there is no clear consensus yet regarding policy for the care of those who are under the age of 3 and who

have parents, or a sole parent, who work. This is the key family policy issue selected for comparative analysis.

FAMILY POLICY ANALYSIS

To identify the most significant policy options concerning this question, the authors did extensive preliminary work in a large number of European countries, interviewing government officials, researchers, and practitioners. Five options emerged as offering a full range of actions that societies could take in response to the issue in question. These options are as follows:

1. To offer direct subsidies that would allow a parent to remain at home and care for a young child.
2. To subsidize out-of-home child care services, thus permitting both parents (or a sole parent) to be employed outside the home.
3. To offer parents the choice between staying at home or being employed by allowing them to select either of the subsidies described above.
4. To encourage the restructuring of work and family life so as to permit parents to manage both roles simultaneously without undue stress.
5. To leave the issue for individuals to handle themselves.

Five countries were selected as best representing each of these policy options: Hungary, East Germany (the German Democratic Republic), France, Sweden, and West Germany (the Federal Republic of Germany). In effect, a natural experiment in child care policy was identified, and these five nations were then used as the units for comparative analysis. The focus was on how children aged 3 and under were cared for during the day, why certain countries stressed one or another policy, and what the consequences were for families, women, men, children, and the society generally. The study's ultimate concern was with (1) the nature of society's response to the major changes occurring today in work and family life and (2) the consequences that these developments and responses have for families and children.

As would be expected in analyzing a family policy question, the final comparative analysis involved assess-

ments of several policy domains in each country. In this case, the domains included

■ income maintenance policies (social insurance, cash assistance, in-kind supports, tax benefits)
■ employment and labor market trends and policies
■ demographic trends and population policies
■ child care programs and services, including family day care, day care centers, and preschool programs
■ health and medical care policies.

Here, too, the analysis was focused on the family-related effects as well as costs, of different strategies in each policy domain. Again, the basic question was, In the total societal context, which policies would be viable and could best make it possible for adults to bear and rear children while remaining productive members of the labor force?

BENEFIT-SERVICE PACKAGES

What follows is a summary of the benefits and services offered in the countries that were surveyed.[7] It should first be noted that no country is a "pure" type. Indeed, in the course of the study it became clear that most countries are already moving toward the adoption of some kind of program that includes a mixed group of family income benefits and out-of-home child care services. These national benefit-service packages may continue to reveal a particular inclination toward one or another model of policy. However, they also reflect a growing international agreement on the need for a combination of policies—a package rather than a single policy option.

Hungary To the extent that any model is typified by any one country, Hungary's child care policy represents the option of subsidizing women to remain at home to care for their own young children. The government assures the replacement of income for employed women for a period of time following childbirth and provides a partial substitute for earned income for a still longer period, as long as the woman remains at home.

"Family life remains an appropriate area of concern for government, if only because virtually all governmental actions affect families—indirectly, if not directly. Therefore, the critical issue is not whether we should have family policy . . . but what kind . . . to have."

Hungary has been attempting since World War II to deal with problems resulting from the extensive participation of women in the labor force. The present Hungarian policy was established in 1967. At that time there was an oversupply of unskilled women in the labor force, and the economy was not growing rapidly enough to absorb them. Because the country was committed to providing jobs for all, there was a problem in the placement and training of workers. Moreover, there appeared to be a high incidence of illness and absenteeism among working women with young children and an equally high incidence of illness among children being cared for in large day care centers. Furthermore, high-quality care for infants was expensive, and there was still a shortage of preschool day care facilities for children aged 3 to 6.

Under present policy, the basic package of benefits includes

■ a cash maternity benefit paid in a lump sum to the mother when a child is born

■ a maternity leave at full pay, with complete job protection, for the 20 weeks following childbirth

■ a flat-rate cash allowance payable to the mother for up to thirty-one months after the conclusion of the maternity leave if the woman leaves work to care for her own child.

The flat-rate allowance for one child is equal to about 40 percent of the wage of an unskilled worker and is accompanied by a guarantee of job protection, seniority, and pension entitlements. Since 1974, this allowance has been higher for women having their second and third children than for those having their first because the government is attempting to increase the birthrate. Also, as a result of a tight labor market and a shortage of women in certain industries, the government now permits women receiving

child care benefits to interrupt their leave and return to work for part of each year. Working mothers with young children are also entitled to thirty days of paid sick leave to care for an ill child at home.

Almost all eligible women use the maternity leave, and about 80 percent of those eligible avail themselves of the child care grant. However, the extent of use varies. Thus, it is largely women in unskilled jobs who use benefits for the entire allowable period. Professionals and administrators are more likely to return to work when their child is about eighteen months old. Such women may find that the benefit payments are inadequate, or they may become concerned about the loss of their careers, or restlessness may simply set in. Regardless of the reasons, the use of child care allowances varies, and well-educated women with high-status jobs remain at home for much shorter periods than others.

Day care centers in Hungary have been improved and expanded in recent years, too, so that at present about 12 percent of the children 3 years of age or younger are in care, most of them aged 18 months to 3 years. They receive high-quality care, with a maximum of 15 children in a group, and a recommended ratio of two trained staff members to every ten children. Current plans are to enroll 15 percent of this age group in day care facilities within the next few years. In contrast, 75 percent of children aged 3 to 6 are in all-day preschool programs.

This, then, is the policy in Hungary: an income maintenance program designed to replace earned income completely for five months and to substitute for a portion of wage income for almost three years. Because the benefits are contingent on prior employment, they provide young women with an incentive to join the labor force; when the payments eventually ex-

pire, women are also expected to return to work.

The attempts to use the program to influence the birthrate, although increasingly strong in recent years, have had little impact thus far. More important is that the condition of the labor market has changed substantially since the inception of this policy. But like many similar efforts in other countries, the program of child care allowances has developed its own constituency and a life of its own. It is a popular policy and could not now be eliminated without incurring a strong negative reaction.

At the same time, it should be remembered that 33 percent of the mothers of children under 3 are in the labor force, even when mothers on child care leave are excluded (the rate is 82 percent when mothers on leave are included—the highest rate for any group of Hungarian mothers, regardless of the ages of their children). This is the same proportion that is found in West Germany, and a higher rate than exists in many other countries. Some of the employed women in this category are those who are interrupting their child care leaves. Most are not using benefits for the full entitlement period.

These and other women are exerting pressure to bring about changes in policy. Proposals have been made to expand the facilities for day care, to lower the age at which children may enter preschool programs to 2½, to make the child care allowance wage related instead of a flat grant, and to permit fathers to qualify for the program if they remain at home to care for a young child or alternate periods of care with the mother.

East Germany This nation has the most extensive participation of females in the labor force among the countries described here and among the highest rates anywhere in the industrialized world. Eighty-five percent of all adult women work, including those with young children. East Germany is also the best illustration of the extensive use of publicly supported out-of-home child care.

Like Hungary, East Germany has

made extensive use of women in the work force since World War II and has a long history of trying to solve the problems that working women have in caring for young children. It has also discovered that there are negative consequences not only to programs involving all-week residential care of children but also to any approach requiring the use of extremely large facilities. However, in contrast to Hungary, East Germany has had a tight labor market, and every adult has been needed in the labor force. As a consequence, the East German government assumed that the mothers of young children would have to work, and it concentrated on the improvement of child care facilities. The government has made an extensive investment of financial resources, personnel, and research in its efforts to improve these facilities, and it is appropriately proud of the results.

Each East German day care center serves a maximum of ninety children in six groups of fifteen. The children range in age from a minimum of 6 months (more usually about 1 year) to between 2½ and 3. Two or three trained staff members serve each group, depending on the age of the children. Sixty percent of all East German children aged 3 or younger are cared for during the day in these centers. This includes about 80 percent of those aged 1 and 2, who are the major participants in the program. Over 90 percent of these children aged 3 to 6 attend the full-day preschool program, which is often conducted in buildings adjacent to day care centers. Regulations require that new housing developments include day care and preschool facilities, along with schools and other services. Current plans are to expand day care to cover 70 percent of children below the age of 3.

In addition to making this extensive provision of day care, East Germany has expanded its social benefits for mothers. Women are entitled to twenty-six weeks of maternity leave at full net pay, with six weeks to be taken before childbirth and twenty after. Women are also entitled to remain at home on an unpaid but job-protected leave until the child is a year old. If a day care placement is unavailable,

single parents are provided a cash benefit at a flat rate equal to about 40 percent of the average wage so that they may provide home care until a placement is available.

Also, the government has recently instituted several policies designed to increase the birthrate. One of these provides that women having a second or subsequent child can remain home after the conclusion of their maternity leave until the child is a year old, while receiving their standard sickness benefit. Mothers are also entitled to three personal leave days per month.

Thus, in East Germany, out-of-home child care service is the dominant policy mode governing care for the children of working women. In addition, health benefits assure women the right to remain at home just before and after childbirth. An income maintenance policy protects women against income loss for at least six months after giving birth, and children therefore do not need out-of-home care until they have reached the age of 6 to 12 months.

France This country best illustrates the third policy option: a partial subsidy through which parents can obtain either out-of-home child care or income replacement, thus making it theoretically possible for them to exercise individual choice more freely than would be possible otherwise. In France, the overall employment rate for females is lower than in the United States. However, the percentage of working women with children under the age of 3 (43 percent) is slightly higher in France, and almost all these women work full time.

France has long had an extensive system of family allowances, monthly cash grants to parents of second and subsequent children in a family. The level is among the highest in Europe. Although the family allowance was established and supported initially to encourage a growth in population, the French birthrate has fallen steadily over the last thirty years, except during a brief period following World War II.

French analysts are convinced that the decision of how many children to have is based on a complicated amal-

gam of factors (including the general state of the economy, employment, housing, and individual preferences), rather than on the availability of a cash benefit. On the other hand, inadequate family income creates unnecessary and potentially harmful stress on families with children. Thus, the French strongly support income maintenance policies designed to reduce the financial burdens borne by families, especially families with young children.

For low-income families with at least one child under the age of 3, the French government provides an income-tested cash benefit in the form of a special supplementary family allowance (*complément familial*). This allowance can be used as the parents wish—to purchase child care so that both parents can work or to supplement family income when only one parent works. In addition, the government provides a sixteen-week maternity leave at full net pay for employed women and gives them the option of taking some of this leave time before childbirth. The program also provides a flat-rate cash grant to mothers on the birth of a child.

The government supplements these benefits with the most extensive out-of-home child care services offered in any Western European country. The first feature of this program is an extraordinary free preschool system that serves 95 percent of children aged 3 to 6 (and 27 percent of 2 year olds) on a voluntary basis, whether or not their mothers work. A substantial number of these schools also provide the children of working mothers with some sort of care before and after normal school hours, at lunchtime, and on school holidays. The second feature is the unusually wide coverage provided for children under the age of 3, in a combination of preschool programs, day care centers, and family day care arrangements. Almost one-third of this age group—and half the children of working mothers—are served through these various programs. This includes 12 percent who are enrolled in some form of group program and 20 percent who receive licensed family day care.

The quality of the care varies enor-

"The . . . high quality of Sweden's publicly subsidized programs is known throughout the world. Its facilities for child care are beautifully designed, well equipped, and extensively staffed. What is less well known is that . . . enrollment in these programs is relatively low."

mously, however. Moreover, the French are quick to acknowledge that private family day care, which is unsubsidized, is expensive and difficult to monitor. Subsidized family day care provided by a social agency, although of higher quality, better supervised, and less expensive for parents, is as expensive for government to provide as care in a center. Good-quality centers or group facilities are expensive to provide and cannot be expanded rapidly.

Some people have argued that French policymakers are trying to achieve contradictory objectives: to support the at-home mother as well as the working mother, in the guise of supporting parental preferences. Others suggest that the French are trying to accomplish too much, considering their limited resources and the current state of the economy and labor market. Because the *complément familial* is designed to supplement low incomes, it does not offer an alternative for families with moderate incomes. It will take time before it is known whether the plan offers a real alternative to work, even for unskilled, poorly paid women.

The French position seems to be based on the assumption that cash transfers are an essential foundation to child care policy. However, direct payments may attenuate financial pressures on low-income families, but they can never fully replace wages over an extended period during the productive years. A program of income maintenance can be supplementary, but adequate child care services must ultimately be provided too. Thus, the debate in France is not over the expansion of these programs, but rather over which type of program offers the optimum environment for the development of young children: a group experience or a familylike, surrogate-mother experience. Most French

policymakers believe a group experience is essential to the adequate development of children aged 2 or older, regardless of whether the child's mother is working; the debate has to do primarily with children younger than 2.

What makes French policy unusual is that issues related to the labor market seem to play a less important role —and family policy considerations a larger role—in comparison to policies in other countries surveyed in this study. And this is true even though trends in the labor market are comparable in all five nations.

Sweden Policy in Sweden illustrates the fourth option: the restructuring of social conditions to permit a closer integration of work and family life for all adults. The proportion of females in the Swedish labor force (69 percent) is the highest among all the Western European countries and is clearly the highest for women with children under age 3 (58 percent). However, half the working women in Sweden are employed only part time. Nevertheless, nonworking mothers with young children, in addition to those women now working part time, might be the only significant source of labor available if a tight employment market should return.

Historically, Sweden's concern has been with population policy, and it established maternity benefits and maternity leaves within that context. However, the issue of population growth became secondary when the economy expanded and a tight labor market developed. These conditions encouraged women to enter the labor market and subsequently stimulated popular pressure on government to expand its programs of child care. The exceptionally high quality of Sweden's publicly subsidized programs is known throughout the world. Its facilities for

child care are beautifully designed, well equipped, and extensively staffed.

What is less well known is that even now, enrollment in these programs is relatively low—certainly the lowest among the five countries considered in this survey. About half the children from the age of 3 to the age of 7 (which is the age at which compulsory school attendance begins in Sweden) are served by day care centers or preschools, and about 23 percent of children under the age of 3 are covered by these programs or by family day care. In addition, Sweden is expanding its supplementary programs for children in primary schools.

In the late 1960s and 1970s, another factor became significant in Swedish family policy: a growing stress on equality between the sexes. This factor has taken many forms in the society in general, including an emphasis on economic equality. Sweden is unusual in that the median wage for females is about 85 percent of the median for males, in contrast to the ratio of 60 to 65 percent that is characteristic of the other countries considered in this study. A concern for equality, which initially addressed poverty and inequities in the distribution of family income, has surfaced in other areas, including the area of child care policy.

It is in this context that the government instituted a system known as Swedish Parent Insurance in 1974 to replace the maternity benefit formerly provided under health insurance. The new system of coverage, which has been expanded somewhat since being introduced, provides a parent with a taxable cash benefit equal to full wages for 9 months following the birth of a child. (A minimum benefit, derived from health insurance, is provided for women who are not in the labor force.) A portion of the benefit can be taken by the mother prior to the expected time of the birth. Except for any portion paid before childbirth, the benefit is available to either parent, if both parents are employed.

Moreover, parents can share the benefit or, if they prefer, use it to cover part-time work. For example, a woman might use the benefit to cover four months of full-time leave after childbirth. Her husband might then take two months of full-time leave. Each might then, in turn, work two months at half time, and then two months at three-quarters time (a 6-hour work day). Employers are required to grant part-time employment to workers who have young children.

In this way, both parents can actively participate in caring for the baby until his or her first birthday, or even a litttle after. As most people would acknowledge, the year following the birth of a child (especially the first child) is particularly trying for parents. If they are able to share this responsibility with each other, the experience is much more gratifying and may contribute significantly to the child's development.

Even though few men have made use of the parent insurance benefit in Sweden thus far (10 percent of those eligible in 1976), the mere fact that such an arrangement is possible has made young women more acceptable to potential employers. Moreover, an additional social insurance benefit that grants paid leave to a parent to care for an ill child at home is used extensively by men.

Thus, influenced by the needs of the labor market as well as by family policy considerations, the Swedish program provides income replacement for either parent, together with out-of-home child care services and special work-related benefits. Thus far, the government has emphasized income replacement and the payment of cash benefits. However, policymakers are continuing their effort to expand child care services, especially group programs, for children above the age of about 7 months. Nevertheless, it is expected that family day care will continue to be an important part of the system. The emphasis on expanding group programs grows out of the Swedish conviction that such an approach provides children with the best opportunity for development. At the same time, the Swedes are continuing to press for a shorter workday (6 hours)—at least for parents of very young children—so that employed parents may take a more ac-

tive part in the care and rearing of their children.

West Germany This nation represents the fifth of the options considered here: to allow individuals to handle the issue of child care by themselves, with little assistance from government. The proportion of females in the West German labor force is lower than in the other four countries considered in this survey, and is a little lower than in the United States. Because of its current concern about unemployment, the West German government is interested in policies that would discourage women from working.

The government has historically supported and encouraged traditional family roles. Unlike several other countries, West Germany actively imported foreign labor in the 1960s instead of fostering the employment of its women. There is extensive political support for the "woman at home" role, and this attitude is intensified by anxiety about the current low birth-rate. Despite all this, West German women are working in greater numbers than ever before.

Because of a variety of pressures urging the expansion of preschool programs, the government passed legislation encouraging the school system to make kindergarten facilities available to 75 percent of children aged 3 to 6. This rate of enrollment has been reached. As is true at all levels in West German schools, the kindergarten hours are short (from 8 A.M. to 1 P.M.). However, in working-class neighborhoods, there is a growing tendency for schools to extend their hours to provide care for the children of working parents. As in the United States, there is no systematic provision of care for infants and toddlers. Working mothers prefer to arrange for some type of family day care, if one can talk of preferences in a country in which only 20 percent of the young children of working mothers are cared for out of the home. Almost half (46 percent) the children in this category are cared for by their grandmothers.

Women are entitled to a 6-month

paid maternity leave, with the basic cash benefit paid under the terms of health insurance. The employer must supplement this payment for a portion of the time to bring the sum up to the employee's wage level. As a result, some employers may prefer not to hire young women. Employed parents are also entitled to a paid leave to take care of an ill child at home.

Given the current situation in connection with the labor market, population trends, and the economy generally, the probability is that if West Germany gives extensive support to any child care policy, it will be to a system subsidizing women to care for their children at home. The qualification is that it is likely to be akin to a "mothers wage" that is provided for about one year and is directed primarily toward the unskilled, poorly educated, low-income woman, to supplement existing family allowances and single-parent benefits. This payment would probably be provided whether or not the mother had been in the labor force. There are some who believe that such a policy would establish one more obstacle to employment for women and that it would not assure women that child care would be available should they find jobs.

PROPOSED POLICY PACKAGE

This brief overview does not begin to provide the full details of the analysis. Before offering conclusions and recommendations for a comprehensive benefit-service package, it is essential to identify the types of criteria used in choosing from among the alternative policies. The most significant factors considered were these:
- the effects of the policy on children, on family units, and on adult members of the family, both men and women
- costs, including direct costs to governments at different levels and to individuals, indirect costs to individuals and families through the tax system, and social and opportunity costs
- preferences of various groups
- historical traditions and national ideologies.

It should also be noted once more

that there is a trend toward convergence in the policies of the countries discussed here. Hungary is expanding its child care services, East Germany is expanding both benefits and services, France is expanding benefits for low-income women and services for all, Sweden has planned expansion of services and is considering new benefits, West Germany is expanding benefits and experimenting with services, and the United States is beginning to consider the issue.

The following elements are recommended for a family policy benefit-service package for families with very young children:

- A universal, statutory cash benefit that replaces wages for either parent following childbirth for up to one year and that may be applied in conjunction with part-time employment. An example of this would be a social security benefit similar to that provided under Swedish Parent Insurance.

- A lowering of the age of entry into existing subsidized, preschool programs or the establishment of new programs, either as part of the public education system or as an independent operation. Such programs should serve children from the ages of 2 or 2½ to 5 or 6 and should cover at least the hours of the normal school day.

- The subsidizing of diverse child care programs (involving centers as well as supervised family day care) for children aged 6 months to 2½ years, but mainly for children aged 1 and 2.

- Special work-related benefits such as flexible working hours or a certain amount of paid leave each year for employees who have to care for an ill child at home.

FAMILY POLICY ANALYSIS

The issue discussed in this article could have been approached more conventionally as either a "women and work" issue or a "child care–day care" issue. The basic research question might have been posed in the following form: As more and more women with young children enter the labor force, what steps—if any—should society take to assure that the children of these women will be well cared for?

It seems preferable to place the issue in the context of an emerging pattern in which it is assumed that (1) all adults, regardless of gender, are increasingly likely to be in the labor force, (2) labor is important to the society, (3) the society needs children if it is to survive, and, (4) most adults want to have and rear children.

Such an approach underscores the larger implications of this social revolution for families and society generally. When the problem is approached as a "family policy" issue, the number of factors to be analyzed, as well as the number of policy options that are proposed, go well beyond those that would be involved in a simple "child care–day care" problem, which might be solved by the creation of more day care centers or the issuing of a tax credit for child care expenses.

The policy suggestions presented in this article represent an attempt to make full use of the social strategies available at this time. Ultimately, of course, the precise mixture of elements in a policy must fit the particular requirements of the country that is attempting to implement it. However, such a policy will not function well unless it is also related to the larger goals of assuring an adequate supply of jobs and family income and bringing about some modification of the relationship of work to family life. Women and men otherwise will find it difficult to reconcile the conflicting demands of work and family life—if they reconcile them at all—and children as well as the society at large will inevitably suffer. Indeed, a family policy perspective, by definition, requires constant attention to the larger picture of the interrelationships of social change, public policies, families, and children.

NOTES AND REFERENCES

1. Sheila B. Kamerman and Alfred J. Kahn, "Explorations in Family Policy," *Social Work*, 21 (May 1976), pp. 181–186.

2. *See Toward a National Policy for Children and Families* (Washington, D.C.: National Academy of Sciences, 1976); and *Families and Public Policies in the United States* (Columbus, Ohio: National Conference on Social Welfare, 1978).

3. *See* Sheila B. Kamerman and Alfred J. Kahn, *Family Policy: Government and Families in Fourteen Countries* (New York: Columbia University Press, 1978), pp. 15 and 476–503.

4. The labor market data included in this paragraph are derived from the following sources: Congressional Research Service, *Women in America: A Source Book* (Washington, D.C.: Library of Congress, 1979); appendix to the statement of Alexis Herman, director of Women's Bureau, U.S. Department of Labor, in U.S., Congress, Senate, *The Coming Decade: American Women and Human Resources Policies and Programs*, Part 1, January 31 and February 1, 1979, Hearings before the Committee on Labor and Human Resources (Washington, D.C.: U.S. Government Printing Office, 1979), pp. 319–362; U.S. Bureau of the Census, "Population Profile of the United States: 1978," *Current Population Reports*, Series P-20, No. 336 (Washington, D.C.: U.S. Government Printing Office, 1979); U.S. Bureau of the Census, "Perspectives on American Husbands and Wives," *Current Population Reports: Special Studies*, Series P-23, No. 77 (Washington, D.C.: U.S. Government Printing Office, 1978); and Paul C. Glick and Arthur J. Norton, "Marrying, Divorcing, and Living Together in the U.S. Today," *Population Bulletin*, 32 (October 1977).

5. For a description and analysis of child care policies and programs in Europe, *see* Alfred J. Kahn and Sheila B. Kamerman, *Social Services in International Perspective* (Washington, D.C.: U.S. Government Printing Office, 1977), chap. 5.

6. For a discussion of child care in the United States, *see* Sheila B. Kamerman and Alfred J. Kahn, "The Day Care Debate: A Wider View," *Public Interest*, No. 54 (Winter 1979).

7. For a full report of this study, *see* Sheila B. Kamerman and Alfred J. Kahn, *Child Care, Family Benefits, and Working Parents*. Unpublished manuscript, New York, 1979. For a partial report of the study and its implications, *see* Sheila B. Kamerman, "Work and Family in Industrialized Societies," *SIGNS Journal of Women in Culture and Society*, 4 (Summer 1979). ◀